"Jesus began his ministry by blessing the 'poor in spirit' (Mt 5:3), and none are better qualified for that designation than people with mental disorders. Yet they remain profoundly stigmatized to this day, even in the church. There is a tremendous need, therefore, for books like this one. An accessible overview of mental disorders written for the church, it offers a welcome dose of scientifically informed common sense, undergirded with sound, biblically based wisdom. It deserves a wide circulation and will make an excellent gift for friends, family members, and ministers looking for a sympathetic Christian guide to this complex area."

**Eric L. Johnson,** Lawrence and Charlotte Hoover Professor of Pastoral Care, The Southern Baptist Theological Seminary

"Having been a pastor for almost four decades and having an undergraduate degree in psychology has created a personal interest in both theology and psychology for many years. I'm well aware of the deep division between these two disciplines. That being said, Dr. Matthew Stanford does a masterful job of showing the truth in how these two seemingly divided groups can find a common and honest intersection. Dr. Stanford skillfully shows how Scripture applies to real life and speaks truth about deep psychological issues. *Grace for the Afflicted* is written in a way that is understandable and applicable. I believe this book will minister to many in the days ahead."

**Frank S. Page,** president and CEO, Executive Committee of the Southern Baptist Convention

"*Grace for the Afflicted* offers the church an account of mental illnesses from a medical and biblical perspective. Stanford speaks a word of hope and grace to those who bear the burden of mental illnesses—patients and families alike. He examines illnesses not often covered in such studies: from traumatic brain injuries caused by accidents, violence, and strokes to personality disorders and dementia. A highly significant addition to the pastor's bookshelf."

**Kathryn Greene-McCreight,** Christ Church, New Haven, Connecticut, author of *Darkness Is My Only Companion*

"Matt's deep commitment to the gospel, coupled with his preparation as a scholar-practitioner, makes him a trusted voice to me and so many others."

**Ed Stetzer,** executive director, Billy Graham Center for Evangelism, Billy Graham Distinguished Endowed Chair for Church, Mission, and Evangelism, Wheaton College

"When responding to mental illness, our churches often start from a place of ignorance, faulty assumptions, or simple hopelessness. Matthew Stanford uses his knowledge and experience to battle all three. As a fellow believer that the Christian community has much to offer people affected by mental health challenges, I applaud and recommend this book, which offers much-needed education, sound biblical thought, and practical ways to help. It's a must-read for every pastor, ministry leader, and concerned Christian who wants to be informed, wise, sensible, and truly helpful."

**Amy Simpson,** author of *Troubled Minds*

"I wholeheartedly recommend *Grace for the Afflicted* for any pastor or church leader who is looking for a reliable resource on understanding mental illness and treatment from a biblical perspective. Dr. Matthew Stanford's extensive background as a neurobiologist is shaped by his vibrant and personal faith in God as our wounded healer who has compassion on his children who suffer."

**Kay Warren,** cofounder Saddleback Church, Lake Forest, California

# GRACE

*for the*

# AFFLICTED

## A Clinical and Biblical Perspective on Mental Illness

### Revised & Expanded

# Matthew S. Stanford

**IVP Books**

An imprint of InterVarsity Press
Downers Grove, Illinois

*InterVarsity Press*
*P.O. Box 1400, Downers Grove, IL 60515-1426*
*ivpress.com*
*email@ivpress.com*

*Second edition ©2017 by Matthew S. Stanford*

*First edition ©2008 by Matthew S. Stanford*

*InterVarsity Press® is the book-publishing division of InterVarsity Christian Fellowship/USA®, a movement of students and faculty active on campus at hundreds of universities, colleges, and schools of nursing in the United States of America, and a member movement of the International Fellowship of Evangelical Students. For information about local and regional activities, visit intervarsity.org.*

*All Scripture quotations, unless otherwise indicated, are taken from the New American Standard Bible®, copyright 1960, 1962, 1963, 1968, 1971, 1972, 1973, 1975, 1977, 1995 by The Lockman Foundation. Used by permission.*

*While any stories in this book are true, some names and identifying information may have been changed to protect the privacy of individuals.*

*Cover design: Cindy Kiple*
*Interior design: Daniel van Loon*
*Images: orchid in broken bottle: © Jose A. Bernat Bacete / Getty Images*
        *broken glass: © matejmm/iStockphoto*
        *white orchid: © pilotL39/iStockphoto*

*ISBN 978-0-8308-4507-1 (print)*
*ISBN 978-0-8308-9080-4 (digital)*

*Printed in the United States of America* ∞

**Library of Congress Cataloging-in-Publication Data**

*A catalog record for this book is available from the Library of Congress.*

| P | 25 | 24 | 23 | 22 | 21 | 20 | 19 | 18 | 17 | 16 | 15 | 14 | 13 | 12 | 11 | 10 | 9 | 8 | 7 | 6 | 5 | 4 | 3 | 2 | 1 |

| Y | 35 | 34 | 33 | 32 | 31 | 30 | 29 | 28 | 27 | 26 | 25 | 24 | 23 | 22 | 21 | 20 | 19 | 18 | 17 |

# CONTENTS

# PREFACE

SINCE THE PUBLICATION of *Grace for the Afflicted* in 2008, significant changes have occurred both in my personal life and in the mental health care system. Ten years after its publication, I find myself in full-time ministry and part of a national conversation on the role of faith communities in mental health care. This has given me the opportunity to meet and talk with thousands of individuals around the country who live with mental illness and their families. Those conversations have given me greater insight into the topic and a better feel for the role that faith communities might play in the lives of those broken by mental health difficulties and disorders.

Within the mental health community, the publication of the fifth edition of the *Diagnostic and Statistical Manual of Mental Disorders* (DSM-5) in 2013 dramatically changed how mental disorders are classified and diagnosed. These two factors have led me to revise and expand *Grace for the Afflicted.*

This new edition is consistent with DSM-5 diagnoses and includes updated neurobiological and treatment information on all disorders. There is a new section on neurological disorders (e.g., dementia), more examples and discussion of madness and mental health problems in the Bible, and new chapters on suicide, bipolar disorders, and trauma. Finally, I have included step-by-step information for setting up a holistic mental health recovery plan and a detailed guide on equipping congregations to better serve those living with mental disorders and their families.

These changes have been made so that *Grace for the Afflicted* might continue to be helpful for those ministering to the "least of these."

# PSYCHOLOGY, PSYCHIATRY, *and* FAITH

# 1

# FEARFULLY AND WONDERFULLY MADE

*The Spirit of God has made me,*
*And the breath of the Almighty gives me life.*

JOB 33:4

"THE SCRIPTURES TELL US that in Christ we have everything we need for life and godliness, correct? So can you explain to me why Anna's bipolar disorder and her dependence on medication is not an issue of weak faith or sin?"

Only two of us stayed after the church meeting that morning, talking over coffee. I was a deacon in the church at the time, and the man who asked the question was a friend and respected elder. The question took me by surprise, and initially I was speechless. If you have a loved one with a mental illness—or you yourself struggle with the debilitating symptoms—your first reaction to such a question may have been more along the lines of sadness, disgust, or anger.

But in my friend's defense, he sincerely wanted to understand something he saw as alien and frightening. Was Anna sick, or was she spiritually weak? We know from 2 Peter 1:3 that we do have "everything we need for a godly life" (NIV). Yet, even though Anna professed Christ as Savior, her life was a mixture of family problems, shame, suffering, and strange behavior. How should the church respond?

Mental illness is a frightening experience, not only for the one afflicted but also for those who witness the individual struggling to control strange thoughts and behaviors. In the United States one out of every five adults (18.6 percent of the population) suffers with a mental disorder in a given year.[1] The annual prevalence of mental illness in adolescents thirteen to eighteen years old is even greater, at 21.4 percent.[2] I believe that the first step in understanding how to effectively minister to and support someone living with mental illness is to recognize how God has created us.

## *How Are We Created?*

We are "fearfully and wonderfully made" (Psalm 139:14), created in the very image of God (Genesis 1:26). Humans are complex beings, unlike any other living creature: the union of a physical body with an immaterial (nonphysical) mind and spirit. Jesus himself describes the complexity of the self in Mark 12:30-31. When asked about the greatest of all the commandments, Jesus, quoting Deuteronomy 6:5, responds by saying, "LOVE THE LORD YOUR GOD WITH ALL YOUR HEART, AND WITH ALL YOUR SOUL, AND WITH ALL YOUR MIND, AND WITH ALL YOUR STRENGTH. . . . [AND] LOVE YOUR NEIGHBOR AS YOURSELF." In other words, love God with all aspects of your being (your whole self) and through your relationships.

---

[1]"Any Mental Illness Among U.S. Adults," *National Institute of Mental Health*, accessed January 25, 2016, www.nimh.nih.gov/health/statistics/prevalence/any-mental-illness-ami -among-us-adults.shtml.

[2]"Any Disorder Among Children," *National Institute of Mental Health*, accessed January 25, 2016, www.nimh.nih.gov/health/statistics/prevalence/any-disorder-among -children.shtml.

The four facets of the self are clearly outlined in Luke 2:52. Describing the development of the young Christ, Luke writes, "Jesus kept increasing in wisdom [mental] and stature [physical], and in favor with God [spiritual] and men [relational]." So you and I, like the incarnate Christ, are a unity of physical, mental, spiritual, and relational facets, with each aspect affecting and being affected by all the others.

*Physical.* We exist in a physical body so we can interact with the material world around us. Our bodies have been specifically designed to take in information from the environment and relay it to our brains. We see, hear, taste, smell, and touch the world around us. The processing of sensory information by our brains produces thoughts, feelings, and emotions, which then result in some outward behavioral display. We are God's creative masterpiece: a miracle of skin, bone, and blood formed from the dust of the ground (Genesis 2:7). But at the same time we are so much more. We reason, we love, and we pray.

*Mental.* Are our thoughts, feelings, and emotions merely the product of neurochemical changes and electrical discharges in our brain? Or is our mind something more—something immaterial, more than the sum of our parts? The truth is probably somewhere in the middle. While the functioning of our brain is integral to the existence of our mind, that alone is not sufficient to explain it. Similarly, to imagine our mind as completely separate and unrelated to the brain doesn't seem correct either. Body and mind are intimately connected, each affecting the other. We retrieve a past memory of a fearful event in our mind, and our physiology reacts with a racing heart and sweaty palms. Our sensory receptors are activated by familiar stimuli in the environment and past thoughts, and feelings rush to consciousness.

We think and choose with our mind. Our mind controls our actions. And God changes our mind through the process of sanctification, conforming us ever closer to the image of his Son

(Romans 8:29). A physical body formed by the hands of the Maker in union with an immaterial mind that controls and plans our behavior is a truly miraculous concept, though a difficult one to grasp. The Scriptures go further and teach us that we have an even more amazing level of being, a spirit (1 Thessalonians 5:23; Hebrews 4:12).

*Spiritual.* It is not uncommon for neuroscientists to talk and debate about the mind. They might use fancy words like *consciousness* or *self-awareness* to make it sound more "scientific," but they are still talking about an immaterial, invisible aspect of our being. Things that can't be seen make scientists uncomfortable. They don't like to say something is beyond their understanding or can't be measured. They may admit that they don't understand something presently but qualify that admission by saying that with enough study and the continued advancement of science they will one day. So to describe us as having a spirit, in addition to a mind and a body, seems almost heretical from a scientific perspective.

God created us as a unity of parts, much like himself. In our inmost being we are spirit, the very breath of God placed into a shell of dust (Genesis 2:7; Ecclesiastes 12:6-7). That is how we differ from the other living creatures: both were created from the ground (Genesis 2:7, 19), but only humanity is created in the image of God (Genesis 1:26). I like the way Paul Brand and Philip Yancey describe it in their book *In His Image*:

> "And the Lord God formed man from the dust of the ground and breathed into his nostrils the breath of life, and man became a living being" (2:7). When I heard that verse as a child, I imagined Adam lying on the ground, perfectly formed but not yet alive, with God leaning over him and performing a sort of mouth-to-mouth resuscitation. Now I picture that scene differently. I assume that Adam was already biologically

alive—the other animals needed no special puff of oxygen, nitrogen, and carbon dioxide to start them breathing, so why should man? The breath of God now symbolizes for me a spiritual reality. I see Adam as alive, but possessing only an animal vitality. Then God breathes into him a new spirit, and infills him with His own image. Adam becomes a living soul, not just a living body. God's image is not an arrangement of skin cells or a physical shape, but rather an inbreathed spirit.[3]

As a spirit being, it is possible for us to be in an intimate spiritual union (Proverbs 20:27; Romans 8:15-16) with our Creator, who is also Spirit (John 4:24). No other living creature, not even the angels, has been given such an opportunity.

**Relational.** We were created to be in relationship. God himself said that it is not good for us to be alone (Genesis 2:18). While our first and greatest relational need is to know God, we should never underestimate the importance of being in fellowship with other believers. The topic of relationship is common throughout the Scriptures. The Bible offers us guidance on a variety of relationships, including marriage (Ephesians 5:22-33), parenting (Psalm 127:3-5), siblings (Proverbs 17:17), friendships (Proverbs 27:9), and with those who are not so friendly (Matthew 5:25). Relationship is one of the reasons why Jesus gave us the church, so that we might be together and never be alone (Acts 2:42; 1 John 1:7).

## *Bringing It All Together*

So how does all this work together—physical, mental, spiritual, and relational? Let's look at a simple visual representation that I use with clients to help them understand how mental illness affects our whole being. Figure 1.1 shows the spiritual, mental, physical, and

---

[3]Paul Brand and Philip Yancey, *In His Image* (Grand Rapids, Zondervan, 1987), 22.

relational facets of our being, each separate but interacting with the others. Our physical body interacts with stimuli and individuals (relationships) in the environment outside and the mind within. The mind, connected to the body through the functions of the brain and nervous system, is also in contact with our immaterial spirit.

Our body senses and reacts to the external environment, and our mind uses that information to perceive, understand, and interpret our surroundings. The mind forms our thoughts and plans out our actions. Our spirit, when connected to God, works to transform the mind into the very image of Christ (2 Corinthians 3:18). This interaction within our being allows us to be involved in healthy, meaningful relationships with others.

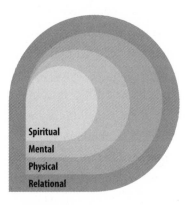

**Figure 1.1.** The holistic self

Since we were created as a unity, dysfunction or disorder in one aspect of the self negatively affects all levels of our being. For example, in individuals diagnosed with a mental illness, a neurochemical dysfunction in the brain (physical) results in abnormal thoughts and feelings (mental) leading to broken relationships (relational) and difficulty connecting with God and other believers (spiritual).

### How Have We Been Affected by the Fall?

After the shock had worn off, I thought for a minute about how to respond to my friend's question about Anna. I asked him, "Do you know anyone who has heart disease and regularly takes medication?"

He said that he did, but before I could continue, he asked me whether I was trying to say that Anna's bipolar disorder and heart disease were somehow the same. Throughout this book, I will try to answer that question. How are they the same? How do they differ? But first we need to answer a more foundational question: What are the results of human sin on the four aspects of our being?

When a follower of Jesus Christ is asked that question, they will often quote Romans 6:23: "The wages of sin is death, but the free gift of God is eternal life in Christ Jesus our Lord." Such a response correctly points out that spiritual death, or separation from God, is the result of sin. As children of Adam, we are sinful by nature and therefore spiritually dead and separated from God at birth (Romans 5:12).

I have always thought it strange, however, that the answer to the question rarely goes beyond the spiritual. Clearly, spiritual death resulted from our sin. But what about the other aspects of our being, particularly our bodies and minds? How were they affected by the fall? I have suggested that the Scriptures describe us as a multipart being, with each part interacting with and affecting the others. If that is true, then our sin must have also adversely affected our mind and body. I'm not saying that this truth is completely unknown in the church today. Plainly, the Bible teaches us that we are fully defiled by sin—caught in what some theologians call "total depravity" (see Romans 3:12). Yet the church emphasizes the spiritual effects of sin while minimizing or disregarding the mental and physical effects. I believe this results from a misunderstanding of what the Scriptures teach about how we have been created.

**Birth.** At birth we are physically alive but spiritually dead. We are born with an imperfect body, scarred as the result of generations of sin. Genetic defects, biological predispositions, and anatomical abnormalities are all the consequences of being conceived in sin (Psalm 51:5). On the day that Adam and Eve fell, they forfeited their intimate relationship with God, and they became mortal. And we were placed at the mercy of the environment and natural biological processes that wreak havoc on our bodies and minds. But as Jesus teaches in the story of the man born blind, each time we struggle with illness and physical weakness is an opportunity for "the works of God" to be "displayed" in us (John 9:1-3).

**Growth.** As we grow and mature, our body and mind learn to interact with and react to our fallen environment, all the while spiritually separated from God by our sin. The body, physically affected by the fall, gathers sensations and stimuli from the earthly environment. Our mind, knowing only sin because of our separation from God, chooses to satisfy itself by the "if it feels good, do it" lifestyle, or what we in psychology call the pleasure principle. Relationally we are egocentric and selfish, thinking only of ourselves. We choose to sin in our *mind* (2 Corinthians 10:5), and with our *body* (Ephesians 2:3) or "members" (Romans 7:23) we act out our sinful thoughts. This process is altered only in the individual who comes to a saving faith in Christ Jesus, and even then that believer will continue to struggle with a sinfully programmed mind and body (Romans 7:14-25). In addition to the sinful desires that attempt to control us, another result of sin is physical death and decay.

**Physical death.** God told Adam that in the day he ate from the forbidden tree he would surely die (Genesis 2:16-17); and while he certainly meant this in a spiritual sense, he also meant it in a physical sense. The moment Adam disobeyed, he began to age and decay (Genesis 3:19). Physical death came a little closer each day of his life, and so it continues for us. In fact, the Scriptures tell us that the whole of the physical creation was affected by our sin and longs for the day of redemption (Romans 8:19-22). Our bodies are damaged because of sin. We age. We get sick. We suffer physically and die because the physical creation has been affected by the fall.

However, while we were all born "dead in sin," which damaged us physically, mentally, spiritually, and relationally, there is an amazing truth for those who have been "born again": we are new creations in Christ; the old things have passed away; the new has come (2 Corinthians 5:17)!

## *Our Identity in Christ*

Have you ever thought about what it means that you are a "new creation"? It means that you have been fundamentally changed; what you were before becoming a Christian no longer exists. That is not how I used to see myself. I lived Sunday to Sunday, holding on to some kind of faith-based fire insurance that I could turn in at my death in order to get into heaven. I certainly didn't see myself as Paul describes the believer in Ephesians 1, having every spiritual blessing. I now recognize that as a believer in Jesus Christ I was chosen before the foundation of the world; predestined for adoption as a son of the living God; purchased out of slavery to sin and death; forgiven of all my sins—past, present, and future; given spiritual wisdom and revelation; and marked as such until the day that I stand before him holy and blameless.

Do you see yourself that way? If you believe in Jesus Christ, then that is exactly how God sees you—whether you accept it or not. It doesn't matter if you are struggling with mental illness. You are a new creation in Christ if you have received him by faith. And we who minister to those who struggle with mental illness should remember that they are his chosen children if they are in Christ, and they should be treated as such.

## A Transformed Life

We were born with a fallen nature, which we received from our ancestral father Adam. But when a person comes to faith in Jesus Christ, they are "crucified"! The "old self" is nailed to the cross with Christ, never to return (Romans 6:6; Galatians 2:20). God gives us his Spirit; Christ's very life takes up residence in us (Colossians 3:1-3). We have his righteousness (1 Corinthians 1:30; 2 Corinthians 5:21; Philippians 3:9) and a new, Christlike nature (Ephesians 4:24). Spiritually, we sit at the right hand of God Almighty (Ephesians 2:6).

So, just like my friend said, as believers we are complete in Christ, having everything we need for life and godliness in him (2 Peter 1:3). That is true in the spiritual realm, but remember that we are a unity of parts. What happens to our body, mind, and relationships after we are transformed in the spirit?

## Being Conformed to the Image of Christ

We were born affected by sin, and we lived some period of time before coming to Christ. Consequently, we have habits, thought patterns, and biological predispositions that are the result of our old self. This "sinful flesh" does not disappear because we have been given a new life. But change is now possible, whereas before it was not.

The Scriptures teach us that we are to submit ourselves to Christ through the indwelling Holy Spirit, allowing him to transform our minds (Romans 12:1-2). As our minds are transformed and our thoughts are taken captive to Christ, he begins to take control of the "members" of our body, changing our behavior and transforming our relationships (Colossians 3:5-10).

## Why Write This Book?

For those struggling with a mental health difficulty or disorder, even in one of the world's richest and most developed countries, obtaining proper care is hindered by a wide range of barriers that are difficult and often times impossible to overcome. Too few mental health care professionals, a shortage of psychiatric facilities, no transportation, limited financial resources, a lack of knowledge and education, stigma and shame, and misguided cultural beliefs all serve as significant barriers to individuals trying to access care. This inability to access proper care leaves the afflicted individual and their family confused, frustrated, and hopeless.

The difficulty in accessing mental health care is one of the reasons individuals in psychological distress are more likely to seek out a member of the clergy *before* a mental health care provider.[4] Viewed through the eyes of faith, it is obvious that this is not an accident but a heavenly orchestrated, divine opportunity for the church. Recognizing that mental health is an open mission field, one goal of this book is to equip clergy and faith communities to better minister to and serve those struggling with mental illness. A second and related goal is to provide individuals affected by mental illness (and their families) with a detailed road map for recovery. There is hope if you or your loved one is struggling with a mental illness. Recovery is possible!

## Final Thoughts

I hope this chapter has shown you that we have been affected by sin at all levels of our being. Both believers and nonbelievers carry the physical, mental, and relational effects of sinful programming.

---

[4]Philipp S. Wang et al., "Patterns and Correlates of Contacting Clergy for Mental Disorders in the United States," *Health Services Research* 38 (2003): 647-73.

Fortunately, believers have been transformed spiritually and are righteous before their Maker. But that does not instantaneously remove the sinful "flesh" we still carry around. Sanctification is a process by which our minds are transformed through submission to Christ. Biological defects and weaknesses do not go away by themselves, no matter how much we want them to or have faith that they will. God can certainly choose to heal us supernaturally, and in some cases he does, but can we embrace our weaknesses as an opportunity to grow in our faith (2 Corinthians 12:7-10; James 1:2-4)? Like the man born blind, we are all flawed so that "the works of God might be displayed" in us (John 9:3).

# 2

# THE ADVERSARY

*I have bipolar [disorder] and was counseled by a pastor
who suggested that I was possessed by demons.*

SHERRY, DIAGNOSED WITH BIPOLAR DISORDER

A PASTOR FRIEND OF MINE recently shared that during a regular
Wednesday night service he spontaneously decided to have a time
of sharing. He asked those in attendance if anyone would like to
share, and a young man near the back of the church got up and
moved forward. My friend did not recognize this young man as
one of his church members. The young man said that he knew this
was a "Bible-believing church" and that they were "praying for
Christ's second coming." He just wanted to let everyone know that
Christ had returned. This young man was schizophrenic and believed himself to be Jesus. He was having what is called a delusion
of grandeur, believing himself to be a famous or powerful person.

This incident ended well, since my friend took the young man to
a local psychiatric facility where he received treatment. Several of
the congregants, however, thought this might be the work of demons.

It is easy to understand how people of faith, who believe in fallen
angels, might attribute the bizarre thoughts and behaviors of individuals with mental illnesses to the demonic, especially when

religious delusions or hallucinations are present. A man with paranoid schizophrenia shot and killed a retired policeman in Florida. At his murder trial the man testified that he "had to kill" the victim, believing the retired policeman was the antichrist because of the University of Alabama *A* on his baseball cap. Many know of the Texas case of Andrea Yates, who, in a delusional state, drowned her five young children, saying that she wanted to protect them from going to hell. You may also be familiar with the tragic story of Sister Maricica Irina Cornici.

In June 2005 Sister Irina, a twenty-three-year-old Romanian Orthodox nun, died of dehydration and suffocation following an exorcism ritual at the Holy Trinity convent in the northeast Romanian village of Tanacu. She had been gagged with a towel and chained to a cross for several days without food or water during the ritual led by Daniel Petru Corogeanu, a monk who served as the convent's priest, and four nuns. Prior to coming to the convent, Sister Irina had been treated by a psychiatrist for schizophrenia. Shortly before her death she had begun hearing voices again—which she believed were the devil telling her that she was sinful. Irina's brother asked the priest to perform the exorcism ritual because he did not believe the medical treatment was working.

When asked by a reporter at his trial whether Sister Irina was mentally ill and in need of psychiatric treatment, Father Daniel replied, "You can't drive the devil out of people with pills. God has performed a miracle for her; finally, Irina is delivered from evil."

The Romanian Orthodox Church condemned the ritual as "abominable" and excommunicated the priest and the four nuns who assisted him. In February 2007 Father Daniel and the nuns were convicted of causing the death of Irina Cornici and given lengthy prison sentences.

These are all truly tragic events, but are they the work of demons?

## Satan and Demons

As a clinical neuroscientist and a Christian, I am often asked questions concerning mental disorders and matters of faith. One of the most common questions I am asked regards the role of the demonic in mental illness. While you may imagine that this is not an easy question to answer, it is made even more difficult by the fact that the typical believer's view of Satan and the demonic has been influenced more by Frank Peretti's novels and movies like *The Exorcist* than by the Bible. My goal in this chapter is to stay true to the biblical text and simply ask, What does the Bible say about the demonic, and how might that relate to mental illness?

The name Satan comes from a Hebrew word (*satan*) that means "adversary," "accuser," or "opponent." The term *devil* (*diabolos*), sometimes used to refer to Satan in the New Testament, is from the Greek and means "slanderer," "traitor," or "false accuser." Satan is a minor figure in the Old Testament, mentioned explicitly in only three passages (1 Chronicles 21:1, Job 1–2, and Zechariah 3:1-2). He is also seen in Genesis 3, where he is referred to as "the serpent." In comparison, Satan and his demonic cohorts are much more prominent in the New Testament. The New Testament writers use a number of different terms to refer to Satan. In the Gospels he is referred to as "the tempter," "the evil one," "Beelzebul," "the ruler of the demons," "the enemy," and "the ruler of this world."

Recognizing that we have a limited set of verses that refer to Satan, what can we know for sure?

First, we know from the biblical texts that Satan is a living, conscious being. He is not a symbolic personification of evil in the world. In the prologue to the book of Job, Satan questions Job's allegiance to God. In the Gospel of Luke, he asks to attack Peter (Luke 22:31). In the Gospel of John, he is said to have desires, to speak lies, and to have an evil nature (John 8:44). In 2 Corinthians, we are told that he can disguise himself as an angel of light (2 Corinthians 11:13-15). These are the actions of a conscious being, not a symbolic representation.

Second, Isaiah 14:12-15 and Ezekiel 28:12-19, which pertain to the kings of Babylon and Tyre, respectively, seem to point beyond their immediate context to a scene in which a magnificent angelic being (Satan) chose to rebel against God and as a result was cast out of heaven. Second Peter 2:4 mentions the angels (plural) who sinned, leading to the conclusion that there were many angels who assisted Satan in his rebellion and were therefore banished from heaven (see also Matthew 25:41). Given that Satan is a fallen angel, it is also important for us to understand that he is a created being. While his power in human terms may appear awesome, it is insignificant in comparison to the power of God the Creator.

Jesus refers to Satan as "the evil one" (Matthew 13:19) and tells us that he has an evil nature, that he is a murderer, and that he is the father of lies (John 8:44). Even though he has been cast out of heaven, Satan continues to plot and scheme against God by attacking the ones he loves (2 Corinthians 2:10-11; Ephesians 6:11-12; 1 Peter 5:8). Satan's goal is to disrupt or limit the relationship God has offered us through his Son Jesus Christ (Mark 4:15).

Satan is not alone in his evil mission; he is assisted by an army of fallen angels the Scriptures commonly refer to as "demons" (Matthew 8:31; James 2:19; Revelation 18:2). The work of Satan and demons as described in the Bible includes deception and false teaching (2 Corinthians 4:4; 1 Timothy 4:1), hindering prayer (Daniel 10:12-13), and causing human affliction and torment (Matthew 17:14-18; Mark 5:1-5). Satan is also referred to as the ruler, or prince, of this world (John 12:31; 14:30; 16:11). God originally gave Adam and Eve dominion over the world

(Genesis 1:26-28), but they abdicated that role when they sinned. This fallen world is so contrary to God because of Satan's control (Ephesians 2:2; 6:12; 1 John 5:19).

A final characteristic the Scriptures teach us about Satan is perhaps the most important: he was defeated by Christ's death and resurrection (Hebrews 2:14; 1 John 3:8). Satan is a defeated foe; and as children of the living God, we must recognize that fact and understand that truly "greater is He who is in you than he who is in the world" (1 John 4:4).

## Demonic Attack

Most believers would likely agree with what I have just written. The nature of Satan is not usually a topic argued among evangelical Christians. What is often hotly debated within the church, however, is the topic of demonic attack. How exactly do Satan and his demonic angels affect and influence human thoughts, behavior, and circumstances? What can they do? What are their limitations?

Satan is an evil being, full of rage and jealousy toward God. He would like nothing better than to overthrow God and place himself in power as the ruler of the universe. But because Satan is a created being, limited in his power, and God is the almighty, eternal, sovereign King, Satan can do nothing directly to God. So he chooses instead to attack humanity, the beloved creation of the One he hates. The goal of all demonic attack is to turn a person's thoughts and behaviors away from Christ and toward self and sin. The Scriptures describe five ways by which Satan and his demonic angels attack humans: temptation, deception, accusation, infirmity, and possession.

***Temptation.*** To be tempted is to be tested. Temptation is a type of demonic attack all believers have personal knowledge of and struggle with daily. The most well-known temptation in the Bible is that of Jesus himself (Matthew 4:1-11; Mark 1:12-13; Luke 4:1-13). After fasting in the wilderness for forty days, Jesus was hungry and in a physically weakened state. That is when Satan usually attacks. He and his demonic cohorts are always looking to exploit our weaknesses, be they physical or mental (Matthew 26:41; 1 Corinthians 7:5; Ephesians 4:26-27).

Temptation may be direct or indirect. By "direct" I mean that Satan or some demonic spirit purposely places before you an enticement meant to draw you into sin. It may be shopping and spending, drugs, or a beautiful woman at work, but the enticement is chosen specifically for you and your unique set of weaknesses. An "indirect" temptation would be a more general enticement that is commonly presented to everyone in a given culture, for instance, pornography. These indirect temptations permeate all cultures, since Satan is the "ruler of this world."

But as in all things, God is sovereign over demonic temptation. He uses these opportunities of testing to grow our faith and draw us closer to Him (James 1:2-4). He has promised that he will not allow us to be tempted beyond our ability to resist and that he will provide a means of escape (1 Corinthians 10:13). So while Satan and his demonic cohorts may be the actual agents of temptation, in times of testing we must recognize that it is God who is fully in control and working within us.

*Deception.* Jesus tells us that Satan is "the father of lies" and that deception is his very nature (John 8:44). The demonic forces in opposition to the people of God would like nothing better than for you to believe a lie. Satan uses deception to keep nonbelievers from seeing the truth of the gospel (2 Corinthians 4:4; Revelation 13:14) and to draw us into sin (Genesis 3:13). The Scriptures tell us that false teaching is another form of demonic deception Satan uses to alter the truths of God (Colossians 2:8; 1 Timothy 4:1). We know that Satan disguises himself as an angel of light (2 Corinthians 11:14) for the purpose of making people believe that his deception is a message from God himself. To recognize the extent and seriousness of demonic deception in our world, we need to look no further than the many false religions and cults that blind the minds of millions from seeing the light of the gospel.

Jesus said, "I am the way, and the truth, and the life; no one comes to the Father but through Me" (John 14:6). It is our abiding in the truth of Christ and staying in his Word that helps shield us from being drawn away by demonic deception (John 8:31-32).

*Accusation.* I mentioned earlier that Satan is explicitly referred to in the Old Testament only three times. In two of those references he is standing before the Lord and accusing one of God's faithful of sin (Job 1–2; Zechariah 3:1-2). Satan is referred to as the "accuser of our brethren" (Revelation 12:10). One aspect of demonic accusation is what we see in Job and Zechariah: Satan continually stands before the throne of God, in a court-like setting, and accuses each believer of being sinful and unworthy of God's affection. Thanks be to God that we have an advocate before the Father, Jesus Christ (Hebrews 7:25; 1 John 2:1), who counters every satanic accusation and promises us that there is no condemnation for those who are in him (Romans 8:1).

A second aspect of demonic accusation is unyielding guilt over past sins and failures. When, by faith, we received Christ into our lives, we were instantly forgiven of all our sins—past, present, and future. But how often have you felt unforgivable? How often have you thought that because you still have sin in your life God could not possibly love you? Those thoughts are examples of demonic accusation. Satan would like nothing more than for us to believe that we are not forgiven, that Christ's sacrifice somehow was not sufficient. By redirecting our attention onto our past sins and failures, Satan is able to affect the level of intimacy in our relationship with the Father. We must accept God at his word—that, indeed, Christ's sacrifice was sufficient and that we are completely forgiven (Acts 10:43; Ephesians 1:7; Hebrews 10:16-18). If we do fall into sin, we know that the disharmony in our relationship with the Father that comes as a result can be repaired through repentance (1 John 1:9).

As in all things, God is sovereign over demonic accusation.

*Infirmity.* The types of demonic attack I have discussed thus far are all mental in nature, meaning they happen within the mind. Infirmity or sickness is a physical form of demonic assault. You may be asking yourself, *Is he suggesting that Satan and demons can make us sick?* The Scriptures do give several examples of individuals suffering with sickness or physical disabilities attributed to the actions of the demonic.

We find two examples in the Old Testament: Job and Saul. After receiving divine permission, Satan caused Job to become ill. Job is described as having boils from the soles of his feet to the top of his head, blackened skin that itched incessantly, running sores infested with worms, fever, foul-smelling breath, weakened bones, and constant pain. All these were the result of Satan's assault. We read in 1 Samuel 16:14 that an evil spirit tormented Israel's king Saul. While the exact nature of the infirmity is unclear, it certainly caused him to suffer and to behave violently at times (1 Samuel 18:10-11).

The New Testament describes at least five instances in which Jesus healed an individual whose sickness was the result of demonic influence. In four of these individuals—a mute man (Matthew 9:32-33; Luke 11:14), a blind and mute man (Matthew 12:22), a Syrophoenician woman's daughter (Matthew 15:22-28; Mark 7:25-30), and a boy suffering from seizures (Matthew 17:14-18; Mark 9:17-27; Luke 9:37-42)—Jesus cast out an evil spirit, resulting in their healing.

In the fifth case, Jesus heals a crippled woman and then tells the crowd that Satan had caused the woman's eighteen-year-long condition (Luke 13:10-16).

So what are we to make of this? I believe we should understand these cases just as they are presented: demonic forces can and do cause individuals to become ill and disabled. But we also must consider this in the broader context. The four Gospels and the book of Acts describe thirty-one specific instances of healing by Jesus or his apostles. Only five of those illnesses (all found in Matthew, Mark, and Luke) are said to have resulted from demonic influence. So while Jesus and his apostles certainly did encounter demonically influenced illnesses, this appears to be less prevalent than what we might refer to as naturally occurring illnesses. In fact, the Scriptures differentiate between natural illness and demonically caused infirmity (Matthew 8:16; Mark 1:32-34), although the Gospel writers clearly blur the lines between the two and describe both as requiring healing (Matthew 4:24). In addition, a number of other passages simply refer to Jesus or his disciples casting out demons, without describing the nature of the individuals' affliction (Mark 1:39; 6:13; Luke 4:41; 8:2; 13:32).

In his second letter to the Corinthians, Paul describes being tormented by "a thorn in the flesh" that he says was "a messenger of Satan" (2 Corinthians 12:7-10). While it is unclear what the exact nature of this "thorn" was, it is generally accepted that it was some type of physical illness. Given the Old Testament and New Testament examples I have just described, it doesn't seem strange that Paul would have an illness resulting from demonic influence; but what *is* very different about this case is God's response. Paul says he prayed three times that God would remove the thorn, and God's response was "My grace is sufficient for you" (vv. 8-9). Paul is told this infirmity would be used in his life in such a way that Christ's power would be manifested and his faith would be perfected. Instead of healing Paul, God supplied him with sustaining grace so that he might endure this trial in his life.

It is unclear from the Scriptures how one can differentiate between a natural illness and one caused by demonic influence, since, as I mentioned earlier, the biblical writers very much blur the line between the two. In both instances the afflicted person is described as requiring healing. And some relief seems possible through physical remedies, even for demonically caused illnesses. We see that music was therapeutic in Saul's case (1 Samuel 16:23), while Job found some relief by draining his boils (Job 2:8). Though the biblical accounts don't mention this, it is possible that Paul's relationship with Luke, a physician, may have resulted from Paul seeking treatment for his "thorn in the flesh." In the end, the root cause of an infirmity doesn't seem to matter to the biblical authors as much as the fact that Christ is sovereign over illness, whether or not it has demonic origins (Acts 10:38). God is able to heal all illnesses, regardless of the cause, but in cases in which he chooses not to heal, he provides sustaining grace to those who turn to him.

*Possession.* Now we turn to a level of demonic attack that is quite controversial in the church today: possession. First, let me define what I mean by demon possession. Demon possession occurs when an individual loses control of his or her mental faculties to an evil spirit. In other words, the demon fully controls the person's thoughts and behaviors. The demonic control may occur intermittently or be continual. We find two detailed examples of demon possession in the Gospels, while the book of Acts briefly describes a possessed slave girl who can predict the future and gives a secondary reference to a failed exorcism.

The first example is described in both Mark 1:21-28 and Luke 4:31-37. Early in his ministry, Jesus was teaching in the synagogue at Capernaum and was confronted by a man with an "unclean spirit." The demon recognized Jesus as "the Holy One of God" and, crying out in the man's voice, asked if Jesus had come to destroy it. Jesus rebuked the evil spirit, and it came out of the man.

The second example of demon possession is probably the most well known: the story of Legion (Matthew 8:28-34; Mark 5:1-20; Luke 8:26-39). After crossing the Sea of Galilee and calming the storm, Jesus was immediately confronted by a man (two men in Matthew) who was said to be demon possessed. This man is described as being naked, extremely violent, and possessing superhuman strength. The biblical accounts tell us that he lived among the tombs, cried out day and night, and cut himself with sharp stones. Similar to the first example of possession, the demons within this man recognized Jesus as the "Son of the Most High God" and were concerned that he had come to torment them. In a brief conversation between Jesus and the demon, we learn that the man was actually possessed by numerous demons who referred to themselves collectively as Legion. With a simple command, Jesus cast out the demons, and they entered a herd of pigs that immediately rushed into the lake and drowned.

While in Philippi, the apostle Paul and Silas encountered a slave girl possessed by an evil spirit that gave her the ability to predict the future (Acts 16:16-19). She followed them around the city for several days crying out, "These men are bond-servants of the Most High God, who are proclaiming to you the way of salvation" (v. 17). Paul commanded the evil spirit, in the name of Jesus Christ, to leave the girl. The girl was freed of the demon and lost her ability to tell the future (vv. 18-19).

The fourth example of demon possession is a secondary reference to an exorcism in Acts 19:13-16. While Paul was in Ephesus, some Jewish exorcists apparently began using the name of Jesus to try to cast out demons. In one such instance, the seven sons of a Jewish chief priest named Sceva tried unsuccessfully to cast a demon out of a man by calling upon "Jesus whom Paul preaches." The demon responded, through the man's voice, "I recognize Jesus, and I know about Paul, but who are you?" The demon possessed man then leaped on the brothers and beat all seven of them badly.

If we compare these examples to those of individuals with demonically caused illnesses (discussed earlier), we find a number of clear differences. In the examples of possession, the demons spoke through the voice of the inhabited individual, which is not seen in those with an illness caused by an evil spirit. Unlike the sick who sought Jesus out for healing, the demon possessed recognized Jesus as the Messiah and were fearful of him. Another difference not seen in the demonically infirmed is the presence of supernatural abilities. For example, two of the possessed individuals displayed superhuman strength, while another had psychic abilities that allowed her to accurately predict the future. In addition, the Gospel writers describe those with illnesses caused by demons as being healed by Jesus, while very different language is used to describe what occurs to the possessed. So it seems clear from these examples that the biblical writers considered demon possession something qualitatively different from simply an illness that resulted from demonic influence.

We need to look at possession in a broader biblical context, much like we did with demonically caused illness. Demon possession, as I have defined it here, is mentioned even fewer times in the Scriptures than individuals with illnesses caused by demons. In fact, we find no reference to demon possession outside of the Synoptic Gospels (Matthew, Mark, and Luke) and Acts. Exorcism is not mentioned in any of the New Testament letters, suggesting that it may not have been an issue. Many people have wondered whether it is even possible for a believer to be demon possessed.

The Scriptures give no examples of demon possessed believers, though two examples of believing individuals with demonically caused illness are described: a crippled woman (a righteous Jew described by Christ as "a daughter of Abraham" in Luke 13:10-16) and the apostle Paul (2 Corinthians 12:7-10). It seems unlikely that Satan or any demon could take up residence in an individual who has been born again. The Bible tells us that our bodies are the temple of God indwelled by the Holy Spirit (1 Corinthians 6:19) and that "greater is He who is in you than he who is in the world" (1 John 4:4). These and many other verses suggest that demon possession of the believer is not possible, since we are indwelled by the Spirit of the sovereign Creator, who makes no room for darkness (1 John 1:5).

## Demons in the Twenty-First Century

So where does that leave us today? Are demons still active? Do they play a role in mental illness? Three possibilities have been suggested to explain the level of demonic activity we see in the Scriptures versus today. The first is that *in biblical times individuals were inclined to attribute to "demons" unusual behavior and untreatable illnesses that, because of their prescientific worldview and naive understanding of disease and mental illness, could not otherwise be explained.* While this was certainly true in some instances (and still is), the problem with this argument is that it causes us to question Jesus' integrity (and perhaps his divinity), since he believed that demons were at work in the specific examples we have discussed.

A second possibility that has been suggested is that *incidences of demon possession and infirmity were limited to biblical times and the ministry of Jesus and the apostles.* Again, there is surely some truth to this suggestion. Exorcism appears to have been a major component of Jesus' earthly ministry and clearly showed the sovereignty of the anointed Messiah and the coming kingdom of God over Satan's kingdom of darkness. However, the New Testament gives us no reason to believe that demonic activity would cease with the apostolic age but, in contrast, often speaks of the evil schemes of Satan and his demonic cohorts toward the church (Ephesians 6:11-12; 1 Peter 5:8). And the continued schemes of Satan and his demons against believers are mentioned in the writings of several of the early church fathers, including Ignatius (c. AD 35–107), Justin Martyr (c. AD 100–165), Tertullian (c. AD 155–230), and Origen (c. AD 185–254).

A third possibility is that *demonic infirmity and possession still occur today much as they did in biblical times.* The first question often asked when this possibility is suggested is, Why, then, does it appear from the Scriptures that this demonic activity (possession and infirmity) was common in biblical times and yet it is not common today? We must remember that the Gospels do not consist of a moment-by-moment account of Jesus' life on earth, and any single event the Gospel writers, by divine inspiration, chose to include may seem to occur frequently when in actuality it was quite uncommon. In comparison to natural illnesses, demonic infirmity and possession are rare in the biblical text and are not even mentioned in a majority of the Scriptures.

In addition, we must understand that demon possession is not possible for those who are born again, and thus exorcism would not play a significant role in the church either today or in the first century. It is possible that demon possession does still occur today in some nonbelieving individuals and is likely to be encountered in missionary or evangelistic settings (much like in Jesus' day). The simplest—and most effective—way to deal with or rule out demon possession would be to lead the individual to faith in Christ Jesus. Exorcism rites or prayers for deliverance may be appropriate if the afflicted individual is an unbeliever and supernatural indicators of possession (e.g., superhuman strength, paranormal occurrences) are clearly present.[1]

I believe that demonically caused illness, in contrast to possession, does commonly occur today in and out of the church. However, the difficulty—if not outright impossibility—of differentiating a demonically caused illness from a natural illness leads us to treat all sickness the same. The infirmed require healing, which may come through medical intervention or through an answer to healing prayer. In either case, healing is the focus, rather than deliverance.

## What About Mental Illness?

Mental disorders are complex states that result from an interaction of biology and environment. If we accept the argument that demons are presently active, then it is likely they are involved in some cases of mental illness. Demons are involved at many levels of our existence, and it certainly isn't necessary for demonic powers to purposefully cause a given mental illness in a person for us to be able to say that they were involved in the disorder. As I said in chapter one, we are born dead in our sins, and even after we are transformed in the spirit by faith, we still live in a body and have a mind that is corrupted by original sin. Satan was involved in that corruption (Genesis 3:13). The world in which we live is demonic. I can say that because I know that Satan is "the ruler of this world," and anything related to the world system has been tainted by his presence (John 12:31; 2 Corinthians 4:4).

---

[1] T. Craig Isaacs, "The Possessive States Disorder: The Diagnosis of Demonic Possession," *Pastoral Psychology* 35 (1987): 263-73.

All mental disorders result from the interaction of biological and environmental factors. We have a biology that is broken because of sin, and we live in an environment infected by the evil one. From this perspective the demonic is involved in all illness, including mental illness, at some level, and that reality may be why the Gospel authors so blurred the lines between natural illness and demonic infirmity.

## Encountering the Demonic

Melissa, a mature believer and a longtime friend of my wife's family, recently told me the story of a demonic encounter she had many years ago. She and her family moved to Denver from Chicago, and not knowing many people Melissa and her husband joined a Saturday night couples' card group. Through that group they became acquainted with Bill and Cindy.

Late one stormy evening, Melissa received a frantic phone call from Bill: "Cindy has gone crazy! She is running up and down the street in the rain, screaming! Can you come over?"

Melissa suspected that Bill called her because they had recently talked about a new women's Bible study Melissa had started. She quickly drove over to the house. The scene was just as Bill had described it. Cindy, wearing only her underwear, was running around in the street, screaming and yelling in the rain. All attempts to get her to come inside were ignored, so Bill grabbed his wife and carried her into the house against her will. He then restrained her in a large chair in the living room. Cindy's eyes were glazed over, and her face was contorted into an angry scowl as she struggled to get free. Melissa tried to talk to Cindy, but Cindy just ignored her. Suddenly Cindy yelled out, "This whole God thing is crazy!"

Melissa told Cindy she was going to pray for her, which brought another angry response. "No prayer! Don't pray for me!"

While Bill continued to hold Cindy down in the chair, Melissa began to pray. Cindy maintained her angry outburst. "I hate my mother!" she yelled. "I'm mad at God. I wanted a baby, and I never got a baby!"

Melissa kept praying, asking in Jesus' name that Cindy would be set free from her bondage. After about fifteen minutes of Melissa praying, Cindy went suddenly and completely limp in the chair. As she began to come around, she looked at Melissa as if she hadn't seen her before. Cindy asked, "Why am I all wet?"

Melissa recounted that Cindy was like a different person. Slowly she remembered some but not all of what had occurred. Cindy was never able to explain what had happened to her. She was not a Christian at the time, and Melissa believes that she was under some type of demonic oppression or perhaps possession. Cindy subsequently accepted Christ and became active in ministry. She had never had a similar experience before that night, and she never had one again. Melissa said she really didn't know what she was doing when she started to pray for Cindy. "All I knew was that Jesus has authority over the powers of darkness, and in him I have that same authority. So that is how I prayed."

## A Biblical Response to the Demonic

The Scriptures are quite clear on how we are to respond to the demonic powers. We are to pray, submit ourselves to God, and resist (stand against) the devil. We are unable to stand against Satan in our own strength, but our response to the demonic is based on one absolute truth: God is sovereign. Through prayer we are able to draw near to God and build an intimate relationship with him (Mark 9:29; Luke 22:40; 2 Corinthians 12:8-9; James 5:13-16). Through submission we recognize that we are unable to accomplish anything apart from him (John 15:5). He is our very life, and through submission we allow his indwelling Spirit to transform our mind and body.

In their writings, Paul, James, and Peter call us to resist or stand against the devil (Ephesians 6:10-17; James 4:7; 1 Peter 5:8-9). That stand is taken by faith through submission to God. Paul tells us that we will be able to stand by putting on the full armor of God: truth, righteousness, peace, faith, salvation, and the Word. Only by living our life *in Christ* are we able to stand against the devil, because Jesus is the truth (John 14:6), our righteousness (2 Corinthians 5:21), the Prince of Peace (Isaiah 9:6), the pioneer and perfecter of our faith (Hebrews 12:2), the author of our salvation (Hebrews 2:10), and the Word made flesh (John 1:14).

Does a biblical response always result in healing from demonic powers? We can use Paul's thorn as an example. Paul prayed three times and asked God to heal him, and the divine sovereign of the universe chose not to remove the thorn. Instead, he willed that the thorn be used to manifest Christ's power in Paul's life and to mature his faith (2 Corinthians 12:7-10). Our response to the demonic is simply to pray, submit to God, and stand in Christ. Whether God chooses to heal us or to supply us with sustaining grace, we can rest in knowing he is sovereign over all things (including demons) and he cares for us.

# 3

# THE SECULAR AND
# THE SACRED

*There is nothing so secular that it cannot be sacred, and
that is one of the deepest messages of the Incarnation.*

MADELEINE L'ENGLE

IN TODAY'S SOCIETY we use psychological terms and phrases very casually. We talk about self-esteem, hyperactive behavior, and dysfunctional families. When we are sad, we say that we are depressed; when we are stressed or worried, we imply that we have an anxiety disorder. Psychiatric medications are regularly prescribed by family physicians for what some would say are normal changes in mood, leading many to wonder what a mental illness really is.

In psychology and psychiatry, we define a mental illness as a clinically significant disruption of a person's *thoughts, moods, behavior,* or *ability to relate to others*, severe enough to require treatment or intervention. While many people will have significant changes in their thoughts, emotions, and relationships during a normal lifetime, those changes are usually not severe enough to require treatment or intervention. A mental illness, on the other hand, is a debilitating experience in which the person is simply unable to function normally over an extended period of time. Given the broad definition, one might wonder exactly how a person is diagnosed with a specific mental disorder such as schizophrenia.

For the purposes of diagnosis and treatment, mental disorders have been categorized into groups according to their common symptoms in the *Diagnostic and Statistical Manual of Mental Disorders*, fifth edition (DSM-5), published by the American Psychiatric Association. Within the DSM-5 there are nineteen primary diagnostic categories. Some categories contain large numbers of disorders, while others contain few.

The following are the primary diagnostic categories of DSM-5:

- neurodevelopmental disorders (e.g., autism spectrum disorder)
- schizophrenia spectrum and other psychotic disorders
- bipolar and related disorders
- depressive disorders
- anxiety disorders (e.g., panic disorder)
- obsessive-compulsive and related disorders
- trauma- and stressor-related disorders (e.g., posttraumatic stress disorder)
- dissociative disorders (e.g., dissociative identity disorder)
- somatic symptom and related disorders (e.g., conversion disorder)
- feeding and eating disorders (e.g., anorexia nervosa)
- elimination disorders (e.g., enuresis)
- sleep-wake disorders (e.g., narcolepsy)
- sexual dysfunctions (e.g., erectile disorder)

- gender dysphoria
- disruptive, impulsive-control, and conduct disorders (e.g., kleptomania)
- substance-related and addictive disorders
- neurocognitive disorders (e.g., delirium)
- personality disorders (e.g., borderline personality disorder)
- paraphilic disorders (e.g., pedophilia)

Within each category, the criteria are listed that must be present for a person to be diagnosed with a specific mental disorder (e.g., major depressive disorder). The decision by a mental health professional to diagnose a person as suffering from a mental illness is not a subjective one but rather is based on the presence of observable mood, behavioral, and cognitive criteria described in the DSM-5. The specific criteria for many of these disorders will be outlined in later chapters.

## What Causes Mental Disorders?

Mental disorders result from a complex interaction of biological (nature) and environmental (nurture) factors. All people are born with differing degrees of biological vulnerabilities or predispositions for developing mental health difficulties and disorders. Some individuals have a greater set of biological vulnerabilities than others. Having a biological predisposition toward developing a mental disorder is not enough by itself to trigger the illness. Instead, an individual's biological vulnerability must interact with stressful life events (e.g., trauma) in order to prompt the onset of the illness. The greater the underlying biological vulnerability an individual is born with, the less stress is needed to trigger the onset of the illness. Conversely, in individuals born with a smaller biological predisposition, greater life stress is required to produce the disorder. Until this critical level of life stress has been reached, people will generally function normally, and their biological vulnerability will remain hidden.

## The Bible and Madness

What we call "mental illness" today—a set of abnormal, extreme, and debilitating moods, thoughts, and behaviors—was referred to as "madness" or "insanity" in biblical times. Madness and insanity are referred to twenty-seven times in the Bible (nineteen times in the Old Testament, eight times in the New Testament) and seven times in the deuterocanonical books.[1] Much like modern-day believers, the people of biblical times struggled with understanding the spiritual aspects of mental illness. The ancient Hebrews knew that God had promised madness as one of the possible divine punishments for not obeying his commands (Deuteronomy 28:28; Zechariah 12:4), but they struggled with differentiating madness as a result of divine punishment and madness as a result of natural causes. So individuals deemed mad or insane were generally seen as unrighteous and suffering under divine punishment.

In the Old Testament, two Hebrew words are most often used to identify this condition, *šaga'* and *hālal*. In 1 Samuel 21:12-15, these words are used interchangeably to describe David's behavior before King Achish.

David took these words to heart and greatly feared Achish king of Gath. So he disguised his sanity before them, and

---

[1]The deuterocanonical books are a set of ancient texts that primarily describe events that took place in the period between the Old and New Testaments. These writings are considered part of the biblical canon by some denominations of Christianity. The word *deuterocanonical* means "second canon."

acted insanely [*ḥālal*] in their hands, and scribbled on the doors of the gate, and let his saliva run down into his beard. Then Achish said to his servants, "Behold, you see the man behaving as a madman [*šāgaʿ*]. Why do you bring him to me? Do I lack madmen [*šāgaʿ*], that you have brought this one to act the madman [*šāgaʿ*] in my presence? Shall this one come into my house?"

David feigned madness in the presence of King Achish so he would not be harmed by the Philistines. King Achish did not consider a person with mental illness a threat, and thus David was able to escape. These verses show us that individuals with mental illness were so common in Old Testament times that a person could mimic abnormal thoughts and behaviors, and others would easily recognize the general condition.

In the New Testament, the Greek word *mainomai*, the origin for the English word *maniac*, is used to describe this same condition. By Jesus' time, insanity was still thought to be primarily spiritual in nature but was more closely associated with the work of demons than divine punishment. We see this illustrated in John 10:20, where Jesus is accused of having a demon and being insane (*mainomai*). The clear implication here is that the people of Jesus' time believed demonic possession to be at least one, and likely the primary, cause of insanity.

In Acts 26:24-25, Festus, the Roman governor of Judea, called Paul "mad" when Paul described Jesus' death and resurrection.

While *Paul* was saying this in his defense, Festus said in a loud voice, "Paul, you are out of your mind [*mainomai*]! Your great learning is driving you mad [*mainomai*]." But Paul said, "I am not out of my mind [*mainomai*], most excellent Festus, but I utter words of sober truth."

Today Festus's response to Paul would be equivalent to calling someone "crazy" or saying "you're nuts," both of which are negative references to the mentally ill.

Individuals displaying abnormal moods, thoughts, and behaviors—the mentally ill—were clearly known throughout biblical history. Today those same abnormal thoughts and behaviors have been categorized into a set of specific mental disorders for which many effective interventions and treatments have been developed. Mental health research and practice have made significant strides in relieving the mental and physical suffering of those afflicted with mental illness. Yet there continues to be a high level of suspicion, distrust, and even fear in the church when it comes to psychology and psychiatry. The simple fact is that Christians develop mental illness at the same rates seen in the general population,[2] and admonitions such as "You need to pray more" or "This is just the result of a lack of faith" are ineffective in dealing with this problem.

### How the Mentally Ill Were Viewed in Biblical Times

The people of the Bible were culturally and religiously very different from modern-day believers. Lacking knowledge of science and the functions of the brain, they struggled to understand the strange and extreme behaviors displayed by individuals they referred to as mad or insane. Despite the enormous differences between biblical times and today, the views of modern believers toward those living with mental illness are, unfortunately, quite similar to their biblical counterparts.

For example, we commonly use derogatory terms such as *crazy*, *nuts*, and *retard* in our everyday language. These terms express contempt and disrespect toward individuals living with mental health

---

[2]Edward B. Rogers et al., "The Defects of Mental Illness on Families Within Faith Communities," *Mental Health, Religion and Culture* 15 (2012): 301-13.

difficulties even if we are not speaking directly to them. Two pejorative references to mental illness appear in the Bible. These include the one attributed to the Roman governor Festus (Acts 26:24-25) and another in Acts 12:15, where the slave girl Rhoda is said to be "out of your mind" when she says the imprisoned Peter is knocking on the door. These examples suggest that the mentally ill of biblical times were shamed and stigmatized because of their illnesses much like they are today.

Prior to the advent of effective treatments for mental illness, individuals suffering from these conditions were often physically restrained out of fear or to keep them from harming themselves or others. We see two references of this in the Scriptures. Jeremiah 29:26 suggests that madmen be controlled with stocks and iron collars, while the story of the Gadarene demoniac (Mark 5:1-20) describes a demonically afflicted mentally ill individual who had been bound for a time with shackles and chains. While it is true that today in many parts of the world the mentally ill are treated humanely, this is more of a recent occurrence and is not true everywhere. In many countries the mentally ill are still either physically restrained by their families with ropes or chains, or warehoused in asylums. I have personally toured the asylums of northern Africa, where the mentally ill live in unairconditioned concrete block rooms and blankly stare at you from behind iron bars. Prior to the 1960s and deinstitutionalization, it wasn't much different in the United States.

## Scientific Fact and Biblical Truth

Before going any further, I would like to clarify that God's revealed Word—not science or the DSM-5—is the final authority on truth. Through the Scriptures the Holy Spirit reveals to us the character of God, human nature, the consequences of sin, our redemptive history, and the humanity and divinity of Christ, who is the way, the *truth*, and the life. The Scriptures teach us who God is and who we are, but their purpose is not to give us *all* factual truth. For instance, they don't tell us how our heart or liver work. While the truths of the Scriptures go beyond the theological (e.g., to include historical facts), the Bible, as a colleague of mine once accurately but flippantly said, "is not a science book, nor is it a manual on how to fix your car." The Bible was never meant to be an encyclopedia of all factual knowledge, but it does instruct us in the most important of truths: there is a God who loves us completely and who sacrificed himself for us.

St. Augustine said, "All truth is God's truth." This statement has often been misused and abused by those who would hold human "truth" to be equal with God's. What Augustine meant was that the way my heart functions, the process by which a seed grows into a mature plant, and the fact that the earth is in an elliptical orbit around the sun are all truths based in the creative power and majesty of God. Romans 1:20 says, "Since the creation of the world His invisible attributes, His eternal power and divine nature, have been clearly seen, being understood through what has been made." God's majesty is reflected in how our brain cells function, the biological and environmental factors that affect the formation of our personalities, the mechanism by which memories are brought to our minds, and the precise balance of brain chemicals that are the foundation of our thoughts and behaviors. So we must be like the Bereans, ever examining the Scriptures (Acts 17:11) as we look at the interplay between psychology/psychiatry and faith.

## *Psychiatry*

While both priests and physicians have struggled to care for individuals with "madness" since the beginning of civilization, psychiatry as a medical discipline is actually quite young. In 1808 the German physician Johann Christian Reil coined the term *psychiatry*, which means the "medical treatment of the soul." As was true of much of medicine at the time, treatments were undeveloped, harsh, and generally ineffective. For most of the first century of its existence, psychiatry concerned itself with severely disordered individuals confined to asylums or hospitals.

A significant change occurred in psychiatry at the beginning of the twentieth century. Sigmund Freud's development of psychoanalytic psychotherapy for the first time gave psychiatrists a treatment to use with mentally ill individuals functioning well enough not to be institutionalized, giving birth to outpatient psychiatry. The later 1950s saw the second major change in psychiatric treatment with the development of psychoactive medications. For the first time an effective treatment was available for the most severely ill institutionalized patients. As a result, state mental hospitals rapidly emptied as medicated patients returned to the community. Today we refer to this event, which occurred primarily in the 1960s and 1970s, as deinstitutionalization.

Until the 1990s all psychiatrists were trained in talk therapy (psychotherapy) as well as the prescribing of psychiatric medications to treat mental disorders. Today, due to advances in neuroscience and the massive proliferation of medications, psychiatric training focuses on understanding how the brain works and prescribing medications to treat mental disorders. Few psychiatrists are still trained to use psychotherapy in their practices. However, research has shown that in the treatment of mental disorders often the best course of action is a combination of medication and psychotherapy. That is why a team approach to treatment that includes both a psychiatrist and a clinical psychologist is so important.

## Clinical Psychology

Clinical psychology can be defined as a field of practice and research that applies psychological principles to the assessment, treatment, and prevention of psychological distress and dysfunctional behavior. Clinical psychologists also work to enhance psychological and physical well-being. The basic mission of clinical psychology is to help people live healthier lives.

Clinical psychologists treat clients who have mental illness or struggle with psychological problems by using some form of talking therapy, generally referred to as psychotherapy. Psychotherapy can be done by many different types of mental health professionals, including clinical psychologists (those with a doctoral degree: PhD or PsyD), or therapists such as clinical social workers (LCSW) and licensed counselors (LPC, LMFT).[3]

During treatment the client and therapist meet regularly in private sessions to talk about concerns and issues related to the client's disorder or problems. More than just a free-flowing discussion, the therapy is guided by the theory and goals associated with the specific psychotherapeutic approach used. There are numerous approaches a psychotherapist can take. Most therapists are trained in several forms of therapy, but typically concentrate on one in their daily practice. The following are descriptions of what are often considered the four most common approaches to psychotherapy.

*Humanistic-existential approach.* In this approach psychological problems are believed to result from an incongruence between the self-concept (how one sees oneself) and the ideal self (how one

---

[3]Common graduate degrees related to clinical psychology include doctor of philosophy (PhD), doctor of clinical psychology (PsyD), licensed clinical social worker (LCSW), licensed professional counselor (LPC), and licensed marriage and family therapist (LMFT).

would like to be). The effects of the client's past, present, and future experiences and influences are given equal emphasis. This approach is nondirective, giving the client the opportunity to discover their own problems and to make choices to correct them. The self-healing capacities of the client are emphasized. The therapeutic relationship in this model is seen as an authentic meeting of equals.

*Cognitive-behavioral approach.* In this approach psychological and emotional problems are believed to result from the client's negative thought patterns and behaviors. The major aim of the therapy is to help the client eliminate negative beliefs or behaviors and replace them with positive ones. Symptom reduction is seen as an end in itself. Understanding the underlying cause of the problem is either secondary or irrelevant. This approach is extremely directive, focusing on things that can be measured and observed (e.g., behavior, reported mood), and avoids theoretical abstractions and speculations.

*Psychoanalytic approach.* Also called psychodynamic therapy, this type of treatment helps a person look within to discover and understand emotional conflicts that may be contributing to emotional problems. The therapist helps the client uncover unconscious motivations—unresolved problems from the past, particularly childhood—in order to resolve present issues by becoming aware of how those motivations influence current actions and feelings. In this nondirective approach the therapist may say very little but instead will listen, occasionally reformulating or interpreting what is reported by the patient. The underlying belief is that the patient, through a process of free association and given enough time, will stumble upon what is important. This is a lengthy process, typically taking several years.

*Integrative approach.* Many clinical psychologists and therapists do not tie themselves exclusively to any one approach. Instead, they blend elements from different psychotherapeutic approaches and adapt the treatment according to the client's needs.

## Christians and Psychotherapy

A Christian who seeks out a therapist for help with a mental illness or psychological problem must remember that the ultimate goal of psychotherapy is to change one's thoughts and behaviors. Psychotherapy comes into conflict with the Scriptures most often as a result of the personal beliefs of the therapist. A study by two research psychologists found that a therapist's personal religious beliefs affected the psychotherapeutic approach they chose to practice. Therapists who held to more Eastern or mystical beliefs tended to take a humanistic-existential approach. This is easy to understand, since this approach emphasizes self-healing. Therapists with conservative Christian beliefs were more likely to practice cognitive-behavioral therapy, while those who used a psychoanalytic approach were best described as nonreligious.[4] So although the type of therapy a client receives is important, the more important factor is the personal religious beliefs held by the therapist.

As the study indicates, therapists' personal religious beliefs affect the type of therapy they practice. If a therapist is not a Christian, it is likely that their beliefs concerning faith will be contrary to Scripture, and they will not be able to recognize that true change is grounded in Christ. I recommend that a Christian seeking therapy find a therapist who shares their same faith. I'm not saying that Christians should go only to therapists who designate themselves as a Christian counselor. Whether the therapist overtly integrates biblical principles into their particular psychotherapeutic

---

[4]Dyer P. Bilgrave and Robert H. Deluty, "Religious Beliefs and Political Ideologies as Predictors of Psychotherapeutic Orientations of Clinical Counseling Psychologists," *Psychotherapy: Theory, Research, Practice and Training* 3 (2002): 245-60.

approach is not the most important criteria for choosing a psychologist. It *is* important that the therapist be sensitive to the spiritual issues that may be part of the recovery process and that they guide the client down a pathway of change in line with God's Word.

# 4

# A CAKE OF FIGS

*When I was looking to God to heal me, my pastor explained that healing from God can come in the form of doctors and medication. She has taken me to the hospital when I required inpatient care, and has been there to support me and remind me of God's enduring love and lasting grace when I was feeling poorly.*

JANET, DIAGNOSED WITH SCHIZOPHRENIA

WHEN PEOPLE I MEET find out I am a clinical neuroscientist, they often ask me questions about the brain and mental illness. It is a topic almost everyone is interested in, and I of course love to talk about what I do. Science is cool! I have been asked all kinds of questions, such as "Is it true that we only use 10 percent of our brain?" and "What causes a person to be a serial killer?" A common question I am asked by people of faith is "Should a Christian take psychiatric medication to treat a mental problem?" I have found over the years that when people ask that question they actually are interested in knowing two things: (1) Are mental disorders real illnesses with a biological basis? and (2) Does the use of medication to treat a mental disorder show a lack of faith in the healing power of God?

Now you may be saying to yourself, *This really can't be a contro-versy. Medications are helpful; they relieve suffering. Only an extremist would believe that you shouldn't take medication for a mental illness.* But I can assure you this is a serious matter in the church that impacts mentally ill believers and their families every day.

In an online survey I conducted of nearly three hundred Christians who are mentally ill or who have a family member who is mentally ill, approximately 25 percent said their church either discourages or forbids the use of psychiatric medications.[1] That percentage equals one out of every four churches. Think how many people that affects! Some of my own friends have been told by their pastor that they did not need to take medication for illnesses such as bipolar disorder. This is a serious and potentially life-threatening issue we as the body of Christ must come to terms with.

What is the answer? Should a Christian take medication to treat a mental illness? To answer this question, let's begin by looking at the biology of behavior.

## *The Brain and Behavior*

Made up of billions of individual neurons and weighing about three pounds, the human brain is an amazing example of God's creative power and genius. Our brains are similar in many ways to other organs in our bodies. All of our organs, including the brain, require nutrients and oxygen from our blood. Like the heart, many of the brain's functions are electrical in nature. Similar to the liver, the brain is sensitized to being damaged by environmental toxins and addictive substances such as alcohol.

But while similar in many respects, the brain is also quite different from our other organs. Neuroscientists, myself included,

---

[1]Matthew S. Stanford, "Demon or Disorder: A Survey of Attitudes Toward Mental Illness in the Christian Church," *Mental Health, Religion & Culture* 10 (2007): 445-49.

have barely scratched the surface in our attempts to understand its complexity. It is, in a very real sense, the master organ, controlling our physiology (e.g., heart rate, respiration) and producing our thoughts and feelings. I can understand how people may think of the brain in a much different way than they think of the stomach or pancreas. There is an immaterial aspect to the brain that is difficult to comprehend.

As I discussed in the first chapter, it is in the brain that our physical self interacts with our immaterial or nonphysical self (mind and spirit). Far too often in the Christian community we have ignored or minimized how our biological processes influence our behavior. We have wrongly defined behavior as having solely an immaterial origin. This misunderstanding tends to be where the controversy around treating mental illness begins.

To better understand the biological aspects of our behavior, let me use an example of a disorder that we will all agree has a solely biological origin: Alzheimer's disease. Alzheimer's disease (AD) is not a mental illness; it is a neurodegenerative disorder. A neurodegenerative disorder results from the deterioration of cells in the brain. Common neurodegenerative disorders include Parkinson's disease, multiple sclerosis, and Huntington's chorea. AD is characterized by multiple cognitive deficits that include memory loss, language disturbances, impaired movement, and problems with planning, organization, and abstracting. In addition, patients with AD may show behavioral disturbances such as restlessness and mood swings.

While presently there is no specific test for AD, it is thought to result from an accumulation of abnormal clumps (amyloid plaques) and tangled bundles of neural fibers (neurofibrillary tangles) composed of misplaced proteins in the brain. These neurological abnormalities appear to be a common byproduct of normal aging and are present in the brains of all elderly people. In patients with AD, however, there is a significantly higher concentration of them, suggesting that they may be related to the cognitive decline seen in these individuals. Unfortunately, these plaques and tangles can only be identified postmortem via an autopsy, so it is impossible to know with 100 percent certainty that the cognitive decline or dementia seen in an elderly person is caused by Alzheimer's disease until after they have died.

So why am I writing about AD if it isn't a mental illness? Because no one tells an AD patient that there is no such thing as AD or that they shouldn't take medication to slow the progression of the disease. We all recognize that AD causes physical damage to the brain, which in turn results in changes to thoughts, feelings, and actions. The same could be said about stroke, a traumatic brain injury, or a brain tumor. All result from physical damage to the brain, causing changes in behavior. Argued from the example of neurodegenerative diseases, it is obvious that brain functioning and behavior are intimately associated. Therefore, what about mental illnesses? Why are they often seen as so different by people of faith?

## Is Mental Illness a Real Illness?

In my experience I have found that there are five common reasons why people in the Christian community tend to deny the legitimacy of mental disorders and attribute the abnormal thoughts and actions of the mentally ill to sin or a lack of faith.

**Denying the legitimacy of mental disorders.** The following are common reasons Christians deny the legitimacy of mental disorders.

- No specific medical tests exist to diagnose an individual with a given mental disorder.

- There does not seem to be consistency in diagnoses across individuals.

- Psychiatric medications are not always effective in treating mental disorders.

- Not all abnormal behavior is the result of a brain disorder.

- Psychiatry and psychology are secular by nature and legitimize sinful behavior.

Let's look at these concerns individually. The first is the belief that no specific medical tests exist that can diagnose an individual with a given mental disorder. In other words, there is no brain blood pressure or mental blood test that can tell us a person has, for instance, major depressive disorder. Some in the Christian community have said there are no such things as chemical imbalances or neuroanatomical abnormalities among psychiatric diagnoses. This is simply not true.

While it is true that presently we do not have a blood test or brain scan specific enough to be used on individual patients for diagnosis, a number of chemical imbalances and neuroanatomical abnormalities have been shown to contribute to mental disorders. These will be discussed in detail in later chapters. In fact, as I stated earlier, the same could be said of the neurodegenerative disorders Alzheimer's and Parkinson's, but these clearly have a biological origin. The lack of a medical test for a disorder is not evidence the disorder does not exist. Mental disorders and traditional medical diseases are diagnosed in a very similar manner, using a set of scientifically derived symptoms or criteria. Blood tests and brain scans are often used to rule out potential causes of the mental illness (e.g., infection, brain tumor, epilepsy). Psychiatry and psychology aren't voodoo; they are science. And science insists on verifiable data. That being said, even science can be abused and misused, so the accuracy of the diagnosis will always be contingent on the quality and training of the mental health care provider.

A second reason people of faith tend to deny the legitimacy of mental disorders is that a diagnosis in one person may look very different from the same diagnosis in another. In other words, there does not seem to be consistency in diagnoses across individuals. Given the variability between people in physiology and environment, there can also be variability in how a particular disorder may manifest itself. This occurs not only in psychiatric disorders but also in traditional medical diseases. However, no matter how variable the manifested behaviors and thoughts may seem, the core features of the disorder will always be present.

A third reason people of faith tend to deny the legitimacy of mental disorders is that psychiatric medications do not always seem to be effective in treating them. In fact, prescribing psychiatric medications often appears to be a guessing game, with the patient trying a large number of medications before an effective treatment is found. Like many traditional medical problems, a given mental disorder may have a number of potential causes. The vast complexity of the brain makes it possible for a disorder to result from an imbalance in a single neurotransmitter or a combination of several. Thus disorders such as depression, anxiety, and psychosis are better thought of as general categories, each describing a number of underlying subdisorders with a common set of core symptoms. These variables make tailoring treatment to the individual patient necessary.

Another cause of this apparent ineffectiveness in treatment is related to the problem of overprescribing. Given present societal trends and the direct marketing practices of pharmaceutical companies, many people experiencing minor mood changes seek psychiatric medication from their regular physician. This has led to massive overprescribing of antidepressants, especially to women, for brief periods of sadness and of psychostimulants to poorly behaved, noncompliant children. The overuse of medications is not a problem unique to psychiatry. Two decades of overprescribing antibiotics to children for nonbacterial infections has led to an increased drug resistance in certain illnesses.[2] This problem is again related to the quality and training of the mental health professional. A *quality* assessment leads to an *accurate* diagnosis that results in an *effective* treatment, whether it is for an ear infection or bipolar disorder.

A fourth reason people of faith tend to deny the legitimacy of mental disorders is that not all abnormal behavior is the result of a brain disorder. And this is true. A person can learn to think and behave abnormally with a perfectly normal brain. For example, children exposed to abuse or high-stress environments (e.g., poverty, high crime) have higher rates of psychological problems later in life. Our brains are designed to adapt our thoughts and behaviors to our environment, so sometimes exposure to bad environments results in the development of what we consider a mental illness. The bias of the current approach to mental disorders, or what some would call the medical model, insists that all mental illnesses are brain diseases that must be treated with medication. But I would say that if wrong behavior can be learned, it can also be unlearned, and appropriate psychological treatment can play an important role. Again, the origin of the problem (i.e., learned or biological) does not dismiss the fact that it is a serious problem that must be addressed.

A fifth and final reason I believe Christians tend to deny the legitimacy of mental disorders is they are concerned that the

---

[2]Linda F. McCaig, Richard E. Besser, and James M. Hughes, "Trends in Antimicrobial Prescribing Rates for Children and Adolescents," *Journal of the American Medical Association* 287 (2002): 3096-102.

designation "mental illness" is simply another tool the world uses to dismiss or legitimize sinful behavior. Although I believe this is a legitimate concern, we need to be careful to separate sin from illness. It is not a sin to be ill, even mentally ill. On the other hand, mental illness, whether it is a learned pattern of abnormal thinking or a biological disorder, does not dismiss sinful behavior (Leviticus 5:17).

In summary, the concerns Christians have about mental disorders vary from the incorrect to the legitimate. Mental disorders are indeed real illnesses that in many instances have a biological origin. Science's limited understanding of the causes of these disorders is not a reason to dismiss their existence. And Christians must always allow Scripture, not the world, to define what is sinful, whether in their own lives or in the lives of others.

## *The Sovereignty of God*

Now to the second question we began this chapter with: Does the use of medication to treat a mental disorder show a lack of faith in the healing power of God? I would say this is no more the case than using insulin for diabetes minimizes God's sovereignty. And isn't the sovereignty of God what we are really talking about? Is God in control of all things, or can a physical remedy somehow override his authority? Who is the ultimate agent of healing—God or medicine? The Scriptures are full of examples of God using physical remedies to heal illness in his people. Let's look at a few.

You may have wondered about the title of this chapter: "A Cake of Figs." It comes from one of my favorite stories in the Bible, the story of King Hezekiah's illness and recovery (2 Kings 20:1-7; Isaiah 38:1-22). Hezekiah was one of Judah's greatest kings, perhaps second only to the great King David himself. He became king of Judah at the age of twenty-five, after the death of his evil father,

Ahaz. Hezekiah inherited a kingdom far from the Lord, filled with idolatry and pagan religious practices, but he changed all that. The Scriptures tell us that he removed pagan worship from the land and did what was right in the sight of the Lord (2 Kings 18:3-4). Although he had moments throughout his reign when he doubted God's faithfulness, 2 Kings 18:5 tells us that no king of Judah, before or after, trusted the Lord like he did. He was truly God's humble servant.

At the age of about thirty-nine Hezekiah became very sick with some type of boil or skin ulcer. The Bible tells us he was "mortally ill," at the point of death. God sent the prophet Isaiah to tell Hezekiah to "set [his] house in order" because he was going to die. As Isaiah was leaving, Hezekiah prayed a very simple and beautiful prayer in which he reminded God of how he had been faithful to God's ways. Before Isaiah left the palace, God told him to return to Hezekiah and tell him he would extend Hezekiah's life by fifteen years. Then Isaiah instructed those attending the king to put a cake of figs on his boil, and Hezekiah recovered.

A cake of figs, or what some translations refer to as a poultice of figs, was a hot, soft mass of figs and other ingredients commonly used in ancient times to treat lesions and infections of the skin. What I find so interesting about this story is that God used a common treatment of the day, a physical remedy, to bring about Hezekiah's recovery. God healed Hezekiah; the cake of figs was merely the means by which God extended his healing grace.

The New Testament tells us that Jesus used a very unconventional physical remedy to bring healing on three occasions. He healed three different men by applying his own saliva to their damaged eyes, ears, or tongue (Mark 7:32-35; 8:22-25; John 9:1-7). Why did he use spit in these instances, when he typically spoke and the person was healed?

The Talmud, an ancient record of Jewish laws and traditions, says the spittle of the firstborn son has healing powers. Now you and I know, as Jesus knew, that saliva from a firstborn son does not heal blindness, deafness, or mutism, but the tradition of the day held that it could. Perhaps Jesus used a physical treatment in these instances as a faith-building tool. What I do know is that Jesus the Messiah healed these men, and he chose to do it using a common remedy of the day.

So what is my point? Should we start using figs and spit as treatments for modern illnesses? No, of course not. But we should recognize that God is sovereign in all things, including healing. He created a part of us to be biological, and he can choose to remedy problems in that part through biological treatments if he wills. Taking medication for any illness is simply making wise use of the abundant resources provided to us by a loving God (Ezekiel 47:12). He is the almighty God of the universe who made us, saved us, and sustains us (Colossians 1:16-17). As people of faith, we must always remember that God is the ultimate agent of healing, and we should turn to him in times of illness (2 Chronicles 16:12).

## Ultimate Healing

Have I convinced you? Mental illnesses are real disorders that have their origins in faulty biological processes. The Bible even supports this by listing madness along with physical problems like boils, tumors, scabs, and blindness (Deuteronomy 28:27-28). Mental disorders do not discriminate according to faith, but rather affect believers and nonbelievers alike. While God is always the ultimate agent of healing, he may choose to use physical remedies, including medication, to bring about recovery. And in those times when healing is not part of his plan, we can rest in the fact that he will provide the endurance and perseverance necessary to perfect and complete our faith (James 1:2-4).

Those of us who know Christ as Savior were once the recipients of a physical remedy for a terminal illness from which we had no hope of recovery. There was simply no other way we could be healed except through a perfect physical sacrifice. The illness was sin, and the physical remedy was God incarnate, Jesus Christ. As we walk alongside our brothers and sisters suffering from mental illness, let us draw on the grace that we as followers of Christ have received, so that we might be a healing presence in their lives.

# MENTAL
# DISORDERS

# 5

# A LOST MIND

## Schizophrenia Spectrum and Other Psychotic Disorders

*I do not know what we would do without the Lord and his people. They have strengthened us and helped carry this incredible burden. They have made us see that our child can be used mightily by God to reach others that no one else without a mental illness could possibly reach.*

Jennifer, mother of a son diagnosed with schizophrenia

To people in her small Texas town, Jillian was the All-American girl everyone wished to be. Led to Christ by her grandfather at the age of six, she remembers always being involved in the church. A straight-A student who enjoyed competing in beauty pageants, she hoped to attend the same Christian college as her older sister. At home, however, not everything was as it appeared. Conflict in her parents' marriage and the traumatic effects of childhood sexual abuse had set the stage for mental health difficulties to come. After graduating from high school, Jillian moved away from home for the first time to attend college. It wasn't long before she recognized that something was wrong. She lacked motivation; everything was an effort. She was depressed and avoided people. In addition, her grades were not at her usual level of achievement. She started restricting when and what she ate, and became obsessed with exercise. Her college friends voiced their concerns to her. The second semester of her freshman year was even worse. Her depression deepened, her grades dropped further, and her problems with food increased. She says, "I felt like I was falling apart." A hoped-for rest during the summer was replaced by a rollercoaster of emotional highs and lows. Her parents suggested that she transfer to the local college so she could live at home and go to school. The move changed nothing; she continued to struggle.

The voices started in the spring. By July she was sitting in her room at home motionless and unable to respond to questions from her family. That month she was hospitalized for the first time. Eight days in the psychiatric hospital brought a diagnosis of schizoaffective disorder. After being discharged, Jillian admits she wasn't compliant with taking her medication over the next several months. "I didn't think I really needed it." By the fall, she had lost so much weight that she had to spend four months at a facility that specialized in eating disorders. After leaving the eating-disorder facility, she finally felt like things were on the right track. Her eating problems were under control, and she was not experiencing voices due to her daily medication. She moved back in with her parents, found a part-time job and began attending an intensive discipleship-training program at her church. It was several months later, just before she left on a short-term mission trip to Tunisia, that she noticed the voices starting to return. Several months passed; the voices intensified.

The stress of her first serious romantic relationship, the pain of working through her childhood sexual abuse in therapy, and not taking her medication regularly were the perfect storm that threw her into a delusional state. She found herself hospitalized once again. After two weeks she was discharged. The next few months were some of the most difficult as her psychiatrist worked to find the right mix of medication to manage her symptoms. The emotional highs and lows, suicidal thoughts, auditory hallucinations and delusions finally ended. That was three years ago.

Today Jillian is finishing up college and expects to graduate this year. She takes medication daily and receives regular psychotherapy. She told me her illness has strengthened her faith.

During the difficult times I did ask God, "Why do I have to go through this?" He simply told me, "I haven't asked you to understand why, but I love you and I'm with you." That's when I really started believing God was with me in the struggle. This illness has taught me that I don't have to have it all together for God. I can rely on him to get me through. My disorder drives me to God; it has caused me to be more dependent on him.

## Characteristic Symptoms

The symptoms of the schizophrenia spectrum disorders fall into two broad categories: positive and negative. Positive symptoms are abnormal thoughts, perceptions, and behaviors that most individuals do not normally experience. These include delusions, hallucinations, disorganized thinking, and grossly disorganized behavior.

**Delusions.** Delusions are strongly held false beliefs despite evidence to the contrary. Several delusional themes are commonly seen in schizophrenia, including *persecution* (the belief that one is going to be harmed or harassed by another), *reference* (the belief that certain gestures, comments, or environmental cues are directed at you), *grandiosity* (the individual believes they have exceptional abilities, wealth, or fame), *erotomania* (the individual falsely believes that another person is in love with them), *jealousy* (the belief that the individual's spouse or lover is unfaithful), *nihilism* (the belief that a major catastrophe will soon occur), and *somatic issues* (preoccupation with one's health and organ function).

**Hallucinations.** Hallucinations are experiences involving the apparent perception of something not present. These experiences can occur in relation to any of the senses, but auditory hallucinations are the most common in the schizophrenia spectrum disorders. Auditory hallucinations are usually experienced as voices perceived as distinct from an individual's own thoughts.

**Disorganized thinking.** Disorganized thinking is typically recognized in the speech of the individual with schizophrenia. They may show loose associations by switching from one topic to another. Answers to questions may be tangentially related or completely unrelated. In rare instances, speech may be so severely disorganized that it is incomprehensible.

**Grossly disorganized behavior (including catatonia).** Grossly disorganized behavior may manifest itself in a variety of ways, ranging from childlike silliness to unpredictable agitation. Individuals with schizophrenia often have difficulty formulating and producing goal-directed behavior. Catatonic behavior is a marked decrease in reactivity to the environment. Individuals exhibiting catatonia appear to be completely unaware of their environment, maintain a rigid posture, and resist efforts to be moved.

**Negative symptoms.** Negative symptoms are the loss or decrease of an ability that is normally present. Common negative symptoms seen in schizophrenia include diminished emotional expression, decreased motivation (avolition), lack of speech (alogia), lack of interest in social interactions (asociality), and a decreased ability to experience pleasure from enjoyable activities and experiences (anhedonia).

## Diagnoses

The Swiss psychiatrist Eugen Bleuler introduced the term *schizophrenia* to the world of psychiatry in 1908.[1] Schizophrenia means a "splitting of the mind" and was used by Bleuler to describe a group of patients who showed a "breaking up or splitting of psychic functioning," including thoughts, feelings, and perceptions. Today individuals who show psychotic symptoms are diagnosed along a gradient, or spectrum, reflective of the duration and intensity of their disorder.[2]

***Schizotypal personality disorder.*** Schizotypal personality disorder is a pervasive pattern of social and interpersonal deficits, including reduced capacity for close relationships, cognitive or perceptual distortions, and eccentric behavior. Abnormalities of beliefs, thinking, and perception are below the threshold for the diagnosis of a psychotic disorder. This is the lowest end of the schizophrenia spectrum.

***Delusional disorder.*** Delusional disorder is characterized by at least one month of delusions but no other psychotic symptoms. If hallucinations are present, they are not prominent and are related to the delusion. Apart from the impact of the delusion or its ramifications, functioning is not markedly impaired, and the individual's behavior is not obviously bizarre or odd.

---

[1]Eugen Bleuler, "Die Prognose der Dementia praecox (Schizophreniegruppe). Allgemeine Zeitschrift für Psychiatrie und psychischgerichtliche," *Medizin* 65 (1908): 436-64.

[2]*Psychosis* is a general psychiatric term meaning "a break from reality," which is often used when describing the symptoms of schizophrenia. An individual suffering with psychosis is said to be psychotic.

***Brief psychotic disorder.*** Brief psychotic disorder is characterized by the presence of one or more of the primary symptoms of psychosis (delusions, hallucinations, disorganized thinking, and grossly disorganized behavior). The duration of the disturbance is at least one day but less than one month, with an eventual return to a normal level of functioning.

***Schizophreniform disorder.*** Schizophreniform disorder is characterized by the presence of two or more psychotic symptoms. The duration of the disturbance is at least one month but less than six months.

***Schizophrenia.*** Schizophrenia is characterized by the presence of two or more psychotic symptoms, each present for a significant portion of time during a one-month period. For a significant portion of the time since the onset of the disturbance, the individual's level of functioning in one or more major areas, such as work, interpersonal relations, or self-care is noticeably below normal. Continuous signs of the disturbance must persist for at least six months.

***Schizoaffective disorder.*** Schizoaffective disorder is characterized by the symptoms of schizophrenia as well as a major mood episode. There are two subtypes of schizoaffective disorder, bipolar and depressive. The essential feature of the bipolar subtype is the presence of a manic episode during the illness, while the depressive subtype is characterized the presence of a major depressive episode. Schizoaffective disorder is the highest and most severe end of the schizophrenia spectrum.

## Prevalence and Age of Onset

It is estimated that schizophrenia affects 0.3–0.7 percent of the population.[3] The onset of schizophrenia occurs between the late teens and early thirties. The disorder affects men and women

---

[3]Lifetime prevalence is the proportion of individuals in the population who have ever manifested a disorder and who are alive on a given day. American Psychiatric Association,

equally, although symptoms generally appear earlier in men (in their late teens or early twenties) than in women (in their late twenties or early thirties). Schizoaffective disorder appears to be less common than schizophrenia, with a lifetime prevalence estimated at 0.3 percent of the population.[4] The age of onset for schizoaffective disorder is the late teens to early twenties. Schizoaffective disorder is more common in women than men.

## Developmental and Psychosocial Risk Factors

Like all mental disorders, the schizophrenia spectrum disorders result from the cumulative effects of a number of biological, developmental, and psychosocial factors. Research has shown the following factors to be associated with a higher risk of being diagnosed with a schizophrenia spectrum disorder as an adult. Prenatal risk factors include exposure to infections (e.g., rubella, influenza), exposure to toxins (e.g., lead), malnutrition, maternal diabetes, and maternal stress. Exposure to a range of obstetric complications including prematurity, low birth weight, and hypoxia have also been shown to increase risk. Other risk factors include place of birth (higher rates in urban areas), migrant status (higher rates for migrants compared to native born), advanced paternal age, and season of birth (higher rates in those born in the late winter and early spring). Childhood risk factors include the presence of neurological soft signs, mixed handedness, physical or sexual abuse, social and cognitive abnormalities, and early cannabis abuse.[5] The

---

*Diagnostic and Statistical Manual of Mental Disorders*, 5th ed. (Washington, DC: American Psychiatric Association, 2013); hereafter DSM-5.

[4]Jonna Perala et al., "Lifetime Prevalence of Psychotic and Bipolar I Disorders in a General Population," *Archives of General Psychiatry* 64 (2007): 19-28.

[5]Alan S. Brown, "The Environment and Susceptibility to Schizophrenia," *Progress in Neurobiology* 93 (2011): 23-58; Stuart J. Leask, "Environmental Influences in Schizophrenia: The Known and the Unknown," *Advances in Psychiatric Treatment* 10 (2004): 323-30; and Colm

first episode of psychosis is often associated with a major life-changing event, such as going to college or being involved in war. This suggests that psychological stress may play a role in the onset of the disorder.

## Neurobiology

**Heritability.** There are two sources from which we can assess the heritability of a disorder: twin studies and adoption studies. In twin studies the rates of a disorder in identical and fraternal twins are examined. Identical twins develop from the same fertilized egg (monozygotic) and so they are genetically identical, whereas fraternal twins develop from two different eggs (dizygotic) and therefore are fertilized by different sperm; subsequently, they are like any traditional set of siblings and share only 50 percent of the same genes. The heritability of a disorder can be determined by looking at affected twins and determining the rate with which the other twin is also affected. If there is a higher rate of concordance in identical twins compared to fraternal twins, then we can infer that genes play a role in the disorder.

Twin studies have consistently found a higher concordance rate for schizophrenia in identical twins (approximately 48 percent of twin pairs both have schizophrenia) when compared to fraternal twins (approximately 17 percent share the disorder).[6] Adoption studies in which identical and fraternal twins are reared apart are used to control for environmental influences such as parenting style that may affect the expression of a disorder. Adoption studies looking at schizophrenia have found

McDonald and Robin M. Murray, "Early and Late Environmental Risk Factors for Schizophrenia," *Brain Research Reviews* 31 (2000): 130-37.
[6]Irving L. Gottesman, *Schizophrenia Genesis: The Origins of Madness* (New York: Freeman, 1991).

similar results suggesting a genetic contribution to the expression of schizophrenia.[7] Several studies have also shown that the risk of developing schizophrenia in family members increases with the degree of biological relatedness to an affected individual; greater risks are associated with higher levels of shared genes.[8]

**Neuroanatomy.** The schizophrenic brain is clearly and reliably different anatomically and functionally from a nonschizophrenic brain. Studies looking at the cellular structure of the brain in schizophrenics have found significant cellular disorganization. Some brain areas have too many neurons (brain cells) while other areas have too few. Neurons are oriented in the wrong direction and neural connections are misaligned.[9] These results suggest a problem in brain development beginning within the first few weeks of life. The effect of this type of disruption in the brain's neural circuitry is an inability to coordinate mental processes. Individuals with schizophrenia also have a reduced volume of gray matter in the brain, especially in the temporal and frontal lobes. This reduction in gray matter is progressive throughout the disorder, with patients losing approximately 5 percent per year. Research has shown that

[7]Irving L. Gottesman and James Shields, *Schizophrenia: The Epigenetic Puzzle* (New York: Cambridge University Press, 1982).

[8]The lifetime risk of developing schizophrenia in the general population is about 0.5 percent. If your first cousin (with whom you share 12.5 percent of your genes) has schizophrenia, then your risk increases to 2 percent; if your half sibling (with whom you share 25 percent of your genes) has schizophrenia, your risk increases to 6 percent; if one of your siblings (with whom you share 50 percent of your genes) has schizophrenia, your risk increases to 9 percent. See Loring J. Ingraham and Seymour S. Ketty, "Adoption Studies of Schizophrenia," *American Journal of Medical Genetics* 97 (2000): 18-22.

[9]Nancy C. Andreasen et al., "Defining the Phenotype of Schizophrenia: Cognitive Dysmetria and Its Neural Mechanisms," *Biological Psychiatry* 46 (1999): 908-20; and Andrew J. Conrad et al., "Hippocampal Pyramidal Cell Disarray in Schizophrenia as a Bilateral Phenomenon," *Archives of General Psychiatry* 48 (1991): 413-17.

the extent of a schizophrenic patient's gray matter loss is significantly associated with the severity of their positive and negative symptoms.[10]

*Neurochemistry.* In schizophrenia, like most mental disorders, there is evidence that an imbalance in a brain neurotransmitter is related to the symptoms of the disorder. The neurotransmitter in this case is dopamine. The dopamine hypothesis of schizophrenia resulted largely from an accidental finding in the 1950s that showed that drugs that block dopamine functioning, called phenothiazines, reduced psychotic symptoms.[11] Because of this, it was suggested that the positive symptoms of schizophrenia may result from an overactive dopaminergic system in the brain. Research has shown this hypothesis to be true.[12] More recently, additional neurotransmitters have also been suggested to play a role in schizophrenia. These include serotonin, glutamate, and acetylcholine.[13]

## Treatment

Given that schizophrenia is predominantly a biologically driven disorder, medication will always be a major component of any

---

[10]Antonio Vita et al., "Progressive Loss of Cortical Gray Matter in Schizophrenia: A Meta-Analysis and Meta-Regression of Longitudinal MRI Studies," *Translational Psychiatry* 2 (2012): e190; and Paul M. Thompson et al., "Mapping Adolescent Brain Change Reveals Dynamic Wave of Accelerated Gray Matter Loss in Very Early-Onset Schizophrenia," *Proceedings of the National Academy of Science* 98 (2001): 11650-55.

[11]Francisco López-Muñoz et al., "History of the Discovery and Clinical Introduction of Chlorpromazine," *Annals of Clinical Psychiatry* 17 (2005): 113-35.

[12]Marta Di Forti et al., "Risk Factors for Schizophrenia: All Roads Lead to Dopamine," *European Neuropsychopharmacology* 17 (2007): s101-7.

[13]Laura F. Martin and Robert Freedman, "Schizophrenia and the Alpha-7 Nicotinic Acetylcholine Receptor," *International Review of Neurobiology* 78 (2007): 225-46; Joseph T. Coyle, "Glutamate and Schizophrenia: Beyond the Dopamine Hypothesis," *Cellular and Molecular Neurobiology* 26 (2006): 365-84; and Herbert Y. Meltzer et al., "Serotonin Receptors: Their Key Role in Drugs to Treat Schizophrenia," *Progress in Neuro-Psychopharmacology and Biological Psychiatry* 27 (2003): 1159-72.

treatment plan. Like diabetes, schizophrenia is a chronic condition that requires constant, lifelong management.

*Antipsychotics.* Antipsychotic medication is the first line of treatment for the positive symptoms of schizophrenia. These drugs can be placed into two broad categories: typical antipsychotics and atypical antipsychotics. The typical antipsychotics (e.g., Haldol, Navane, Thorazine) are older medications that work by blocking the function of the neurotransmitter dopamine in the brain, meaning they are dopamine antagonists. Typical antipsychotics can have serious side effects that mimic the symptoms of Parkinson's disease, such as rigidity, persistent muscle spasms, tremors, and restlessness. After long-term use, a condition known as tardive dyskinesia may appear in the patient, resulting in uncontrollable jerky movements of the arms, legs, and facial muscles. The newer atypical antipsychotics (e.g., Abilify, Geodon, Risperdal, Zyprexa) do not seem to produce the same serious movement-related side effects seen with the older drugs. Atypical antipsychotics modify the functioning of both dopamine and serotonin in the brain. While these medications can greatly improve the patient's quality of life by managing the psychotic symptoms of schizophrenia, they are not a cure.

*Psychosocial therapy.* A positive relationship with a therapist gives the patient a reliable source of information, encouragement, and hope. For those who are stabilized on antipsychotic medication, psychosocial therapy helps deal with issues like communication, motivation, self-care, work, and establishment and maintenance of relationships with others. For example, most people who are recovering from schizophrenia want to become more independent in their daily living. To do so, they may need assistance learning how to better manage everyday activities, such as shopping, budgeting, cooking, clothes laundering, personal hygiene, and social/leisure activities. Psychosocial therapy can provide this type of life skills training. In addition, including cognitive behavioral therapy in the patient's treatment plan has been shown to be effective in the direct reduction of symptoms.

## The Other Side of Schizophrenia

This is not how Nancy had dreamed her life would turn out. Taking care of a thirty-three-year-old schizophrenic son is not something most people consider as a future possibility when they are blessed with a child. Nancy says Daniel was always a difficult child. As an infant, he had a number of allergies, especially to food, and difficulty sleeping. As he grew older and his behavior became more extreme, he was diagnosed with attention-deficit hyperactivity disorder. Not wanting to give him medication, Nancy and her husband decided to use alternative treatments and diet to control his behavior. Despite their best efforts Daniel was always in trouble at school. Nancy tried homeschooling for a time, but ultimately the family sent Daniel off to a Marine military academy for troubled boys. Difficulties in the marriage were only magnified by a child with behavioral problems, and the couple divorced when Daniel was in high school. Daniel dropped out of high school but later earned his GED. He enrolled in a technical college to study computer science but soon dropped out. Several other attempts to earn a degree ended in failure. Daniel made his first suicide attempt at thirty. In the hospital he was diagnosed with schizophrenia. Nancy was shocked. Between high school and the first psychiatric hospitalization, Daniel had bounced around between living with Nancy, his father, and a number of girlfriends. He held few jobs, the longest of which lasted for slightly over a year. "I always just thought he was lazy.

I saw most of his problems as spiritual. I never considered that he might have a mental disorder." Two years later, Daniel was hospitalized again for slashing his throat. At that time Nancy finally reached out for help.

When I first started seeing Nancy, Daniel had been living with her for several months, denied he had a mental illness, and refused to see a psychiatrist or take medication. Working only with Nancy, we were able to bring structure and routine to Daniel's daily life as well as minimize conflict and build effective communication between the two of them. After three months, Daniel agreed to go to a psychiatrist and is presently taking medication. Today Nancy says, "Our relationship is better than it has ever been. When I first called you I had no hope, but today I see things improving, and I have hope for the future."

## Biblical Examples

The Bible describes two individuals whose thoughts and behaviors suggest they were suffering from a psychotic disorder on the schizophrenia spectrum.

*Nebuchadnezzar II.* Nebuchadnezzar II was king of Babylon (c. 605–562 BC) during the second Babylonian Empire. Born in 630 BC, he came to the throne at the age of twenty-five upon the death of his father Nabopolassar. Mentioned over ninety times in the Bible, Nebuchadnezzar extended the Babylonian Empire from modern-day Iraq to northern Africa, and oversaw extensive building projects, including the construction of the legendary Hanging Gardens of Babylon, one of the seven wonders of the ancient world. To students of the Bible, Nebuchadnezzar is best known for his military defeat of the kingdom of Judah. In 586 BC, in their second invasion of Judah, the Babylonians devastated Jerusalem during a year-long siege, looted the temple, and burned it to the ground. Judah's king Zedekiah, the Jewish leadership, and many of the Jewish people, including the prophet Daniel, were taken away into what is commonly known as the Babylonian Exile (2 Kings 25:1-21). Nebuchadnezzar II ruled for forty-three years, dying of natural causes at the age of sixty-eight. He was succeeded by his son Amel-Marduk (2 Kings 25:27).

The book of Daniel (specifically chap. 4) and a Babylonian cuneiform tablet fragment housed at the British Museum describe Nebuchadnezzar's psychosis.[14] Daniel 4 tells us that Nebuchadnezzar had a frightening dream, which he was unable to understand, about a great tree being cut down. He called together all the wise men of his kingdom—the magicians, astrologers, and diviners—but they were unable to explain the dream to him. Finally, the prophet Daniel was consulted, and he interpreted the dream. Daniel told the king that the tree represented Nebuchadnezzar himself, and because of his sin, God was going to remove the kingdom from him for seven years. God would do this by changing Nebuchadnezzar's mind from that of a man to that of an animal (Daniel 5:21). The king would be driven away from people, eating grass and living out in the elements like an animal. The Babylonian cuneiform tablet fragment adds that during this time (likely the twelve months leading up to the beginning of the psychosis), Nebuchadnezzar was depressed and began giving contradictory orders, refused to accept the counsel of his courtiers, was unemotional, neglected his family, and was unable to perform his duties as king. Twelve months after the dream, Nebuchadnezzar became delusional, believing himself to be an animal.

---

[14]British Museum, No. BM 34113 (sp 213). Its translation was published by A. K. Grayson, "Babylonian Historical Literary Texts," in *Toronto Semitic Texts and Studies* 3 (Toronto: University of Toronto Press, 1975).

The delusion that one is an animal, called lycanthropy, while rare, has been documented throughout history, with the description of Nebuchadnezzar's psychosis being the most ancient.[15] Modern psychiatric patients with lycanthropy have been diagnosed with a variety of psychotic disorders, including schizophrenia, schizoaffective disorder, and depressive psychosis.[16] When viewed within a modern diagnostic context (see table 5.1), Nebuchadnezzar appears to meet the criteria for schizoaffective disorder, although a depressive psychosis cannot be completely ruled out.

**Table 5.1.** Biblical example of schizoaffective disorder

| CHARACTERISTIC SYMPTOMS | NEBUCHADNEZZAR'S SYMPTOMS | REFERENCE |
|---|---|---|
| Delusions | Believes self to be an animal | Daniel 4:33; 5:21 |
| | Eats grass | Daniel 4:33; 5:21 |
| | Lives outside with animals | Daniel 4:33; 5:21 |
| Disorganized thinking (speech) | Sanity removed; mind of an animal | Daniel 4:34, 36; 5:21 |
| | Bad counsel to son | Babylonian Tablet Line 5 |
| | Contradictory orders | Babylonian Tablet Line 6 |
| | Refused to accept the counsel of his courtiers | Babylonian Tablet Line 7 |
| Grossly disorganized behavior | No longer able to perform duties as king | Babylonian Tablet Line 14 |
| Negative symptoms | Showed love to neither son nor daughter | Babylonian Tablet Line 11 |
| | Neglected his family | Babylonian Tablet Line 12 |
| Depressive episode | Life had lost all value | Babylonian Tablet Line 3 |

In Nebuchadnezzar's case, God used a mental disorder as discipline. However, we should not generalize this to every case of mental illness. God certainly could choose to bring mental illness into our lives as discipline (Deuteronomy 28:28), but if we were to

---

[15]Effie Poulakou-Rebelakou et al., "Lycanthropy in Byzantine Times (AD 330–1453)," *History of Psychiatry* 20 (2009): 468-79.

[16]Ali Abdul Younis and Hamdy Fouad Moselhy, "Lycanthropy Alive in Babylon: The Existence of Archetype," *Acta Psychiatrica Scandinavica* 119 (2009): 161-65.

mistakenly generalize that mental illness is always the result of God's discipline, then we would also have to consider common problems such as boils, tumors, scabs, and itching (Deuteronomy 28:27) to always be signs of God's discipline.

*Gadarene demoniac.* Although the story is reported in all three of the Synoptic Gospels (Matthew 8:28-34; Mark 5:1-20; Luke 8:26-39), very little information is given in relation to the Gadarene demoniac's background and history. We do know he was from a Gentile region southeast of the Sea of Galilee and that he had been suffering for an extended period of time.

After crossing the Sea of Galilee with his disciples and calming the storm, Jesus was immediately confronted by a man (two men in Matthew) who was possessed by a large number of demons collectively referred to as "Legion." This man is described as being naked and extremely violent. He lived among the tombs, cried out day and night, and cut himself with sharp stones.[17] The people of the nearby town had, in the past, attempted to restrain the man with ropes and chains, but they were no longer able to control him. He was greatly feared by the people and had become a problem in the region because he would not allow anyone to pass through the area where he lived. With a simple command, Jesus cast out the demons. The demons entered a herd of pigs who immediately rushed into the lake and drowned. When viewed within a modern diagnostic context (see table 5.2), the Gadarene demoniac appears to meet the criteria for schizophrenia.

---

[17]This description is similar to the characteristics of the insane outlined in the Talmud. The Talmud is a collection of rabbinical writings written between AD 200 and 500 that interpret, explain, and apply the Torah. In the Talmud the rabbis characterize the insane (*shoteh*) as individuals who (1) go out unaccompanied at night, (2) sleep in cemeteries, (3) tear their garments, and (4) lose everything that is given to them.

**Table 5.2.** Biblical example of schizophrenia

| CHARACTERISTIC SYMPTOMS | DEMONIAC'S SYMPTOMS | REFERENCE |
|---|---|---|
| **Disorganized thinking (speech)** | Not in right mind | Mark 5:15; Luke 8:35 |
| | Crying out day and night | Mark 5:5 |
| **Grossly disorganized behavior** | Lived among the tombs | Matthew 8:28; Mark 5:3; Luke 8:27 |
| | Wore no clothes | Mark 5:15; Luke 8:27, 35 |
| | Extremely violent | Matthew 8:28 |
| | Cutting self with stones | Mark 5:5 |

The Gadarene demoniac's mental disorder was the result of demonic possession and infirmity, but not all mental illness is the result of the demonic. Similar to the case of Nebuchadnezzar, if we were to mistakenly generalize all mental illness to be the result of the demonic, then we would also have to consider common problems such as boils (Job 2:7), back troubles (Luke 13:10-16), blindness (Matthew 12:22), mutism (Matthew 9:32-33; Luke 11:14), and epilepsy (Matthew 17:14-18; Mark 9:17-27; Luke 9:37-42) to always be signs of demonic possession.

## Final Thoughts

I believe there are two consistent themes we see in these biblical examples of psychosis. First, God is actively pursuing his lost sheep in the midst of mental illness. God had long pursued the pagan king Nebuchadnezzar, and Jesus traveled a great distance to encounter the Gadarene demoniac. He longs for relationship with us, and a mental illness should not be seen as a mark of shame but as an opportunity to know him more. Second, we see that mental illness can be a transformational experience, drawing one closer to God. Mental health difficulties do not hinder God's purposes, nor do they in any way affect God's plan for one's life. It was during their psychoses that the pagan king was transformed into a follower of Yahweh and the Gadarene demoniac encountered the long-awaited Messiah.

# 6

# TORMENTED

## BIPOLAR AND RELATED DISORDERS

*My recovery from manic depression has been
an evolution, not a sudden miracle.*

PATTY DUKE

SHIRLEY'S LIFE WAS difficult from the beginning. Her parents divorced when she was young. Raised by an emotionally neglectful and verbally abusive mother and stepfather she was sexually abused by her older brother at the age of twelve. Desperate for love and affection, she became sexually promiscuous in her teen years, leading to a marriage immediately after high school. That marriage lasted only a few years. A second marriage produced a child but also lasted only a few years. Shirley's family and spousal relationships were strained by her ever-increasing mood swings and erratic behavior. During her third marriage she had her second child and was first diagnosed with bipolar disorder. Cycling between dark, depressive episodes and manic delusional states, Shirley struggled to raise her two children, work, and sustain a marriage. Over the next several years, she was hospitalized multiple times for suicidal thoughts and attempts. After ten years of marriage, during a manic state, she left her husband for another man, who would become her fourth husband.

Mark and Shirley's marriage has been difficult, but they have survived twelve years together. Several years ago, Shirley finally began receiving the treatment that she so desperately needed. Mark educated himself about bipolar disorder and began attending a weekly support group for the families of individuals living with mental illness. Shirley is unable to work due to her illness, one of her children refuses to have any contact with her, and she is estranged from both her mother and brother. Bipolar disorder has destroyed most of her past friendships and relationships; however, the last two years have been the best she has known in some time. Her moods are stable, she has a close friendship with a woman in her neighborhood, and her and Mark's relationship is better than ever. While she is unable to maintain regular employment, she serves her local church by doing their landscaping, and visits individuals in local hospitals and convalescent centers. Her desire to serve others is truly inspirational.

## Characteristic Symptoms

The bipolar disorders are characterized by cycling mood changes. The affected individual alternates between severe highs (manic or hypomanic episodes) and severe lows (major depressive episodes), often with periods of normal mood in between. The mood changes can be rapid but most often occur gradually.

*Manic episodes.* A manic episode is a distinct period of increased energy and abnormally elated, irritable, or euphoric mood that is present for most of the day, nearly every day, for at least one week. During the episode, three or more of the following symptoms must also be present: higher than usual self-esteem, significantly reduced need for sleep, an increase in talkativeness, racing thoughts, distractibility, an increase in goal-directed behavior (either socially, at work or school, or sexually) or psychomotor agitation, and excessive involvement in pleasurable activities that are risky or self-destructive (e.g., excessive spending, sexual promiscuity). Mania, left untreated, may worsen to a psychotic state.

*Hypomanic episodes.* A hypomanic episode is less intense and of shorter duration (at least four consecutive days) than a full manic episode. The most important differences between mania and hypomania are that the latter is not severe enough to cause marked impairment in daily functioning or to require hospitalization, and no psychotic features are present.

*Major depressive episodes.* A major depressive episode is characterized by either a persistent depressed mood or loss of interest or pleasure in daily activities over at least a two-week period. Four or more of the following symptoms must also be present: significant weight change or change in appetite, sleeping too much or not being able to sleep, psychomotor agitation or retardation, fatigue or loss of energy, feelings of worthlessness or excessive guilt, an inability to concentrate or indecisiveness, and recurrent suicidal thoughts.

## Diagnoses

In 1854, French psychiatrists Jules Baillarger and Jean-Pierre Falret made separate, independent presentations to the French Imperial Academy of Medicine in which they described a mental illness characterized by periodic shifts between mania and depression. Baillarger referred to this illness as "dual-form insanity," while Falret labeled it "circular insanity."[1] This marked the first appearance

---

[1] Jules Baillarger, "Notes sur un genre de folie dont les accés sont caractérisés par deux périodes régulières, l'une de dépression, l'autre d'excitation," *Bulletin de l'Academie Nationale de Médecine* (Paris) 19 (1854): 340; Jean-Pierre Falret, "Mémoire sur la folie circulaire," *Bulletin de l'Academie Nationale de Médecine* (Paris) 19 (1854): 382-415.

of bipolar disorder in the psychiatric and medical literature. In 1899, the German psychiatrist Emil Kraepelin, expanding on Baillarger's and Falret's earlier work, distinguished between two different forms of psychosis, manic-depressive psychosis (bipolar disorder) and dementia praecox (which would later become schizophrenia).[2] The term manic-depressive illness was used to describe the disorder until 1980 and the publication of the third edition of the *Diagnostic and Statistical Manual of Mental Disorders* (DSM-III), which introduced the term *bipolar disorder*.[3] In the most recent edition of the diagnostics manual DSM-5, bipolar and related disorders are placed between the schizophrenia spectrum and other psychotic disorders and depressive disorders and serve as a bridge between these two diagnostic categories in terms of both symptoms and presentation. The primary bipolar disorders are bipolar I, bipolar II, and cyclothymia.

**Bipolar I disorder.** Bipolar I disorder is characterized by a manic episode that lasts at least seven days, severe enough to cause marked impairment in the individual's daily functioning, hospitalization to prevent harm to self or others, or the presence of psychotic symptoms. Usually major depressive episodes occur as well.

**Bipolar II disorder.** Bipolar II disorder is characterized by a pattern of hypomanic and major depressive episodes, but the criteria for a full manic episode are not met. The hypomanic episode is associated with a clear change in daily functioning that is uncharacteristic of the individual.

**Cyclothymic disorder (cyclothymia).** Cyclothymic disorder is a milder form of bipolar disorder. It is characterized by at least two

---

[2]Emil Kraepelin, *Psychiatrie: Ein Lehrbuch für Studierende und Ärzte* (Leipzig: Ambrosius Barth, 1896).

[3]The term *manic-depressive illness* was changed to *bipolar disorder* primarily to help minimize the stigma associated with referring to individuals living with manic-depression as "maniacs."

years of periodic hypomanic and depressive symptoms. However, the symptoms do not meet the diagnostic criteria for any other type of bipolar disorder.

## Prevalence and Age of Onset

The lifetime prevalence of the bipolar disorders in the United States is estimated to be 1.0 percent for bipolar I disorder, 1.1 percent for bipolar II disorder, and 2.4 percent for cyclothymic disorder.[4] Bipolar I disorder and cyclothymia affect men and women equally, while bipolar II disorder is more common in women. The age of onset for the first manic, hypomanic, or major depressive episode is usually late adolescence to early adulthood, although it can occur at any age. The first episode in men tends to be mania or hypomania, while the first episode in women is most often depression. Some individuals experience rapid cycling between manic and depressive states, meaning they experience four or more episodes of major depression, mania, or hypomania within a year. Rapid cycling is more common in women than men.

## Developmental and Psychosocial Risk Factors

Bipolar disorder results from a complex interaction between biological and environmental factors. The following developmental and psychosocial factors have been shown to increase the risk that an individual will be diagnosed with a bipolar disorder as an adult. Childhood risk factors include maternal loss, emotional abuse, traumatic events such as physical-sexual abuse, and attentional impairments (including a diagnosis of attention-deficit/hyperactivity disorder). Additional risk factors include having a first-degree

---

[4]Kathleen R. Merikangas et al., "Prevalence and Correlates of Bipolar Spectrum Disorder in the World Mental Health Survey Initiative," *Archives of General Psychiatry* 68 (2011): 241-51.

relative with bipolar disorder,[5] lower socioeconomic status, a seizure disorder, and a history of traumatic brain injury. The first manic, hypomanic, or major depressive episode is often associated with an increase in stressful life events. This suggests that psychological stress may play a role in the onset of the disorder.[6]

## Neurobiology

**Heritability.** Twin studies looking at the role that heredity plays in the bipolar disorders have consistently found significantly higher concordance rates in identical twins (approximately 51 percent of twin pairs both have a bipolar disorder) compared to fraternal twins (approximately 6 percent share the disorder). Another way of assessing the heritability of a disorder is to look at the risk of diagnosis in the first-degree relatives of someone with the disorder. As mentioned earlier, the lifetime risk of bipolar disorder in the general population (for unrelated persons) is about 1 percent. In contrast, family studies have shown the lifetime risk for the first-degree relatives of a person diagnosed with a bipolar disorder is 5-10 percent (five to ten times higher).[7]

**Neuroanatomy.** Neuroimaging studies of those diagnosed with bipolar disorders have shown a high frequency of small nonspecific,

---

[5] A first-degree relative is a family member who shares about 50 percent of their genes with a particular individual in a family. First-degree relatives include parents, offspring, and siblings.

[6] Marsal Sanches et al., "Neurodevelopmental Basis of Bipolar Disorder: A Critical Appraisal," *Progress in Neuro-Psychopharmacology & Biological Psychiatry* 32 (2008): 1617-27; Lauren B. Alloy et al., "The Psychosocial Context of Bipolar Disorder: Environmental, Cognitive, and Developmental Risk Factors," *Clinical Psychology Review* 25 (2005): 1043-75; Preben B. Mortensen et al., "Individual and Familial Risk Factors for Bipolar Affective Disorders in Denmark," *Archives of General Psychiatry* 60 (2003): 1209-15; and Kenji J. Tsuchiya et al., "Risk Factors in Relation to an Emergence of Bipolar Disorder: A Systematic Review," *Bipolar Disorders* 5 (2003): 231-42.

[7] Jack Edvardsen et al., "Heritability of Bipolar Spectrum Disorders: Unity or Heterogeneity?," *Journal of Affective Disorders* 106 (2008): 229-40; and Levi Taylor et al., "Family, Twin, and Adoption Studies of Bipolar Disease," *Current Psychiatry Reports* 4 (2002): 130-33.

subcortical lesions throughout their brains. These lesions appear to be most focused within the brain's white matter pathways. This disrupts communication between differing brain areas, particularly the fronto-temporal pathways involved in the regulation of emotion. In addition, individuals with a bipolar disorder also show reduced gray matter volumes in several areas of the brain, including the frontal lobes and hippocampus (an area involved in memory). This neural degeneration appears to be progressive, worsening as the individual ages. It is thought that due to a physiological abnormality, the brain cells of those with bipolar disorder are particularly vulnerable to cellular stress and thus easily damaged. Several studies have found that bipolar disordered individuals demonstrate a heightened physiological fight-or-flight stress response, which may be the cause of this neural damage.[8]

*Neurochemistry.* The neurotransmitter most often associated with the bipolar disorders is norepinephrine (NE). NE is an excitatory neurotransmitter involved in mood, attention, motivation, and stress. Studies in bipolar disordered individuals have shown an increased level of NE in the brain during the manic phase of the disorder. In depression, reduced NE neurotransmission has been associated with lack of pleasure, decreased alertness, low energy, and problems of inattention, concentration, and cognitive ability. In addition, antidepressant medications that increase the amount of NE in the brain (e.g., tricyclic antidepressants, tetracyclic antidepressants, and serotonin-norepinephrine reuptake inhibitors) can cause an abrupt transition from depression into mania in

---

[8]Gareth Nortje et al., "Systematic Review and Voxel-Based Meta-Analysis of Diffusion Tensor Imaging Studies in Bipolar Disorder," *Journal of Affective Disorders* 150 (2013): 192-200; Tadafumi Kato, "Molecular Neurobiology of Bipolar Disorder: A Disease of 'Mood-Stabilizing Neurons'?," *Trends in Neuroscience* 31 (2008): 495-503; and Gregory S. Berns and Charles B. Nemeroff, "The Neurobiology of Bipolar Disorder," *American Journal of Medical Genetics Part C: Seminar in Medical Genetics* 123C (2003): 76-84.

individuals who are genetically vulnerable to bipolar disorder.[9] This is called a "manic switch," and it does not happen as often with antidepressant medications that do not affect the brain's NE levels.[10] As in most mental disorders, dysfunction in several neurotransmitter systems has been suggested to be involved in the illness. In the bipolar disorders, evidence suggests that both dopamine and serotonin may also play a role.[11]

## Treatment

Much like schizophrenia, the bipolar disorders are chronic, biologically driven problems that require medication for effective symptom management. In addition, several forms of psychotherapy (talk therapy) have been shown to be effective in the treatment of the bipolar disorders.

**Lithium.** Unlike other psychiatric medications used to treat mental disorders, lithium carbonate (e.g., Eskalith, Lithobid) is a salt, and consequently it does not have a specific receptor it binds to in the brain. Rather, after administration lithium is widely distributed throughout the central nervous system, where it is transported into the brain's cells (neurons) through sodium channels in the cell membranes. Lithium appears to have a neuroprotective action by reestablishing chemical balance (homeostasis) in the neurons and decreasing their susceptibility to damage from both internal and external stimuli. Second, it has

[9]Tricyclic antidepressants include Anafranil, Elavil, Pamelor, Sinequan, Tofranil, and Vivactil; tetracyclic antidepressants include Asendin, Ludiomil, Norval, and Remeron; serotonin-norepinephrine reuptake inhibitors include Cymbalta, Effexor, Fetzima, and Pristiq.

[10]Isabella Pacchiarotti et al., "The International Society for Bipolar Disorders (ISBD) Task Force Report on Antidepressant Use in Bipolar Disorders," *American Journal of Psychiatry* 170 (2013): 1249-62.

[11]Kato, "Molecular Neurobiology of Bipolar Disorder," 495-503; and Husseini K. Manji et al., "The Underlying Neurobiology of Bipolar Disorder," *World Psychiatry* 2 (2003): 136-46.

been shown to promote neurogenesis (the growth of new brain cells). This medication, while highly effective, has a number of serious side effects, and the range between an effective dose and a toxic dose is quite small.

*Anticonvulsants.* A number of medications originally developed for treating seizure disorders have also been found to have mood-stabilizing effects. These include valproic acid or divalproex sodium (Depakote), lamotrigine (Lamictal), gabapentin (Neurontin), topiramate (Topamax), oxcarbazepine (Trileptal), and carbamazepine (Tegretol). These medications appear to exert their mood-stabilizing effects through a neuroprotective action similar to lithium. Anticonvulsant medications are most often used in combination with lithium, antidepressants, or atypical antipsychotics in the treatment of bipolar spectrum disorders.

*Atypical antipsychotics.* The atypical antipsychotics, which I described in the chapter on schizophrenia, modify the functioning of both dopamine and serotonin in the brain. These medications have been shown to have mood-stabilizing effects and are particularly useful for treating acute mania with or without psychotic symptoms. Atypical antipsychotics commonly used in the treatment of bipolar spectrum disorders include olanzapine (Zyprexa), aripiprazole (Abilify), quetiapine (Seroquel), risperidone (Risperdal), and ziprasidone (Geodon).

*Psychotherapy.* During psychotherapy, a patient receives assistance from another individual in understanding and resolving problems that may be contributing to their disorder. The therapy sessions may focus on a number of issues, including helping the patient unlearn behavioral patterns that contribute to or result from their disorder, mend disrupted personal relationships, change negative thinking styles, or resolve conflicted feelings and emotions.

Four psychotherapeutic approaches have been shown to be effective in treating bipolar spectrum disorders.

The major aim of cognitive-behavioral therapy (CBT) is to help the client eliminate negative beliefs or behaviors and replace them with positive ones. Symptom reduction is seen as an end in itself. Family-focused therapy includes family members. This approach helps enhance family coping strategies, improves communication, and teaches effective problem-solving skills. Interpersonal and social rhythm therapy helps people with bipolar disorder identify and maintain the regular routines of everyday life. Regular daily routines and sleep schedules help protect against the onset of difficult symptoms. Interpersonal issues and problems that may arise, which directly impact the person's routines, are also part of the therapy. The principal goal of psychoeducation is to provide accurate and reliable information about the disorder, including ways of dealing with mental illness and its effects. Helping individuals to become more knowledgeable and aware of their disorder gives them more control over their condition. This can help reduce the severity of symptoms and how often they occur.

## The Other Side of Bipolar Disorder

Michael and Linda met in college. Both were highly involved in college ministry and each felt called to the unreached nations of the earth. After graduating they were married and began training for life together as missionaries. After a few years in Asia they served for eight years in a Muslim country in Africa. "For the longest time we didn't realize the extent of Linda's mental health problems because depression and anxiety are common issues among missionaries." It was only after she was actually diagnosed with bipolar I disorder that they were able to look back and see that problems had been cropping up since college.

Before then, Linda's struggles been treated by Michael and the missionary organization as a counseling or ministry issue. "Not until the scary meeting with the psychiatrist did it really hit me for the first time."

As Linda's condition worsened, the family had to leave the mission field and return to the United States for treatment. "I was in complete denial! How could this be happening to us?" What followed was intense despair as Michael watched everything he knew about his wife and best friend slowly slip away. "The worse she became, the more I questioned God's faithfulness. To me God became little more than a distant, silent presence." Their five children began to slip into confusion and despair. "I've never seen my children filled with such extreme sadness and anger. While Linda was hospitalized, I would tuck my children into bed while they cried wondering what's wrong with Mommy and would she ever come back."

Initially Linda's treatment was unsuccessful; even months of hospitalization failed to bring her stability. The family was in financial ruin due to the excessive medical cost. It was not until Michael checked his wife out of the psychiatric hospital against medical advice that her recovery truly began. Having seen the inability of the mental health care system to bring relief to his wife's suffering, Michael purposed himself to help her recovery. He started reading everything he could about bipolar disorder. He attended seminars and made contact with local mental health professionals. His pastor was there to listen and be present during times of distress. A local psychologist came alongside him to provide guidance in how to successfully navigate the mental health care system. A family physician helped him find the right professionals, and a family friend with a mentally ill daughter walked Michael through the realities of caring for a mentally ill loved one. It took about two years, but with Michael's help and the support of their community, Linda fully recovered.

Michael says it has been years since Linda has had any significant manic or depressive episodes, and the numerous medications
she once took have been weaned down to only one at the lowest
dose. "It doesn't mean that she doesn't have rumblings, but she
knows what to do with them, and we as a family know how to
support her. She is an incredible wife and a great mother. On this
side, we are more confident in God, have a greater depth of joy and
a greater sense of rest than we have ever known. This situation
challenged our view of his goodness, but it was the process of recovery that made his love and security truly real to us all. God has
redeemed and strengthened our family."

## A Biblical Example

Historically, among both theologians and psychiatrists, the biblical
character most commonly thought to have suffered from a mental
disorder is Israel's King Saul.[12]

After three years of being led by a set of judges (men and women
called by God to lead his people in times of crisis), the Israelites
asked God for a king to rule over them. God answered their request
by choosing Saul. The son of Kish, from the tribe of Benjamin, he is
described as wealthy, handsome, and taller than all of the other men
of Israel. God tells the prophet Samuel that Saul will "deliver My
people from the hand of the Philistines" (1 Samuel 9:16). At this time
in history, Israel was a set of loosely associated tribes with no central
government. They were easy prey for their stronger, more organized
neighbors. It was Saul's job to take this loose confederation of tribes
and transition them into a centralized monarchy. King Saul ruled

---

[12]Gillian P. Williams and Magdel le Roux, "King Saul's Mysterious Malady," *Theological
Studies* 68 (2012): 906; George Stein, "The Case of King Saul: Did He Have Recurrent
Unipolar Depression or Bipolar Affective Disorder?," *British Journal of Psychiatry* 198
(2011): 212; and Liubov Ben-Noun, "What Was the Mental Disease That Afflicted King
Saul?," *Clinical Case Studies* 2 (2003): 270-82.

Israel for forty-two years, dying by suicide at the age of seventy-two. He was succeeded by his son Ish-bosheth (2 Samuel 2:8-10).

First Samuel 9:1–31:13 and the writings of Titus Flavius Josephus, the first-century Roman-Jewish historian, both give details of King Saul's mental illness.[13] Saul's strange and abnormal behavior is evident from the beginning of his reign. On the same day that he is secretly anointed as king by the prophet Samuel, Saul meets a group of ecstatic prophets and he begins to prophesy. The Scriptures note that this behavior seemed strange to those who knew Saul. The Bible describes two other similar incidences in the life of Saul. Once when prophesying in his house, he tries to kill David with a spear. On another occasion while searching for David, he begins to prophesy, strips off his clothes, and lies naked on the ground in front of the prophet Samuel for a day and a night. Thus we see that to prophesy sometimes indicated abnormal behavior to the Hebrews of the Old Testament. For example, Jeremiah 29:26 refers to mad men who act as prophets. Acting as a prophet and being mad are virtually equated in this verse. In addition, Saul flies into several homicidal rages in which he attempts to kill David on two occasions and his own son Jonathan on another. Taken together, these examples of frenzied and euphoric behavior suggest that Saul experienced several manic episodes during his lifetime.

Twenty-seven years into Saul's reign as king, God informs Saul (through the prophet Samuel) that he will remove the kingdom from him due to his disobedience. At this time, God removes his Spirit from Saul and places it on David. From this point forward in Saul's life, he is intermittently tormented by an evil spirit.[14]

---

[13]Flavius Josephus, *The New Complete Works of Josephus*, trans. William Whiston (Grand Rapids: Kregel, 1999).

[14]It may be troubling to some that the evil spirit that torments King Saul is credited to God (1 Samuel 16:14). This can be explained by the fact that in the perspective of the biblical writers there are no secondary causes. All causes are ultimately traced back to God, who

When the evil spirit torments him, he shows episodes of overexcited mania or dark depression and fear. His physicians suggest music therapy to treat his affliction. This is how Saul is originally introduced to David, who is able to soothe Saul's tormented mind as a harp player during these episodes. I think it is important to recognize that the tormenting evil spirit was not the punishment for Saul's disobedience, the loss of the kingdom was. When God removed his empowering and protective Spirit from Saul, the king became vulnerable to demonic attack. These demonic attacks appear to have taken advantage of Saul's already present mental vulnerabilities and weaknesses. His behavior was odd and abnormal even before the tormenting evil spirit.

As Saul's mind continued to deteriorate over the latter part of his reign, he showed increasing paranoia toward those around him, sudden changes in mood, restlessness, feelings of worthlessness, loss of appetite, difficulty making decisions and poor judgment. The night before his death, during what appears to have been a major depressive episode, he desperately sought guidance from the spirit of dead Samuel through the witch of Endor. The fact that only Saul heard the voice of Samuel, and that only after God would not answer him (1 Samuel 28:6), suggest that he may have been having an auditory hallucination (a symptom of psychosis). The following day, after being wounded in battle against the Philistines, Saul killed himself so he would not be captured by the enemy. When viewed within a modern diagnostic context (see table 6.1), King Saul appears to meet the criteria for bipolar I disorder.

While we often think of the story of King Saul as a tragic tale, the fact is he was a successful ruler who God used powerfully

---

causes all. The writer of 1 Samuel attributing the evil spirit to Yahweh simply assumes that the world is ordered by the direct sovereign rule of God.

within redemptive history. Within the first two and a half years of his reign, he freed the Jewish people from all their enemies except the Philistines. Saul oversaw military victories against Moab, Ammon, Edom, the kings of Zobah, and the Amalekites. With the help of David, he was able to push the Philistines out of Israel's territory. Saul established and trained an army to defend the country from invaders, outlawed pagan rituals (e.g., mediums and magicians), and sought God's guidance until the end of his reign.

In addition, God used Saul to fulfill at least two prophecies mentioned prior to his reign. During the exodus from Egypt, God promised to wipe out the Amalekites because of their aggression toward his people (Deuteronomy 25:19). Hundreds of years later, God uses Saul to fulfill that prophecy (1 Samuel 15). A few decades before Saul was anointed as king, God told the judge and high priest Eli that his house would be cut off from the priesthood due to his family's disobedience (1 Samuel 2:30-31). Again, God uses Saul to begin the fulfillment of this prophecy (1 Samuel 22:18). King Saul prepares the way for Israel's golden age under David and Solomon.

**Table 6.1.** Biblical example of bipolar I disorder

| CHARACTERISTIC SYMPTOMS | SAUL'S SYMPTOMS | REFERENCE |
|---|---|---|
| **Manic episodes** | Prophetic frenzies, euphoria | 1 Samuel 18:10-11; 19:23-24; JA 6.4.2 |
| | Homicidal rage outbursts | 1 Samuel 19:9-10; 20:33; 22:17-19 |
| Inflated self-esteem | Builds monument to self | 1 Samuel 15:12 |
| Increase in goal-directed behavior | Paranoid, obsessive pursuit of David | 1 Samuel 23:14 |
| Anxious distress | Suffocations as were ready to choke him | JA 6.8.2 |
| **Major depressive episodes** | Filled with depression and fear | 1 Samuel 16:14-17, 23 |
| | Under great dread, courage fell | JA 6.14.2 |
| Problems with concentration/ indecisiveness | Foolish order, continually oversteps religious commands, witch of Endor | 1 Samuel 13:13; 14:24; 15:13-15, 20; 28:15 |

| CHARACTERISTIC SYMPTOMS | SAUL'S SYMPTOMS | REFERENCE |
|---|---|---|
| Feelings of worthlessness/ excessive guilt | Hiding in baggage, comparison to David, uncharacteristic guilt over his pursuit of David | 1 Samuel 10:22; 18:8; 24:16; 26:21 |
| Change in appetite | Loss of appetite | 1 Samuel 28:20-23 |
| Suicidal thoughts | Suicide | 1 Samuel 31:4 |
| Psychotic features | Hears voice of deceased Samuel | 1 Samuel 28:15-20 |

JA = Flavius Josephus, *Jewish Antiquities*

## Final Thoughts

There are two lessons to be learned from this biblical example of bipolar disorder. First, the mentally ill are not to be stigmatized, excluded, or neglected. The behavior of David, Saul's court, and Saul's family in response to his madness stands in stark contrast to the shame and stigmatization that presently exist in the church toward those with mental illness. Not only did they care for Saul and continue to accept him as king, but they also included him in decisions concerning his treatment (1 Samuel 16:15-18). This is a wonderful example of how we should treat those living with mental illness among us today. Second, the presence of a mental illness does not alter or thwart the perfect purpose and plan God has for a person's life. God chose Saul to be king knowing his condition. At the appointed time in redemptive history, Saul fulfilled the sovereign plan God had laid out before him. His illness did not alter that plan but rather in some instances was actually a necessary part of God's will being done (1 Samuel 22:17).

# 7

# IN THE VALLEY
# OF DARKNESS

## DEPRESSIVE DISORDERS

*Although I still suffer from depression and even suicidal
thoughts, I have come to understand that God is not
disgusted by me for it.*

CHRIS, DIAGNOSED WITH MAJOR
DEPRESSIVE DISORDER

BLAKE'S MENTAL HEALTH PROBLEMS FIRST surfaced as overwhelming anxiety when he was in the seventh grade. The dark,
depressive episodes started soon after. His parents took him to a
pediatrician who immediately referred them to a child psychologist who diagnosed Blake with major depressive disorder
and obsessive-compulsive disorder. Blake began receiving therapy
from the psychologist and started to take Prozac prescribed by
a psychiatrist.

My parents felt helpless. My illness caused them to worry
about my future. At times they even lost hope, but through it
all they have been my greatest support. They have constantly
been on my side. God blessed me with very supportive parents.

They have supported me in every way possible. They have gone above and beyond to make sure I get the treatment I need. It has certainly been a journey that has taken a toll on them. But even in the darkest of times, they have been by my side.

Because of his depression and anxiety Blake grew up isolated and lonely, with few friends.

My depressive symptoms were often mistaken for laziness. Nobody could see how much I was hurting. At times too much was expected from me. I even pushed myself too hard at times so I would not disappoint my family. After years of suffering, I don't even remember what it feels like to feel normal. Over the years I subconsciously developed ways to hide all the pain, loneliness, and suffering so I could function as normally as possible. Eventually I broke down. The mental pain became too much to handle.

Blake attempted suicide at age twenty-four to end the pain.

Depression and anxiety have been devastating to my life. That being said, I think they have pushed me to cling more strongly to Jesus. I feel that illness has opened my eyes to how much I need God. Only God can possibly know the pain I have experienced. Only the Creator of awareness could be completely aware of every aspect of my struggles. I depend on God to fill so many relational holes. He is a father, a brother, a friend, a constant companion, and somebody who is constantly on my side. I know God does not enjoy seeing me go through so much pain. I recognize illness as ultimately being a product of the fall described in Genesis. God did not afflict me with this illness. He is not sadistic. I have not been completely healed, but I believe that I will be. It may not be during this lifetime, but I am going to pray for it to be and ask others to pray for me to be completely healed as well. The hope of God's healing and the joy he has put in my heart keeps me going. I lean on God's love.

## Characteristic Symptoms

The characteristic symptom of the depressive disorders is a persistently depressed and empty mood. A period of sadness or melancholy that occurs in reaction to personal loss or trauma is often referred to as a reactive depression. While in some instances a reactive depression may be severe enough to require treatment, it is normally of short duration and self-correcting. In the depressive disorders, however, the depressed mood arises spontaneously and is long lasting, the symptoms are severe, and the individual is unable to function normally.

As described in chapter six a *major depressive episode* is characterized by either a persistent depressed mood or loss of interest or pleasure in daily activities over at least a two-week period. Four or more of the following symptoms also must be present: significant weight change or change in appetite, sleeping too much or not being able to sleep, psychomotor agitation or retardation, fatigue or loss of energy, feelings of worthlessness or excessive guilt, an inability to concentrate or indecisiveness, and recurrent suicidal thoughts.

## Diagnoses

Depression has been recognized by humans for millennia. The term *melancholia* (which means black bile in Greek) was first used by Hippocrates to describe the condition around 400 BC.[1] Most

---

[1] Hagop Souren Akiskal, "Mood Disorders: Introduction and Overview," in *Comprehensive Textbook of Psychiatry*, ed. B. J. Sadock and V. A. Sadock (New York: Lippincott, Williams & Wilkins, 2000), 1284-98.

of the major symptoms of depression observed today were known in ancient times. Our modern understanding of depression was heavily influenced by the German psychiatrist Karl Leonhard, who after observing that some of his patients had histories of both depression and mania, while others had histories of depression only, proposed a distinction between unipolar and bipolar depression.[2] Prior to this, depression was not seen as a separate diagnosis but rather listed as a part of other disorders such as manic-depression and psychosis.

The publication of the DSM-III in 1980 first introduced the diagnostic category mood disorders, containing distinct criteria for both the bipolar disorders and depressive disorders as Leonhard had proposed decades earlier.[3] In the most recent edition of the diagnostics manual (DSM-5), the depressive disorders are for the first time separated completely from the bipolar disorders and given their own category. The primary depressive disorders are major depressive disorder and persistent depressive disorder (dysthymia).

*Major depressive disorder.* Major depressive disorder is characterized by a major depressive episode that lasts at least two weeks, severe enough to cause marked impairment in the individual's daily functioning. A person may experience a major depressive episode only once, but more commonly episodes occur several times in a lifetime.

*Persistent depressive disorder (dysthymia).* Persistent depressive disorder is a less severe form of depression characterized by a chronically depressed mood for at least two years. The symptoms of dysthymia, while not seriously disabling, keep

---

[2]Karl Leonhard, *Aufteilung der Endogenen Psychosen* (Berlin: Akademie Verlag, 1957).
[3]William N. Goldstein and Robert N. Anthony, "The Diagnosis of Depression and the DSMs," *American Journal of Psychotherapy* 42 (1988): 180-96.

the individual from functioning well or feeling good. Many people with dysthymia experience major depressive episodes during their lives.

## Prevalence and Age of Onset

The lifetime prevalence of the depressive disorders in the United States is estimated to be 16.6 percent for major depressive disorder and 2.5 percent for persistent depressive disorder.[4] The depressive disorders occur more commonly in women than men. The age of onset for the first major depressive episode is usually late adolescence or early adulthood, although the first episode can occur at any age. A family history of depression increases the likelihood that a child will also have a depressive disorder. Major depressive disorder is the leading cause of disability in the United States and the second leading cause of disability worldwide.[5]

## Developmental and Psychosocial Risk Factors

A number of psychosocial factors and life experiences increase the likelihood that a person will suffer from a depressive disorder. Childhood risk factors include parental loss or separation, abandonment, neglect, or physical or sexual abuse. Individuals who have an extremely negative outlook on life (negative affectivity), marked by low self-esteem and self-defeating or distorted thinking, are more likely to develop depressive episodes in response to stressful life events. Additional risk factors that increase the risk for major

---

[4]Ronald C. Kessler et al., "Lifetime Prevalence and Age-of-Onset Distributions of DSM-IV Disorders in the National Comorbidity Survey Replication," *Archives of General Psychiatry* 62 (2005): 593-602.

[5]Alize J. Ferrari et al., "Burden of Depressive Disorders by Country, Sex, Age, and Year: Findings from the Global Burden of Disease Study 2010," *PLoS Med* 10 (2013): e1001547; and Christopher J. L. Murray and Alan D. Lopez, "Alternative Projections of Mortality and Disability by Cause 1990-2020: Global Burden of Disease Study," *Lancet* 349 (1997): 1498-1504.

depressive episodes include low socioeconomic status, little or no social support, chronic sleep problems, and chronic or disabling medical conditions. Significant stress from negative life events such as the loss of a job, financial difficulties, long-term unemployment, death of a family member, or divorce may also play a role in triggering a depressive episode.[6]

## Neurobiology

**Heritability.** As with all mental disorders, twin studies have consistently found a higher concordance rate for the depressive disorders in identical twins (approximately 52 percent of twin pairs both have a depressive disorder) when compared to fraternal twins (approximately 30 percent share the disorder). First-degree relatives of individuals diagnosed with a depressive disorder have a two to fourfold higher risk of having a depressive disorder themselves when compared to the general population. Similarly, adoption studies have also found evidence for a genetic effect on the transmission of the depressive disorders.[7]

**Neuroanatomy.** Neuroimaging studies have identified several brain structures that are dysfunctional in individuals diagnosed with depressive disorders. Two of these structures, the amygdala and the subgenual anterior cingulate cortex (subgenual ACC), are part of what is called the limbic system.[8] The amygdala is involved in emotionally mediated attention, in assigning emotional significance to stimuli, and along with the hippocampus (another limbic

---

[6]DSM-5.

[7]Ibid.; Jack Edvardsen et al., "Unipolar Depressive Disorders Have a Common Genotype," *Journal of Affective Disorders* 117 (2009): 30-41; and Patrick F. Sullivan et al., "Genetic Epidemiology of Major Depression: Review and Meta-Analysis," *American Journal of Psychiatry* 157 (2000): 1552-62.

[8]The limbic system is a set of structures deep within the brain that controls our most basic emotions (e.g., fear, pleasure, anger) and drives (e.g., hunger, sex, care of offspring).

system structure) in remembering emotionally significant events. The subgenual ACC appears to mediate the subjective experience of emotion. In depressed individuals these two structures have been found to be overactivated. A third structure found to be dysfunctional in the depressive disorders is the dorsolateral prefrontal cortex, which is involved in cognitive control and the regulation of emotion. In depressed individuals this area has been found to be underactivated.[9]

**Neurochemistry.** Dysregulation in two neurotransmitters systems, norepinephrine (NE) and serotonin (5-HT), appear to be involved in the depressive disorders. Studies have consistently found decreased levels of 5-HT and NE in depressive individuals. Alterations in these two neurotransmitters lead to abnormalities in sleep, concentration, attention, and memory. These two brain chemicals also help regulate the limbic-cortical network described earlier. Abnormal regulation of this network results in the symptoms of the depressive disorder; heightened levels of anxiety and irritability, an inability to experience pleasure, excessive worry, and a lack of emotional control.[10] Treatment with antidepressant medications normalizes the levels of these two brain chemicals, resulting in a reduction in depressive symptoms in many individuals.

## Treatment

While depression is a dark and painful disorder, a number of effective treatments have been developed that can bring

[9]Julia Graham et al., "Meta-Analytic Evidence for Neuroimaging Models of Depression: State or Trait," *Journal of Affective Disorders* 151 (2013): 423-31; and Ian H. Gotlib and J. Paul Hamilton, "Neuroimaging and Depression: Current Status and Unresolved Issues," *Current Directions in Psychological Science* 17 (2008): 159-63.

[10]Kerry J. Ressler and Charles B. Nemeroff, "Role of Serotonergic and Noradrenergic Systems in the Pathophysiology of Depression and Anxiety Disorders," *Depression and Anxiety* 12, sup. 1 (2000): 2-19.

significant relief to those who are suffering. More than 80 percent of people with a depressive disorder improve when they receive appropriate treatment.

*Antidepressants.* As previously mentioned, antidepressant medications are given to alter the levels of the neurotransmitters 5-HT or NE in the brain. While some improvement in the symptoms of depression may be seen in just a few weeks, antidepressant medications generally have to be taken for three to eight weeks before the full therapeutic effect is realized. Because of the variability of response, a patient may have to try several antidepressants at different doses over a period of time before an effective treatment is found.

Antidepressant medications are grouped into five classes based on their structure or action in the brain. *Monoamine oxidase inhibitors* (MAOIs) are the oldest class of antidepressants. MAOIs inhibit an enzyme (monoamine oxidase) in the brain's cells that breaks down neurotransmitters (including 5-HT and NE) making them inactive. Dietary restrictions are necessary when taking MAOIs to minimize dangerous side effects. Drugs in this class include phenelzine (Nardil), tranylcypromine (Parnate), isocarboxazid (Marplan), and selegiline (Emsam).

*Tricyclic antidepressants* (TCAs) work by inhibiting the brain's reuptake of 5-HT and NE. They also partially inhibit the reabsorption of the neurotransmitter dopamine (DA). TCAs tend to have more side effects than other antidepressants. Side effects include weight gain, drowsiness, dizziness, nausea, dry mouth, constipation, and increased heart rate. Drugs in this class include amitriptyline (Elavil), clomipramine (Anafranil), desipramine (Norpramin), nortriptyline (Pamelor), and imipramine (Tofranil).

*Selective serotonin reuptake inhibitors* (SSRIs) are the most commonly prescribed class of antidepressants. This class of medications, as the name implies, blocks the reabsorption of 5-HT (serotonin) into the nerve cells. Drugs in this class include fluoxetine (Prozac), fluvoxamine (Luvox), sertraline (Zoloft), paroxetine (Paxil), escitalopram (Lexapro), and citalopram (Celexa).

The *serotonin and norepinephrine reuptake inhibitors* are one of the newest types of antidepressant. These medications block the reabsorption of both 5-HT and NE into the nerve cells. Drugs in this class include duloxetine (Cymbalta), venlafaxine (Effexor), desvenlafaxine (Khedezla), levomilnacipran (Fetzima), and desvenlafaxine (Pristiq).

The *atypical antidepressants* are a class of mostly newer medications that target neurotransmitters other than 5-HT and NE or have unique actions in the brain. Drugs in this class include bupropion (Wellbutrin), trazodone (Oleptro), mirtazapine (Remeron), and vortioxetine (Brintellix).

**Psychotherapy.** Research has found two psychotherapeutic approaches to be effective in treating the major depressive disorder, interpersonal psychotherapy (IPT) and cognitive-behavioral therapy.[11] The foundational idea of IPT is that depression can be treated by improving how a person relates to others. IPT puts an emphasis on the way symptoms of depression are related to a person's relationships. The goals of IPT are symptom reduction, improved interpersonal functioning, and increased social support. As mentioned in chapter six the major aim of cognitive-behavioral therapy is to help the client eliminate negative beliefs or behaviors, and replace them with positive ones.

**Electroconvulsive therapy.** Electroconvulsive therapy (ECT) is a procedure in which electric currents are passed through the brain,

---

[11]Steven D. Hollon and Kathryn Ponniah, "A Review of Empirically Supported Psychological Therapies for Mood Disorders in Adults," *Depression and Anxiety* 27 (2010): 891-932.

intentionally triggering a brief seizure. ECT, also known as "shock treatment," may seem like a frightening prospect for a patient seeking relief from depressive symptoms. In recent years, however, the ECT procedure has been greatly improved, and clinical research clearly shows it to be an effective treatment for major depression. Prior to the procedure the patient is given a muscle relaxant, and the procedure itself is performed under mild anesthesia. Electrodes are placed at precise locations on the head to deliver a low-level electrical current. The electrical stimulation causes a brief seizure in the brain, lasting about thirty seconds. It is not fully understood how ECT is effective in treating depression, although it is theorized that like antidepressants ECT alters the levels of certain neurotransmitters in the brain. For the full therapeutic effect, repeated sessions are usually required over several weeks.

*Transcranial magnetic stimulation.* Transcranial magnetic stimulation is a procedure that uses magnetic fields to stimulate nerve cells in the brain to improve symptoms of depression. During the procedure a large electromagnetic coil is placed against the patient's scalp near the forehead. The electromagnet creates electric currents that stimulate nerve cells in the prefrontal cortex thought to be involved in mood control and depression. The procedure is painless, has no reported side effects, and is usually done as an outpatient procedure in a psychiatrist's office or clinic. Daily sessions are usually required for four to six weeks to obtain the full therapeutic benefit. Each session lasts approximately forty minutes.

## The Other Side of Major Depressive Disorder

Looking back now Brenda sees that her daughter Kelly was struggling even during elementary school. "She was never comfortable spending the night at a friend's house or staying over for a slumber party. She wanted to so badly and might even try but would be terribly anxious for days in advance." As she grew, Kelly's problems with anxiety resulted in a lack of confidence and poor self-worth. She struggled to make friends in junior high and high school. "She was so desirous to have friends." Desperate to be accepted, she associated herself with a negative group of peers that treated her poorly. Kelly shared with her mother that while these girls treated her awful, "any friends were better than none."

Brenda said, "When Kelly graduated from high school, we went through all the motions of getting her ready to start college, but all the warning signs were there for us to see and know something was wrong." Kelly broke down after one quarter at college and had to come home. She refused to see a counselor. Her parents still did not fully recognize that Kelley was struggling with a mental health problem. Brenda said, "We simply changed plans, found her an apartment, and she started attending the local junior college." Kelly broke down several times over the next semester and had to move back in with her parents. This time she agreed to see a therapist.

Kelly was diagnosed with major depressive disorder and panic attacks. Brenda recalls what it was like when she first heard the diagnosis. "I felt helpless and thankful at the same time. With a diagnosis comes information, and with that you feel like there is hope. Hearing and understanding that she has depression and panic attacks made total sense. We were just so thankful to finally have answers."

Brenda says that "this experience has caused me to rely on Christ more and more. It has also made me more sensitive to other people's pain." Support has been very important for Brenda and her husband during this time. "I have a best girlfriend who has walked through this with me, as well as my sister. We also have a group of close friends, three couples, who would do anything for us, but they don't fully understand this, and I have been hurt a few times by their questions or naive advice."

Today Kelly is living at home with her parents, has a job at a local restaurant, and is working on managing her depression and anxiety. "She is gorgeous, inside and out; creative and an amazing artist. When I come upon things she has written, it blows me away how bright and creative she is! It makes me so sad that she is trapped in a mind and body that to this point have prevented her from being everything she could be. She desperately wants friends but still struggles with a lack of confidence and a negative self-image. I pray every day that an amazing woman that loves the Lord will walk into Kelly's life and mentor her. I pray that she will be in community with believers. As a parent this is very hard."

## A Biblical Example

A number of individuals in the Scriptures are reported to have experienced periods of profound sadness and grief that might be considered depression, but none were better documented than Israel's greatest king, David.

**King David.** Born in approximately 1040 BC, David was the youngest of eight brothers. Following the disobedience of King Saul, God chose the youth David, a man after his own heart (1 Samuel 13:14), to be the next king. The son of Jesse, from the tribe of Judah, he is described as "ruddy, with beautiful eyes and a handsome appearance" (1 Samuel 16:12). Upon the death of Saul at the hands of the Philistines, David became king of Judah. He ruled Judah for seven years before uniting all of Israel under a single government. King David ruled the Jewish people for forty years (c. 1010 to 970 BC), dying of natural causes at the age of seventy. He was succeeded by his son Solomon (1 Kings 2:12).

The books of 1–2 Samuel, 1 Kings, and 1 Chronicles give details of David's life and reign. In addition, he authored many of the psalms, which gives us amazing insight into his personal thoughts and struggles. David's military and political achievements are legendary even to those outside the church. As a youth he defeated the Philistine giant Goliath, and once king he united the kingdom, captured Jerusalem and made it Israel's capital, significantly expanded the borders, and made preparations for the construction of the first temple. David, and later his son Solomon, reigned during what we think of as Israel's golden age.

Despite his achievements as king and the fact that he was a man after God's own heart, David struggled in his personal life. His personal sins and family problems are almost as well-known as his successes. He was a polygamist, having at least seven wives and a number of concubines. This lead to significant discord within his family. He committed adultery with Bathsheba and then had her husband, Uriah, murdered to cover it up. This sin further undermined his reign. His firstborn son and likely heir, Amnon, raped his own half-sister Tamar. Absalom, Tamar's brother, killed Amnon, his half-brother, in revenge. Absalom later led a military rebellion against David in an attempt to make himself king. Absalom was killed during the coup. In direct disobedience to God's command David called for a census of his military, which resulted in God sending a plague that killed seventy thousand Israelites. At the end of his life, while David lay dying, his son Adonijah attempted to take the throne. Adonijah would later be killed by his half-brother Solomon, David's chosen successor.

King David knew great personal sorrow, which is clear from his own writings in the Psalms, a set of songs, hymns, or poems that were used in worship by the Jewish people. The psalms can be categorized into various types or genres, which include laments, songs of praise, liturgy, songs of thanksgiving, wisdom psalms, and pilgrim songs. Of the seventy-eight psalms authored by David, over half are laments expressing grief or sorrow. A thorough review of his writings shows that David describes experiencing all of the symptoms of major depressive disorder (see table 7.1).[12]

**Table 7.1.** Biblical example of major depressive disorder

| CHARACTERISTIC SYMPTOMS | DAVID'S SYMPTOMS | REFERENCE |
|---|---|---|
| Depressed mood | Mourning/sorrow all day, weeping | Psalm 6:6-7; 13:2; 31:10; 38:6, 17; 39:13; 69:3 |
| Significant weight loss or decrease in appetite | Forgets to eat, bones cling to flesh, weak from fasting | Psalm 102:4-5; 109:24 |
| Insomnia | Crying all night, no rest at night, couldn't sleep | Psalm 6:6; 22:2; 102:7; 2 Samuel 11:2 |
| Psychomotor retardation | Like a deaf and dumb man, fear and trembling | Psalm 38:13-14; 55:5 |
| Fatigue or loss of energy | Strength dried up/fails, vitality drained away, heart has withered away | Psalm 22:14-15; 31:10; 32:4; 38:10; 102:4 |
| Feelings of worthlessness | A worm, not a man, a reproach to others, no one cares for my soul, song of the drunkards | Psalm 22:6; 31:12-13; 69:12; 109:25; 142:4 |
| Diminished ability to think or concentrate, or indecisiveness | Did not go to war, unable to discipline rebellious sons | 2 Samuel 11:1; 13:21ᵃ; 18:5; 19:1-7; 1 Kings 1:6 |
| Recurrent thoughts of death | Dust of death, terrors of death | Psalm 22:15; 55:4 |

ᵃSeptuagint addition to verse, "but he would not punish his son Amnon, because he loved him, since he was his firstborn."

In his psalms David tangibly expresses the physical pain felt in depression:

> I am bowed down and brought very low;
>     all day long I go about mourning.
> My back is filled with searing pain;
>     there is no health in my body.

[12]Liubov Ben-Noun, "Mental Disorder That Afflicted King David the Great," *History of Psychiatry* 15 (2004): 467-76.

I am feeble and utterly crushed;
  I groan in anguish of heart.

All my longings lie open before you, Lord;
  my sighing is not hidden from you.
My heart pounds, my strength fails me;
  even the light has gone from my eyes.
  (Psalm 38:6-10 NIV)

He describes the overwhelming loneliness of being trapped in a pit of darkness:

I am the utter contempt of my neighbors
and an object of dread to my closest friends—
  those who see me on the street flee from me.
  (Psalm 31:11 NIV)

My friends and companions avoid me because of my wounds;
  my neighbors stay far away. (Psalm 38:11 NIV)

I am a foreigner to my own family,
  a stranger to my own mother's children.
  (Psalm 69:8 NIV)

And he experiences the terrifying spiritual isolation one feels from God.

How long, LORD? Will you forget me forever?
  How long will you hide your face from me?
How long must I wrestle with my thoughts
  and day after day have sorrow in my heart?
How long will my enemy triumph over me?

Look on me and answer, LORD my God.
Give light to my eyes, or I will sleep in death.

(Psalm 13:1-3 NIV)

David's centuries-old descriptions of his depressive experiences are identical to what we hear from those suffering with the depressive disorders today. Depressive disorders negatively affect every aspect of an individual's being: body, mind, spirit, and relationships. Two significant adverse events in David's life described in the Scriptures may have been the result of his depression.

In 2 Samuel 11:1 it says that in the spring, at the time when kings go to war, David sent his general Joab out to lead the army rather than going himself. David is clearly distressed at this time because he is unable to sleep (2 Samuel 11:2). His distress and inability to lead his army may have been the result of a major depressive episode. The symptoms of major depressive disorder cause significant impairment in an individual's ability to function occupationally. Depression also significantly impairs an individual's ability to interact with and relate to others. Three of David's sons, Amnon, Absalom, and Adonijah, violate significant family and relational boundaries, but the Scriptures describe David as being emotionally paralyzed and unable to discipline or correct them (2 Samuel 13:21; 18:5; 19:1-7; 1 Kings 1:6), which results in even greater personal turmoil and tragedy.

## Final Thoughts

There is an important lesson to be learned from this biblical example of depression. In a time before psychological and psychiatric treatments existed, David found relief from his suffering in God's unchanging character, infinite faithfulness, and unconditional love. David took his sorrow and pain to God, and there he found a foundation of hope from which he could re-build. Hope that transcends our circumstances, even depression, is only available in the loving God who created us, sustains us, and made a way for us to be in an eternal relationship with him. David knew this truth well, and he tightly held to it throughout his life. Our first response in times of mental distress should be to seek God. Finding our hope in him is the first step on the journey to recovery.

# 8

# OVERWHELMED

## ANXIETY DISORDERS

*When my anxious thoughts multiply within me,*
*Your consolations delight my soul.*

PSALM 94:19

DIAGNOSED WITH GENERALIZED anxiety disorder at the age of seven, Roger, now twenty-three years old, has struggled since he was an infant to control the anxiety and fear that torment him. It was clear to Roger's parents that something was different about him from the beginning. He cried more than most babies and never seemed content. As a toddler he began to show extreme compulsive behaviors, like lining up all of his shoes in a row and hoarding objects. Anything that disrupted his attempts at order and control, such as a shoe slightly misaligned, resulted in an extreme emotional display.

By the age of seven Roger feared leaving the house and, because of fear, he could not sleep in his own room but instead chose to sleep in the hallway with the light on. Because of his extreme anxiety his family was unable to eat at a restaurant, see a movie, or attend church together. Any change to his routine resulted in a debilitating episode of crying and anxiety. Roger's anxiety varied from normal childhood fears of thunder and lightning (although he feared that he would die because of the storm) to unrealistic fears of falling into quicksand. Roger's parents took him to a psychiatrist, who diagnosed him with generalized anxiety disorder, prescribed the antidepressant Zoloft, and recommended behavior therapy. At first Roger's parents were against him taking the medication. But after more strange and extreme behavior from Roger, they felt they had no choice if they were going to help their son. Roger's mother told me, "It was never smooth sailing. We felt like every time we moved one step forward we got knocked back two. Some months were better than others."

While the medication made a tremendous difference in his life, Roger continued to struggle with anxiety. As a teenager he still had an overwhelming fear of storms and of getting his clothes wet. In high school, Roger did very well athletically and academically, but the anxiety affected him socially. Unable to relax, he attempted to lower his anxiety by incessantly talking and asking questions. His peers grew weary of his constant questions and odd behavior. During this period, under direction from his psychiatrist, Roger's parents attempted to wean him off his medication. His behavior changed dramatically, and he dropped out of all his regular activities. His parents realized he still needed the medication to function normally.

Today, Roger is no longer on medication and has found ways to cope when he feels anxious. Maturity has helped him realize that many of the things he was anxious about simply aren't going to happen such as falling in quicksand. He has a better understanding of what causes him anxiety. For instance, he knows that he struggles when in large crowds with people he doesn't know. By staying away from situations such as those, his anxieties stay in check and he doesn't have trouble. He is able to function like any normal twenty-three-year-old young man, and most people he meets would never suspect he has had issues with anxiety his whole life.

## Characteristic Symptoms

Everyone knows what it is like to feel anxious—that uncomfortable, apprehensive feeling that comes over us when we are stressed. At normal levels, anxiety rouses us to action. It causes us to study more for an exam; it prepares us for action in a dangerous situation; it keeps us on task as we give an important presentation to our boss. Anxiety is a normal cognitive and physiological response that God designed to call our attention to the seriousness of an event or situation, and motivate us to action. With an anxiety disorder, however, the anxiety is not mild and brief, but severe and chronic. Panic attacks, a consuming wave of fear and dread, are a common characteristic of the anxiety disorders.

A *panic attack* is a sudden surge of overwhelming fear and anxiety that reaches a peak within minutes. The DSM-5 lists thirteen potential symptoms of a panic attack: increased heart rate, sweating, trembling, shortness of breath, feelings of choking, chest pain, nausea, dizziness, chills or heat sensations, numbness or tingling, feelings of unreality or depersonalization (being detached from oneself), fear of losing control, or fear of dying. Four or more of these symptoms must be present for the episode to be considered a panic attack. A panic attack may be a one-time occurrence in an individual's life, but many people experience multiple episodes.

## Diagnoses

While severe anxiety has been recognized as a problem since antiquity, it was typically considered only a symptom of melancholia.

This is understandable given that even modern mental health care providers seldom encounter seriously depressed patients who are not also anxious to a significant degree.[1] While the first modern medical description of anxiety appeared in Richard Burton's 1621 compendium *The Anatomy of Melancholia*, it was not until the nineteenth century that anxiety was first recognized as a common thread running through a set of related conditions.[2]

In the DSM-5 the section on anxiety disorders is placed immediately after the depressive disorders in recognition of the strong relationship between these two categories of distress. The primary anxiety disorders are separation anxiety disorder, selective mutism, specific phobia, social anxiety disorder, panic disorder, agoraphobia, and generalized anxiety disorder.

*Separation anxiety disorder.* Separation anxiety disorder is characterized by inappropriate and excessive fear or anxiety concerning separation from home or those the individual is attached to. The fear or anxiety is persistent, lasting at least four weeks in children and adolescents, and six months or more in adults.

*Selective mutism.* Selective mutism is characterized by an inability to speak in some social settings and to some people for at least one month. A child with selective mutism may talk normally at home or when alone with their parents, but cannot speak at all, or speak above a whisper, in other social settings. The disorder is often marked by high social anxiety.

*Specific phobia.* Specific phobia is characterized by extreme and irrational fear or anxiety about a specific object or situation. Specific phobias commonly focus on animals, insects, germs, heights,

---

[1]Marc-Antoine Crocq, "A History of Anxiety: From Hippocrates to DSM," *Dialogues in Clinical Neuroscience* 17 (2015): 319-25.

[2]Gerrit Glas, "A Conceptual History of Anxiety and Depression," in *Handbook on Anxiety and Depression*, ed. J. A. den Boer and A. Sitsen, 2nd ed. (New York: Marcel Dekker, 2003), 1-48.

thunder, driving, public transportation, flying, dental or medical procedures, and elevators.

*Social anxiety disorder.* Social anxiety disorder is characterized by marked fear or anxiety about social situations in which the individual is exposed to possible scrutiny or judgment by others. The fear or anxiety causes clinically significant distress, lasting for six months or more.

*Panic disorder.* Panic disorder is characterized by recurrent panic attacks that strike suddenly and without warning. Persons with panic disorder often develop intense anxiety between episodes, worrying about when and where the next panic attack will occur. To compensate for this anxiety, panic-disordered individuals often begin to avoid places and situations in which they have experienced an attack. Some people's lives become restricted to the point that they avoid even everyday activities such as driving or going to the store.

*Agoraphobia.* Agoraphobia is characterized by the avoidance of situations or places in which it is thought that escape might be difficult or help might be unavailable in the event of a panic attack or other incapacitating or embarrassing symptoms.

*Generalized anxiety disorder (GAD).* Generalized anxiety disorder is characterized by excessive anxiety and worry, even though there is little or nothing to provoke it, occurring for at least six months. In GAD, the anxiety is severe enough to affect the individual's ability to function daily. The anxiety is always more intense than the situation warrants, and the person will often recognize it as such. With GAD, the anxiety is usually accompanied by physical symptoms such as fatigue, sleeplessness, headache, muscle tension, sweating, shortness of breath, irritability, and hot flashes. During the course of the disorder, the focus of worry may shift from one concern to another.

## Prevalence and Age of Onset

Anxiety disorders are the most common mental illness in the United States, affecting approximately forty million adults (18 percent of the population).[3] The lifetime prevalence of the anxiety disorders in the United States is estimated to be 5.2 percent for separation anxiety disorder, 0.5 percent for selective mutism, 12.5 percent for specific phobia, 12.1 percent for social anxiety disorder, 4.7 percent for panic disorder, 1.4 percent for agoraphobia, and 5.7 percent for generalized anxiety disorder.[4] Women are twice as likely to be diagnosed with an anxiety disorder as men. The age of onset of selective mutism is usually before five years, while separation anxiety disorder, specific phobia, and social anxiety disorder usually first manifest in later childhood. The common age of onset for panic disorder and agoraphobia is early adulthood, while generalized anxiety disorder has the latest onset of the anxiety disorders, around thirty years.[5] Individuals with anxiety disorders are at high risk for coexisting conditions, such as depression and substance abuse.

## Developmental and Psychosocial Risk Factors

Like all mental illnesses, anxiety disorders result from a complex interaction of psychosocial, biological, and developmental factors. Research has shown a significant increase since 1950 in anxiety levels of children and college students.[6] This increase has been

---

[3]"Any Anxiety Disorder Among Adults," *National Institute of Mental Health*, accessed February 5, 2016, www.nimh.nih.gov/health/statistics/prevalence/any-anxiety-disorder-among-adults.shtml.

[4]Patricia Wong, "Selective Mutism: A Review of Etiology, Comorbidities, and Treatment," *Psychiatry* 7 (2010): 23-31; and Ronald C. Kessler et al., "Lifetime Prevalence and Age-of-Onset Distributions of DSM-IV Disorders in the National Comorbidity Survey Replication," *Archives of General Psychiatry* 62 (2005): 593-602.

[5]DSM-5.

[6]Jean M. Twenge, "The Age of Anxiety? Birth Cohort Change in Anxiety and Neuroticism, 1952–1993," *Journal of Personality and Social Psychology* 79 (2000): 1007-21.

associated with a lack of social connection and a sense of a more threatening environment. Psychological factors in childhood such as low self-esteem, fear of being abandoned or rejected, feelings of intense loneliness and helplessness, and early onset of depression have all been suggested to increase a person's risk of developing an anxiety disorder. Early life events such as childhood trauma, a negative family environment, death of a parent or sibling, and academic failure appear to be predisposing factors.[7] Major life stressors such as a physical illness, death of a loved one, a move to a new home, loss of employment, relationship problems, financial problems, or the birth of a child may play a role in triggering the onset of an anxiety disorder.

## *Neurobiology*

**Heritability.** Studies using twin pairs have consistently found higher concordance rates for the anxiety disorders in identical (monozygotic) twins when compared to fraternal (dizygotic) twins.[8] The contribution of genetic factors has been estimated to be 67 percent for agoraphobia, 51 percent for social anxiety disorder, 48 percent for panic disorder, 32 percent for generalized anxiety disorder, and 30 percent for specific phobias. Panic disorder, generalized anxiety disorder and specific phobias have been found to have a significantly higher rate of occurrence in first degree relatives of patients with anxiety disorders.[9]

---

[7]Rachel L. Grover, Golda S. Ginsburg, and Nick Ialongo, "Childhood Predictors of Anxiety Symptoms: A Longitudinal Study," *Child Psychiatry and Human Development* 36 (2005): 133-53.

[8]Katharina Domschke and Jürgen Deckert, "Genetics," in *Behavioral Neurobiology of Anxiety and Its Treatment*, ed. Murray B. Stein and Thomas Steckler (New York: Springer, 2010), 63-75.

[9]John Hettema et al., "A Review and Meta-Analysis of the Genetic Epidemiology of Anxiety Disorders," *American Journal of Psychiatry* 158 (2001): 1568-78; and Wolfgang Maier et al., "A Controlled Family Study in Panic Disorder," *Journal of Psychiatric Research* 27 (1993): 79-87.

***Neuroanatomy.*** A number of studies using brain imaging techniques have found abnormalities in specific brain areas in individuals diagnosed with anxiety disorders.[10] These areas include the frontal cortex and three deep brain structures: the amygdala, hippocampus, and anterior cingulate gyrus. The frontal cortex, amygdala, and anterior cingulate gyrus are part of a neural pathway in the brain that helps us determine the threat level of a situation or event. This system activates the body's automatic fight-or-flight response as the body prepares itself for danger. This response is what triggers symptoms like sweating and a pounding heart when we are afraid or anxious. When this system or a component of this system is not functioning correctly, a person may experience high levels of anxiety in situations that are not usually stressful or pose no threat. It has been suggested that this inability to assess the threat related to everyday situations effectively may lead to the development of an anxiety disorder.

The hippocampus, a brain area related to the three structures just discussed, is involved in emotion and in memory storage. Studies have shown that the hippocampus is smaller in people diagnosed with anxiety disorders. It is thought that prolonged exposure to glucocorticoids (adrenal steroids released during stress) causes neuronal cell death within the hippocampus, which results in the atrophy seen.[11]

---

[10]Justine M. Kent et al., "Prediction of Panic Response to a Respiratory Stimulant by Reduced Orbitofrontal Cerebral Blood Flow in Panic Disorder," *American Journal of Psychiatry* 162 (2005): 1379-81; Stefan Urusu et al., "Overactive Action Monitoring in Obsessive-Compulsive Disorder: Evidence from Functional Magnetic Resonance Imaging," *Psychological Science* 14 (2003): 347-53; and Scott L. Rauch et al., "Exaggerated Amygdala Response to Masked Facial Stimuli in Posttraumatic Stress Disorder: A Functional MRI Study," *Biological Psychiatry* 47 (2000): 769-76.

[11]Eva Irle et al., "Reduced Amygdalar and Hippocampal Size in Adults with Generalized Social Phobia," *Journal of Psychiatry and Neuroscience* 35 (2010): 126-31; and Ramon J. L. Lindhauer et al., "Effects of Psychotherapy on Hippocampal Volume in Out-Patients

*Neurochemistry.* Several studies have suggested that an imbalance in certain neurotransmitters may play a role in the development of anxiety disorders. Low levels of the neurotransmitters gamma-aminobutyric acid (GABA) and serotonin have been shown to be related to generalized anxiety disorder.[12] In a normal brain, GABA helps prevent nerve cells (neurons) from overfiring, and serotonin produces feelings of well-being. Low levels of serotonin also appear to play a role in obsessive-compulsive disorder.[13] Individuals diagnosed with anxiety disorders have been shown to have abnormalities in the levels of stress hormones and the neurotransmitter norepinephrine.[14] This may account for their high levels of irritability and tendency to startle easily.

## Treatment

Anxiety disorders, like many psychiatric disorders, are most effectively treated with a combination of medication and psychotherapy. In addition, there are a number of lifestyle changes people can make that will help reduce their anxiety. Anxiety disorders and stimulants such as caffeine or nicotine do not mix. Because stimulants increase the likelihood and severity of panic attacks, they should be avoided. Individuals with an anxiety disorder should increase their level of exercise. Aerobic exercise over fifteen weeks or more has been shown to reduce anxiety significantly. A healthy lifestyle that includes exercise, adequate rest, and good nutrition can help reduce the impact of panic attacks.

with Posttraumatic Stress Disorder: An MRI Investigation," *Psychological Medicine* 35 (2005): 1421-31.

[12]James C. Ballenger, "Overview of Different Pharmacotherapies for Attaining Remission in Generalized Anxiety Disorder," *Journal of Clinical Psychiatry* 62 (2001): 11-19.

[13]Joelle Micallef, "Neurobiology and Clinical Pharmacology of Obsessive-Compulsive Disorder," *Clinical Neuropharmacology* 24 (2001): 191-207.

[14]Elizabeth Martin et al., "The Neurobiology of Anxiety Disorders: Brain Imaging, Genetics, and Psychoneuroendocrinology," *Psychiatric Clinics of North America* 32 (2009): 549-75.

*Anxiolytics.* There are a number of anxiolytic (anxiety relieving) drugs available for health professionals to prescribe. For years the standard medication used to treat anxiety disorders has been a class of medications called benzodiazepines. Examples of this type of medication include Xanax, Klonopin, Valium, and Ativan. The most common side effect of these drugs is daytime drowsiness, or what some have described as a "hung-over feeling." Benzodiazepines lower anxiety by increasing the activity of the neurotransmitter GABA. There is a serious risk of dependency and abuse with these medications, so they are generally prescribed for only short periods of time. Individuals who have had problems with drug or alcohol abuse are not good candidates for treatment with benzodiazepines because they may become dependent on them.

Buspirone (BuSpar) is a unique anxiolytic agent that is in a class of drugs known as the azapirones. Clinical trials have found it to be effective in treating generalized anxiety disorder. While the exact mechanism of action for buspirone is unknown, it is thought that its antianxiety effects are the result of changes produced in the serotonin neurotransmitter system. Common side effects include dizziness, drowsiness, and nausea. Unlike the benzodiazepines, buspirone is not addictive and must be taken for at least two weeks to achieve an antianxiety effect.

*Antidepressants.* Due to the addictive risks associated with benzodiazepines, antidepressant medications—particularly selective serotonin reuptake inhibitors—are increasingly being used as the initial treatment for anxiety disorders. Examples of SSRIs include Prozac, Zoloft, Paxil, and Celexa. As mentioned in chapter seven, these drugs work specifically to increase levels of serotonin in the brain. Older medications such as tricyclic antidepressants (e.g., Anafranil) and monoamine oxidase inhibitors (e.g., Nardil), which affect a wider range of neurotransmitters, are also prescribed for anxiety disorders.

These medications have been shown to be as effective as the SSRIs in treating anxiety disorders, but because the side effects of these medications can be severe, most physicians and patients prefer the SSRIs.

*Psychotherapy.* The psychotherapeutic approach shown to be most effective in treating anxiety disorders is cognitive-behavioral therapy. The focus of CBT is to reduce anxiety by eliminating beliefs and behaviors that help to maintain the disorder. To be effective, the therapy must be directed at the person's specific anxieties. For example, an individual with a specific phobia who is fearful of dirt and germs may be encouraged to actually get their hands dirty during a session. As anxiety builds because of the "contamination," the therapist works with the patient to develop skills for managing the physical sensations and negative thoughts. Over a number of sessions the therapist might encourage the person to wait for increasingly longer periods of time before washing. Treatment usually lasts from twelve to twenty weeks. It may be conducted individually or in a group setting, provided the people in the group have similar problems.

## *The Other Side of Social Anxiety Disorder*

Martha first noticed Hannah's anxiety the summer before seventh grade. "We dropped her off at church camp, and the next morning she called and said I needed to pick her up because she was not feeling well. I didn't think much of it, just thought she was sick. I did think it strange that once in the car all her symptoms disappeared and she felt fine by the time we got home." The next few years Hannah's fears and anxiety increased to the point that she would become virtually nonfunctional in social situations. "Every time she was invited to a gathering or there was some school or church event, she would say she was sick. She would complain of stomach pains and would often have a low-grade fever. We took her to the doctor for a physical with blood work, but he could find nothing wrong. She was fine going to school, but with any other social situation all she wanted to do was lay in the bed and isolate herself."

Hannah's parents found a local therapist for her to see. "Our first interaction with the mental health care system was a disaster. The therapist was very unprofessional, diagnosing Hannah with obsessive-compulsive disorder after only a few minutes of conversation and then focusing on parental conflict as the most significant problem. Hannah refused to go back to the therapist or be involved in any type of treatment or intervention for years." Martha said she cried a lot about Hannah's struggles. "I knew she couldn't change on her own but we just didn't know what to do."

The summer before her sophomore year of high school, Hannah agreed to try medication to control her anxiety. "Our first attempt with medication didn't go well either. Hannah was prescribed Paxil, and instead of lowering her anxiety it actually made it worse. After about a month or so she stopped taking it."

A few more years of suffering, another unhelpful therapist, and another unsuccessful round of medication left Hannah's family feeling frustrated and concerned about her future. "She had socially become a hermit." The summer before her senior year in high school, a referral to a clinical psychologist who diagnosed her with social anxiety disorder and a third try at medication changed everything. "It was almost like a miracle. She turned around so quickly once she received the right treatment." Today Hannah is in college, independent and full of life. "She manages her anxiety very well with medication, an occasional trip to the psychologist, and massages."

## A Biblical Example

The people of biblical times recognized that fear and anxiety had both cognitive (mental) and physiological components. A number of Scriptures describe the mental anguish of anxiety (e.g., Psalm 94:19; Proverbs 12:25), while others illustrate that overwhelming fear can cause a pounding heart, trembling, and physical pain (Job 4:14; Psalm 48:5-6; Isaiah 13:7-8; 21:3-4; Sirach 48:19). While no clear examples of anxiety disorders exists in the Scriptures there does appear to be a description of panic attacks in Psalm 55.

Authored by King David, Psalm 55 describes the betrayal by David's friend and counselor Ahithophel (2 Samuel 15:31). Heartbroken by his son Absalom's attempt to take the throne from him, David appears to begin to have panic attacks when he learns that Ahithophel has also turned against him. The symptoms David describe meet the DSM-5 diagnostic criteria for a panic attack (see table 8.1). Individuals suffering with major depressive disorder like King David (as discussed in chap. 7) often also struggle with clinically significant levels of anxiety.

**Table 8.1.** Biblical description of a panic attack

| CHARACTERISTIC SYMPTOMS | DAVID'S SYMPTOMS | REFERENCE |
|---|---|---|
| Palpitations, pounding heart, or accelerated heart rate | Heart is in anguish within me | Psalm 55:4 |
| Trembling or shaking | Trembling, shuddering | Psalm 55:5 |
| Chest pain or discomfort | Heart is in anguish within me | Psalm 55:4 |
| Fear of dying | Terrors of death | Psalm 55:4 |

*Note:* Verse 4 is variously translated as "My heart is sore pained within me" (KJV), "My heart beats violently within me" (NET), and "My heart is in anguish within me" (NASB). Together these give the sense of an increased heart rate with chest pain.

## Final Thoughts

Anxiety disorders result from a neurobiological dysfunction. They are brain disorders! The overwhelming panic described by David in Psalm 55 is not the same as the normal levels of worry and concern that Jesus talks about in the Sermon on the Mount (Matthew 6:25-34) and the apostles Paul (Philippians 4:6) and Peter (1 Peter 5:7) mention in their epistles. As the body of Christ we must be aware of this difference when ministering to those struggling with anxiety disorders. The Scriptures do not teach that anxiety is a sin but rather anticipate and expect that we will all experience fear and anxiety at some level. The great truth the Bible does teach us about anxiety is that when we struggle, God is present, taking care of our needs and providing the sustaining grace needed to persevere in a fallen world.

# 9

# BROKEN AND CRUSHED

## TRAUMA- AND STRESSOR-RELATED DISORDERS

*Trauma is an expulsive cataclysm of the soul.*

DAVID BROOKS

MONICA IS THE SMALL-TOWN GIRL who always wanted to get out and see the world. As a young child she would chart her uncle's travels in the Navy and drill him with questions about the exotic, faraway places he visited and lived. "I was determined to go there myself one day." Growing up in an extended family with parents, siblings, grandparents, an uncle, and periodically, various cousins under the same roof was chaotic. Monica says, "We were a happy, dysfunctional, enmeshed family." The stress of her home life and hidden abuse took its toll on young Monica, and by ten she was struggling with significant depression, which included suicidal thoughts.

In the midst of her struggle, school was a safe place and an escape. She excelled in academics and graduated with honors from both high school and university. The year after graduating from high school she went to Germany as an exchange student. "My year in Germany birthed the idea that my desire to travel the world and my love for other cultures should be combined with my desire to share the gospel by doing full-time mission work."

After returning from Germany, Monica enrolled in a Christian college with an emphasis on missions. "I wanted to get a degree that would allow me to go anywhere in the world to share the gospel." While working on her degree, she started a ministry for international students and worked with immigrants and the poor through local ministries. "I dove into every mission opportunity possible, both local and abroad. I saw education as the source of empowerment both for myself and for others, and I saw that it was an excellent vehicle for spreading the gospel."

After finishing college Monica enrolled in seminary to continue her education. Her first job after completing seminary was teaching third grade at an inner-city school. After three years of teaching elementary school, she was presented with the opportunity to go to South Asia as a missionary, and she jumped at the chance. This was what she had been waiting for all her life.

Two years later Monica's lifelong dream of traveling the world to share the gospel was shattered in South Asia when she was sexually assaulted. "After the assault and living in an environment in which I was sexually harassed on a regular basis, I started experiencing physical symptoms in addition to emotional ones. It manifested through migraines and ultimately my entire right side went numb. I started not being unable to remember things. Due to the physical symptoms, I underwent a variety of medical tests, which all came out inconclusive." Monica's symptoms worsened to the point that she could not leave her apartment. "I could not function. I would sleep, cry, or watch TV in a trance-like state. I barely ate or overate. I was forced to leave South Asia."

Upon returning to the United States Monica spent a month in a center for wounded Christian workers. She met with a counselor three times a week, with an eye movement desensitization and reprocessing specialist twice a week, and a women's support group and pastoral counselor once a week. During this time she was diagnosed with complex posttraumatic stress disorder (PTSD). The diagnosis came as a relief. "I finally had an explanation for why I felt crazy. I now had hope because I knew recovery was possible and there were resources."

"The effect of the trauma on me has put a strain on my family. They do not understand and at first did not want to even acknowledge that I was struggling. My parents wanted me to get over it and move on. They had expectations of me picking up my life where I left off when I left for South Asia three and a half years before. As part of my recovery process I have had to create healthy boundaries with my family."

Monica says that because of the trauma, she has lost the faith she once had and let go of her understanding of God. In its place she has a new and stronger faith built on surrender and rest. "Mental illness is not something you fight. You ride it like a wave safely back to shore. I have encountered a new God; one who is loving and not out to punish me. My soul is safe with him despite what happens. I am not to blame for my trauma. He grieves for me and those who hurt me. I am learning how to be a wounded healer. I have great hope and long to see how God will use my pain, struggles, and brokenness to bring healing and hope to others."

## Characteristic Symptoms

The trauma- and stressor-related disorders are serious psychological reactions that develop in some individuals following exposure to a traumatic or stressful event such as childhood neglect, childhood physical or sexual abuse, combat, physical assault, sexual assault, natural disaster, an accident, or torture.

The characteristic symptom of psychological distress resulting from childhood emotional neglect is impairment in the child's ability to relate interpersonally to adults and peers. This symptom is unique to disorders resulting from a pattern of insufficient caregiving that limits an infant's opportunities to form stable attachments. The characteristic symptoms of all other trauma- and stressor-related disorders can be placed into four broad categories: intrusion symptom, avoidance symptoms, negative alterations in cognition and mood, and hyperarousal symptoms.

*Intrusion symptoms.* Intrusion symptoms include recurrent, involuntary and distressing memories, thoughts, and dreams of the traumatic event. The individual may also experience flashbacks, a dissociative experience in which they feel or act as if the traumatic event is reoccurring. Exposure to stimuli or cues that resemble some aspect of the traumatic event may also result in marked distress for the individual.

*Avoidance symptoms.* Avoidance symptoms are efforts to avoid internal (memories, thoughts, feelings) or external (people, places, situations) reminders of the traumatic event. Preoccupation with avoiding trauma-related feelings and stimuli can become a central focus of the individual's life.

*Negative alterations in cognition and mood.* Negative alterations in cognition and mood include problems remembering important aspects of the traumatic event, depression, fear, guilt, shame, and feelings of isolation from others.

*Hyperarousal symptoms.* Hyperarousal symptoms are often reported to be some of the most troubling symptoms of the trauma- and stressor-related disorders. These symptoms include being jumpy and easily startled, irritability, angry outbursts, self-destructive behavior, problems concentrating, and difficulty sleeping.

## Diagnoses

It has long been understood that exposure to a traumatic event, particularly combat, causes some individuals to display abnormal thoughts and behaviors that we today refer to as mental illness. The first medical diagnosis for a trauma-related disorder is attributed to Swiss military physicians who in 1678 identified a pattern of symptoms caused by exposure to combat, which they called "nostalgia." This condition was characterized by melancholy, incessant thinking of home, disturbed sleep, weakness, loss of appetite, anxiety, cardiac palpitations, stupor, and fever. Accounts of trauma-related disorders have historically been linked to warfare.

During World War I "shell shock" was a significant medical and military problem. Symptoms included fatigue, tremor, confusion, nightmares, and impaired sight and hearing. Initially it was believed shell shock resulted from physical injury to the nerves due to exposure to heavy artillery bombardment. As medical personnel began recognizing that many soldiers suffered these symptoms without having been on the front lines, a greater emphasis was placed on psychological factors as the cause.[1]

The onset of World War II once again resulted in a number of soldiers exposed to combat showing anxiety, intense autonomic arousal, flashbacks, and sensitivity to stimuli that reminded them of the original trauma. The term most commonly used for this condition at that time was *combat exhaustion*. Unfortunately, while this condition was recognized by medical personnel as psychological in nature, those suffering with the condition were often shamed and reprimanded by their superiors because they were thought to be weak and cowardly.

---

[1]Steve Bentley, "A Short History of PTSD: From Thermopylae to Hue Soldiers Have Always Had a Disturbing Reaction to War," *VVA Veteran*, March-April (2005), www.mycombatptsd.com/threads/a-short-history-of-ptsd-from-thermopylae-to-hue.2989.

The DSM-I, published in 1952, included the diagnosis of "gross stress reaction." The criteria for this disorder were intentionally broad and recognized that exposure to traumatic events other than combat (e.g., natural disaster) could also cause significant distress. Without explanation the DSM-II, published in 1968, omitted the diagnosis of "gross stress reaction." The publication of the DSM-III in 1980 saw the inclusion of "posttraumatic stress disorder" as an anxiety disorder for the first time. Subsequent editions of the diagnostics manual (DSM-III-R, DSM-IV, DSM-IV-TR) continued to include PTSD as an anxiety disorder.[2] In the most recent edition of the manual, DSM-5, all trauma- and stressor-related disorders are for the first time grouped together in a single category. The primary trauma- and stressor-related disorders are reactive attachment disorder, disinhibited social engagement disorder, posttraumatic stress disorder, acute stress disorder, and the adjustment disorders.

***Reactive attachment disorder (RAD).*** Reactive attachment disorder usually presents before age five and is characterized by serious problems in emotional attachment to others. These children rarely seek comfort when distressed and are minimally emotionally responsive to others. RAD results from a pattern of insufficient caregiving or emotional neglect that limits an infant's opportunities to form stable attachments. Children who are adopted from foreign orphanages are commonly affected, particularly if they were removed from their birth parents during the first weeks of life.

***Disinhibited social engagement disorder.*** Disinhibited social engagement disorder is characterized by a pattern of behavior that involves culturally inappropriate, overly familiar behavior with unfamiliar adults and strangers. Like RAD, this disorder results from

[2]Nancy C. Andreasen, "Posttraumatic Stress Disorder: A History and a Critique," *Annals of the New York Academy of Science* 1208 (2010): 67-71.

a pattern of insufficient caregiving or emotional neglect that limits an infant's opportunities to form stable attachments.

***Posttraumatic stress disorder.*** Posttraumatic stress disorder is characterized by significant psychological distress lasting more than a month following exposure to a traumatic or stressful event. Symptoms from all of the categories previously discussed must be present.

***Acute stress disorder.*** Acute stress disorder is similar to PTSD but the duration of the psychological distress is only three days to one month following exposure to a traumatic or stressful event.

***Adjustment disorders.*** Adjustment disorders are characterized by the development of emotional or behavioral symptoms in response to an identifiable stressor (e.g., problems at work, going off to college). Adjustment disorder symptoms vary from person to person but must occur within three months of the stressful event, and once the stressor has ended the symptoms do not persist more than six months.

## Prevalence and Age of Onset

Determining the prevalence of the trauma-related disorders is somewhat difficult because unlike other mental disorders they do not spontaneously occur but are triggered by exposure to a specific traumatic or stressful event. RAD and disinhibited social engagement disorder are thought to be rare in the general population, affecting less than 1 percent of children under the age of five. However, the rates of these disorders are thought to be significantly higher in institutionalized populations. For example, it is estimated that half of all US children adopted from orphanages, along with 40 percent of children in the foster care system, meet criteria for these disorders.[3]

---

[3]Shawnna Balasingham, "An Uncommon Disorder That Is Fairly Common Among Institutionalized Children," *Columbia Social Work Review* (2012): 63-70.

The lifetime prevalence of PTSD in the United States is estimated to be 8.7 percent of the population. PTSD occurs more commonly in women than men and can occur at any age. The prevalence of acute stress disorder varies according to the nature of the traumatic event. For example, significantly higher rates of individuals show acute stress disorder following an assault or rape (20-50 percent) than following a motor vehicle accident (13-21 percent). Acute stress disorder can occur at any age and is more common in women than men.

Adjustment disorders are the least severe and the most common of the trauma- and stressor-related disorders.[4] The prevalence of adjustment disorders varies widely as a function of the population and setting studied. Research estimates that 2.9 percent of primary care patients meet criteria for an adjustment disorder while 5-20 percent of outpatient mental health clients have been found to meet criteria.[5] Adjustment disorders can occur at any age.

## Developmental and Psychosocial Risk Factors

Research has shown that a vast majority (89.7 percent) of the population reports exposure to traumatic events. In fact, exposure to multiple traumatic events in one's lifetime is the norm.[6] However, only a small percentage of individuals exposed to trauma will go on to show a trauma-related disorder. A number of factors have been found that increase a person's risk of significant distress after exposure to a traumatic event. These risk factors include experiencing a prior trauma, preexisting psychological problems, a family

[4]DSM-5.
[5]Anna Fernández et al., "Adjustment Disorders in Primary Care: Prevalence, Recognition and Use of Services," *British Journal of Psychiatry* 201 (2012): 137-42.
[6]Dean G. Kilpatrick et al., "National Estimates of Exposure to Traumatic Events and PTSD Prevalence Using DSM-IV and DSM-5 Criteria," *Journal of Traumatic Stress* 26 (2013): 537-47.

history of mental illness, lower socioeconomic status, high trait anxiety, and a lack of social support.[7]

## Neurobiology

**Heritability.** Like all mental disorders the trauma- and stressor-related disorders would be considered polygenetic disorders. This means they are not the result of variation in a single gene but rather an individual's inherited vulnerability for a trauma-related disorder is likely influenced by multiple genes. Family studies have demonstrated children whose mother or father has been diagnosed with PTSD are five times more likely to receive the diagnosis themselves compared to children whose parents did not develop PTSD.[8] Twin studies have found that 30–40 percent of the variance in PTSD symptoms can be accounted for by genetic factors.[9] Taken together these data indicate that the genetic makeup of some individuals renders them considerably more vulnerable than others to developing distressing symptoms following trauma.

**Neuroanatomy.** The cognitive and social deficits present in children with RAD and disinhibited social engagement disorder are related to underdevelopment of the brain caused by the absence of a nurturing primary caregiver in the first months of life. These developmental brain defects leave the child with a reduced ability to regulate emotions, show empathy, and form and maintain

---

[7]Sharain Suliman et al., "Predictors of Acute Stress Disorder Severity," *Journal of Affective Disorders* 149 (2013): 277-81; and Emily J. Ozer et al., "Predictors of Posttraumatic Stress Disorder and Symptoms in Adults: A Meta-Analysis," *Psychological Bulletin* 129 (2003): 52-73.

[8]William H. Sack et al., "Posttraumatic Stress Disorder Across Two Generations of Cambodian Refugees," *Journal of the American Academy of Child and Adolescent Psychiatry* 34 (1995): 1160-66.

[9]Murray B. Stein et al., "Genetic and Environmental Influences on Trauma Exposure and Posttraumatic Stress Disorder Symptoms: A Twin Study," *American Journal of Psychiatry* 159 (2002): 1675-81; and William R. True et al., "A Twin Study of Genetic and Environmental Contributions to Liability for Posttraumatic Stress Symptoms," *Archives of General Psychiatry* 50 (1993): 257-64.

meaningful relationships. Recovery from these symptoms is thought to be possible if the emotional neglect does not persist beyond the age of six months. Neglect that continues beyond six months is thought to cause permanent damage to the brain, resulting in long-lasting deficits in social and cognitive functioning.[10] Several areas of the brain have been shown to function abnormally in PTSD. Reduced activity in the anterior cingulate cortex (ACC) and medial prefrontal cortex (mPFC) results in a lack of control over emotional regulation. This leads to the problems with cognition and mood seen in PTSD. Increased activity in the amygdala and insular cortex causes nonthreatening stimuli and situations to be experienced as threatening.[11] Overactivation in these areas produces hyperarousal symptoms. Reduced volume in the hippocampus is likely the primary cause of the intrusion symptoms (distressing memories, flashbacks, and nightmares).[12]

*Neurochemistry.* Dysregulation in both hormonal and neurotransmitter systems appears to play a role in the trauma-related disorders. Individuals diagnosed with PTSD have been shown to secrete low levels of cortisol (from the adrenal glands) and high levels of corticotropin-releasing hormone (from the paraventricular nucleus of the hypothalamus). This dysregulation in what is called the hypothalamic-pituitary-adrenal axis (HPA axis) results in an exaggerated stress response.[13] These same individuals have been

---

[10]John P. Kemph and Kytja K. S. Voeller, "Reactive Attachment Disorder in Adolescents," *Adolescent Psychiatry* 30 (2008): 159-80; and Peter M. Lake, "Recognizing Reactive Attachment Disorder," *Behavioral Health Management* 25 (2005): 41-44.

[11]The insula is a cortical area involved in perception, self-awareness, and interpersonal experiences.

[12]Ronak Patel et al., "Neurocircuitry Models of Posttraumatic Stress Disorder and Beyond: A Meta-Analysis of Functional Neuroimaging Studies," *Neuroscience and Biobehavioral Reviews* 36 (2012): 2130-42; and Sarah N. Garfinkel and Israel Liberzon, "Neurobiology of PTSD: A Review of Neuroimaging Findings," *Psychiatric Annals* 39 (2009): 370-81.

[13]The HPA axis is responsible for coordinating the body's hormonal response to stress.

shown to have abnormally high concentrations of dopamine (DA) and norepinephrine in their brain. High levels of these two neurotransmitters likely contribute to the hyperarousal symptoms seen in PTSD. Low levels of the neurotransmitters serotonin (5-HT) and gamma-aminobutyric acid have also been shown to play a role in PTSD. Decreased concentrations of these two neurotransmitters results in increased impulsiveness and high levels of anxiety for the individual diagnosed with PTSD.[14]

## Treatment

As can be seen from the previous description, psychological trauma has destructive effects on both the anatomy and function of the brain. Successful treatment of the trauma-related disorders usually requires both medication and some form of psychotherapy.

*Selective serotonin reuptake inhibitors.* As described in the depressive disorders chapter, these antidepressant medications block 5-HT from being reabsorbed into the brain cells. Currently only the SSRIs Zoloft (sertraline) and Paxil (paroxetine) are approved by the Food and Drug Administration for the treatment of PTSD. There is strong evidence that Prozac (fluoxetine) may also be effective in treating the trauma-related disorders.

*Psychotherapy.* Two forms of trauma-focused cognitive-behavior therapy (TF-CBT) have been shown to be effective in treating the trauma-related disorders. Prolonged exposure therapy is a variant of CBT that has been shown to be effective in treating both anxiety and trauma-related disorders. In prolonged exposure therapy the therapist creates a safe environment in which to expose the individual to the things they fear and avoid. The exposure to the feared

---

[14]Jonathan E. Sherin and Charles B. Nemeroff, "Post-Traumatic Stress Disorder: The Neurobiological Impact of Psychological Trauma," *Dialogues in Clinical Neuroscience* 13 (2011): 263-78.

objects, activities, or situations in a safe environment helps reduce fear and decrease avoidance.

In cognitive processing therapy (CPT) the therapist seeks to help the client gain an understanding of the traumatic event and take control of distressing thoughts and feelings associated with it. Components of CPT include learning about the symptoms of PTSD; exploring how the traumatic event has affected the client's life; learning the connection between trauma-related thoughts, feelings, and behaviors; remembering the traumatic event and experiencing the emotions associated with it; and learning skills to challenge maladaptive thoughts related to the trauma.

## The Other Side of PTSD

Trey's wounds weren't obvious when he returned from a tour of duty in Iraq. His wife, Jane, says, "I noticed small things when he first got back, but we were both young and I never thought much of it. He drove more aggressively, he was quick tempered, and he seemed a little harder. It wasn't until he had been home for almost two years that he had his first major event. We were watching TV and a character in the show was driving her kids to school when she had a war-related flashback of a child strapped to a bomb standing in front of her. Trey started sweating and left. He left the house! At 10 p.m.! I could not figure out what was going on. It wasn't until he came home several hours later that he was able to tell me he couldn't handle those things because they had happened to him. From that point it was a downward spiral for about six years."

During those years Jane describes Trey as "angry, guarded, mean, disconnected, and when he wasn't any of those he was asleep; that's all he ever wanted to do." She says, "I remember thinking a lot of times it may have been better if he had died on the battlefield. I know that sounds harsh, but our life was a living hell! When he was finally diagnosed with PTSD and a mild traumatic brain injury, I was actually relieved. We had struggled for so long not knowing what was going on; it felt good to finally have an answer. I knew things would never be the same, but at least I knew why."

When asked how Trey's illness has affected her faith, Jane said, "In the beginning I prayed a lot, and church was an escape for me and the kids. In the middle, when it was really bad, I hated God. I couldn't understand why Trey was so broken, and he wasn't getting better. I was so angry with God for giving me that life while everyone else around me seemed so happy. That resulted in me being angry with God for about three years. As Trey and I began to get counseling, I began to seek God again and wouldn't you know, things got better!"

Today, after many years of counseling, Jane and Trey's family is doing well. "We still have very tough times, but Trey and I have learned to communicate and get through them. I know him well enough to know when he needs to be quiet or alone. I would love for people to know that Trey is doing great! He adores our three children and is fully active in their lives. He does lots of peer-to-peer support with veterans going through the same types of struggles."

## Biblical Examples

The oldest historical reference to traumatic events leading to mental illness can be found in the Old Testament. While describing the destruction that will come upon the Israelites if they choose not to keep their covenant with God, Moses says that disobedience will result in drought, disease, military oppression, rape, robbery, and slavery. He goes on to say that these events will be so traumatic, so devastating, that "you shall be driven mad by the sight of what you see" (Deuteronomy 28:34). In my opinion, this is a clear reference to what we today call posttraumatic stress disorder. In addition, two individuals described in the Old Testament, Jacob and Job, experience trauma and subsequently display the symptoms of PTSD.

*Jacob.* The events in the life of the third Hebrew patriarch, Jacob, are well-known to followers of both Judaism and Christianity. The son of Isaac and grandson of Abraham, Jacob was born holding on to the heel of his twin brother, Esau. With the assistance of his mother, Rebekah, Jacob stole his brother's firstborn birthright by deceiving his blind and dying father into giving him the family blessing. Despite this deception, God was faithful to his covenant with Abraham and Isaac, and blessed Jacob and his family. With his four wives Jacob had twelve sons, who became the fathers of the twelve tribes of Israel.[15] Jacob died in Egypt of natural causes at the age of 147 (Genesis 47:28).

The story of Jacob's traumatic exposure and subsequent mental health problems are described in the book of Genesis and the writings of Titus Flavius Josephus.[16] The trauma that devastates Jacob is the apparent death of his favored son, Joseph. Although Joseph is actually sold into slavery and alive in Egypt, through the deception of his other sons Jacob believes that Joseph was killed by wild animals. Jacob's sons present their father with Joseph's coat of many colors, torn and covered in blood, as proof of his violent death. Exposure to this event meets the first criterion for posttraumatic stress disorder in the DSM-5.[17]

---

[15]The twelve tribes of Israel are Reuben, Simeon, Judah, Dan, Naphtali, Gad, Asher, Issachar, Zebulun, Benjamin, and Joseph's two sons, Manasseh and Ephraim, who were adopted by Jacob. Levi was set aside for the Lord and did not count as one of the twelve.

[16]Flavius Josephus, *The New Complete Works of Josephus*, trans. William Whiston (Grand Rapids: Kregel, 1999).

[17]Exposure to actual or threatened death in the following way—learning that the traumatic event occurred to a close family member or close friend. In cases of actual or threatened death of a family member or friend, the event must have been violent or accidental.

While a period of profound grief and sorrow would be expected following the death of a child, the effects of this trauma adversely affect Jacob's ability to function for the rest of his life. Following Joseph's apparent death, Jacob goes into a deep depression that lasts years and develops an unrealistic fear that something similar will happen to Joseph's younger brother, Benjamin. This causes Jacob to not allow Benjamin to leave his side even as an adult. When it becomes necessary to allow Benjamin to leave with his brothers to buy food in Egypt due to a famine, Jacob refuses, putting the entire family at risk of starvation. The overwhelming fear that the traumatic death of Joseph will somehow be repeated in Benjamin's life damages Jacob's relationships with his other sons, alters his perception of his surroundings, and limits his ability to make decisions for his family.[18] When viewed within a modern diagnostic context (see table 9.1) Jacob appears to meet the criteria for posttraumatic stress disorder.

**Table 9.1.** Biblical example of posttraumatic stress disorder (Jacob)

| CHARACTERISTIC SYMPTOMS | JACOB'S SYMPTOMS | REFERENCE |
|---|---|---|
| **Intrusion Symptoms** | | |
| Intense or prolonged distress upon exposure to trauma cues | Distressed all day, tired from grief upon Benjamin leaving | JA 2.6.5 |
| **Avoidance Symptoms** | | |
| Avoidance of or efforts to avoid external reminders | Refuses to send Benjamin to Egypt | Genesis 42:4, 38 |
| **Negative Alterations in Cognitions and Mood** | | |
| Persistent and exaggerated negative beliefs or expectations | Believes something bad will happen to Benjamin if he leaves home, foreshortened future, negative view of his life | Genesis 42:4; 45:28; 47:9 |
| Persistent negative emotional state | Prolonged period of depression | Genesis 37:35; JA 2.3.4, 2.6.3 |

[18]Aiton Birnbaum, "Jacob and Joseph: A Biblical Case Study of Posttraumatic Stress Disorder," *Journal of Aggression, Maltreatment and Trauma* 14 (2007): 75-86.

| CHARACTERISTIC SYMPTOMS | JACOB'S SYMPTOMS | REFERENCE |
|---|---|---|
| Feelings of detachment or estrangement from others | Concern is only for Benjamin, detached from other sons | Genesis 42:36; 44:30; JA 2.6.5 |
| **Alterations in Arousal and Reactivity** | | |
| Irritable behavior and angry outbursts | Irritability and anger with sons | Genesis 42:36; 43:6 |
| Reckless or self-destructive behavior | Places Simeon at risk of execution Places family at risk of starvation | Genesis 42:19, 24; JA 2.6.5 Genesis 43:8, 10; JA 2.6.5 |

JA = Flavius Josephus, *Jewish Antiquities*

***Job.*** Living during the time of the patriarchs (Abraham, Isaac, and Jacob), Job was a prominent and wealthy leader of a family clan in the land of Uz. God says that "there [was] no one like him on the earth, a blameless and upright man, fearing God and turning away from evil" (Job 1:8). Because of his great faith Job was assaulted by Satan. In a single day Job lost his wealth and status, all his servants were murdered, and his ten children died in a wind storm. Even after this incredible set of traumatic events Job held strong to his faith, causing Satan to afflict him with painful sores all over his body. Exposure to any of the traumatic events Job experienced would meet the first criterion for posttraumatic stress disorder in the DSM-5.

A period of profound sadness would be expected after such a set of personal tragedies. However, the psychological and physiological effects of these traumas affect Job for at least several months (Job 7:3); Jewish tradition tells us it was a full year. The detail provided in the book of Job offers us clear insight into the thoughts, feelings, and actions of Job as he tries to cope with the devastation that has come upon him. As he debates his friends on the cause of his circumstances, Job describes virtually every symptom seen in individuals suffering with PTSD today (see table 9.2). He has nightmares and fearful visions of the tragic events, he is depressed, irritable, unable to sleep, emotionally numb, and wishes that death might end his suffering.

**Table 9.2.** Biblical example of posttraumatic stress disorder (Job)

| CHARACTERISTIC SYMPTOMS | JOB'S SYMPTOMS | REFERENCE |
|---|---|---|
| **Intrusion Symptoms** | | |
| Recurrent, involuntary, and intrusive distressing memories | Distressing memories | Job 9:27-28 |
| Recurrent distressing dreams | Nightmares | Job 7:14 |
| Dissociative reactions in which the individual feels or acts as if the trauma is recurring | Flashbacks (visions) | Job 7:13-14 |
| Marked physiological reactions to internal or external trauma cues | Thoughts cause trembling | Job 21:6 |
| **Avoidance Symptoms** | | |
| Avoidance of or efforts to avoid internal reminders | Tries to avoid thoughts and memories | Job 9:27-28 |
| **Negative Alterations in Cognitions and Mood** | | |
| Persistent and exaggerated negative beliefs or expectations | Foreshortened future | Job 7:6-7, 16; 9:25; 10:20; 16:22; 17:1 |
| Persistent negative emotional state | Depression, shame, fear | Job 3:24; 6:2-3; 4:5; 7:3-4; 10:15; 30:31 |
| Feelings of detachment or estrangement from others | Feels detached and alone, abandoned by family and friends | Job 12:4; 16:10; 17:6; 19:13-19; 30:1, 9-10 |
| Persistent inability to experience positive emotions | Will never see happiness again, no joy | Job 7:7; 9:25; 10:20 |
| **Alterations in Arousal and Reactivity** | | |
| Irritable behavior and angry outbursts | Anger | Job 15:12-13; 18:4 |
| Hypervigilance | No ease, no quietness, no rest, churning inside | Job 3:26; 30:27 |
| Sleep disturbance | Insomnia | Job 7:4, 13-14 |

## Final Thoughts

The biblical descriptions of PTSD in the lives of Jacob and Job demonstrate to us that mental health problems are no respecter of faith. Simply being a person of faith, even an exemplary faith as in the case of Job, is not enough to keep one from struggling with mental health problems. The unfortunate fact is that mental illness occurs at the same rates in followers of Christ as it is does outside the church.[19] Yet in the midst of trauma and tragedy, faith serves as a stabilizing anchor in an ever-changing sea. Jacob and Job were both overwhelmed by trauma, which psychologically and physically damaged them, yet their faith was a sustaining force that gave them a foundation from which to heal.

[19]Edward B. Rogers et al., "The Effects of Mental Illness on Families Within Faith Communities," *Mental Health, Religion and Culture* 15 (2012): 301-13.

# 10

# DISTRESSED AND DESTRUCTIVE

## PERSONALITY DISORDERS

*My mother rages and alienates everyone, then wonders why she has no friends. She is very intense, makes false accusations, and has even made up lies about me!*

CARRIE, WHOSE MOTHER IS DIAGNOSED WITH
BORDERLINE PERSONALITY DISORDER

TO MANY IT WOULD LOOK LIKE Luis never had a chance. Born into poverty, Luis's father spent the better part of his childhood and adolescence in prison for armed robbery and drug distribution. Luis's mother struggled to support the family and was often not around to provide the supervision her children so desperately needed. Luis found school difficult from the beginning. His poor academic performance angered and frustrated him. He took his frustration out on the younger and weaker children at school and quickly gained a reputation as a bully. Drug use and gang involvement were part of his life by junior high. His addiction progressed quickly from alcohol and marijuana to harder drugs, including methamphetamine and heroin.

Run-ins with the juvenile justice system led to numerous detention centers and boot camps. At seventeen he was arrested for drug distribution, tried as an adult, and spent one year in prison. Luis completed his GED while in prison, but little else positive came from the experience. Upon release he quickly returned to gang life and crime. By the age of twenty-three he was addicted to heroin, had a long arrest record, had physically assaulted numerous people, shot two others, been stabbed twice, and had a baby by a former girlfriend. His parole officer set up the psychological evaluation that first diagnosed Luis with antisocial personality disorder. Much like his previous incarcerations, the diagnosis brought little change to his life.

Coming down off a bad drug trip, Luis ran into an old high school friend who told him about a local church that had changed his life. Luis still isn't really sure why he went to the church on Sunday, but he was curious, and he knew his life was going nowhere. There he met a couple who invited him to lunch despite the fact that they came from two very different worlds. Luis became more involved at the church, enrolled in their drug treatment program, and turned his life around. No more crime, no more gangs, no more drugs. He reconciled with his child's mother, and they were married. For the first time Luis had hope for the future, and he wanted the same for his young son. He started a lawn care and handyman business—his first legal job. He also began to share his transformation experience with his older brother, who was incarcerated and whose life had paralleled his own.

Today, Luis is happily married with three kids. He helps run the treatment program that turned his life around and is active at his church. His brother has also had a life transformation and is clean and sober. Recently Luis visited his father, who has been out of prison only a few years. "I want my kids to know their grandfather.

I know that their life is going to be different than mine because I have chosen to break the generational cycle of crime and pain in my family. Without God's intervention I would most likely be dead today. Instead, he is using my destructive past to help set others free."

## Characteristic Symptoms

Personality disorders are characterized by a long-lasting, rigid pattern of maladaptive thoughts, feelings, and behaviors. This enduring pattern of inner experience and behavior deviates markedly from the expectations of the individual's culture. Because of the inflexibility and pervasiveness of these patterns, they cause serious relational problems and impairment of functioning for the afflicted individual. The characteristic symptoms of the personality disorders fall into four categories: distorted thinking, emotional dysregulation, impulse control problems, and interpersonal difficulties.

***Distorted thinking.*** Distorted thinking is an extreme and inaccurate pattern of perceiving and interpreting one's self, others, and the world around them. Examples of distorted thinking patterns include idealizing then devaluing other people or one's self; extreme black-or-white thinking; distrustful, suspicious thoughts; unusual or odd beliefs that are contrary to cultural norms; and thoughts that include perceptual distortions and bodily illusions.

***Emotional dysregulation.*** Emotional dysregulation is an inability to modulate the range, intensity, lability, and appropriateness of emotional responses. Some personality disorders are characterized by emotional sensitivity and a tendency to experience intense feelings. Other disordered individuals show little or no emotional response, regardless of the circumstance or situation. Still other personality disorders are characterized by emotional extremes: one moment overwhelmed with intense emotions, the next, numb and disconnected.

*Impulse control problems.* Impulse control problems are a third common characteristic symptom of personality disorders. Impulse control is the degree to which a person can regulate their internal drives or impulses to act. Much like the emotional regulation problems described earlier, personality disordered individuals have problems regulating their impulses. Some personality disorders are characterized by behavioral overcontrol (an inability to act), while others are characterized by a lack of behavioral control (acting spontaneously without forethought).

*Interpersonal difficulties.* Interpersonal difficulties are common to all of the personality disorders. As would be expected, the three characteristic symptoms already described (distorted thinking, emotional dysregulation, and impulse control problems) make it difficult for personality disordered individuals to form and maintain healthy relationships.[1]

## Diagnoses

Unlike many of the disorders discussed in this book, descriptions of personality differences and problems are clearly and commonly found in the earliest medical, philosophical, and religious writings of ancient cultures; these societies include Israel, India, China, Babylonia, Greece, and Rome.[2] The modern description of personality disorders is generally attributed to the eighteenth-century French physician Philippe Pinel. In his writings Pinel described a group of patients who were mentally unimpaired but nonetheless

---

[1]DSM-5.

[2]Walid Khalid Abdul-Hamid and George Stein, "The Surpu: Exorcism of Antisocial Personality Disorder in Ancient Mesopotamia," *Mental Health, Religion & Culture* 16 (2013): 671-85; Marc-Antoine Crocq, "Milestones in the History of Personality Disorders," *Dialogues in Clinical Neuroscience* 15 (2013): 147-53; Theodore Millon, "On the History and Future Study of Personality and Its Disorders," *Annual Review of Clinical Psychology* 8 (2012): 1-19; and George Stein, "Lost in Translation: The Biblical Classification of Personality Disorder," *British Journal of Psychiatry* 193 (2008): 337.

engaged in impulsive and self-defeating behavior. He called the condition "*la folie raisonnante*" (the reasoning madness), meaning they understood the irrationality of their behavior but continued with it anyway.[3] Given this extensive history of writings on personality, it is not surprising that the diagnosis of personality disorder has been included in every edition of the *Diagnostic and Statistical Manual of Mental Disorders*.

Within the most recent edition of the diagnostics manual, DSM-5, the ten personality disorders are grouped into three clusters based on similar symptoms and clinical presentation.

*Cluster A personality disorders.* Cluster A, also referred to as the odd-eccentric group, includes the personality disorders paranoid, schizoid, and schizotypal. The common features of the disorders in this cluster include social awkwardness, social withdrawal, and distorted thinking.

*Paranoid personality disorder.* Paranoid personality disorder is characterized by a pattern of distrust and suspiciousness such that others' motives are interpreted as hostile or malicious. Individuals with paranoid personality disorder falsely believe that they are being victimized by others. They are highly critical of others, yet hypersensitive to criticism of themselves.

*Schizoid personality disorder.* Schizoid personality disorder is characterized by a long-standing pattern of detachment from social relationships. Individuals with schizoid personality disorder display a restricted range of emotions, rarely experiencing emotional extremes such as anger or joy. They seldom reciprocate gestures or facial expressions, such nods or smiles. To others they appear cold, aloof, and socially isolated.

---

[3]Philippe Pinel, *Medico-Philosophical Treatise on Mental Alienation*, trans. G. Hickish, D. Healy, and L. C. Charland (1809; repr., Chichester, UK: Wiley-Blackwell, 2008).

*Schizotypal personality disorder.* Schizotypal personality disorder is characterized by a pattern of acute discomfort in close relationships, cognitive or perceptual distortions, and eccentric behavior. Individuals with schizotypal personality disorder often hold odd beliefs or superstitions, distort reality, and are unable to form close relationships. Abnormalities of belief, thinking, and perception in STPD are below the threshold for the diagnosis of a psychotic disorder. As mentioned in chapter 2, this is the lowest end of the schizophrenia spectrum.

**Cluster B personality disorders.** Cluster B, also referred to as the dramatic-erratic group, includes the personality disorders antisocial, borderline, histrionic, and narcissistic. The common features of the disorders in this cluster include a lack of impulse control and problems with emotional regulation.

*Antisocial personality disorder.* Antisocial personality disorder is characterized by a pattern of behavior that involves the manipulation, exploitation, or violation of the rights of others. Individuals with antisocial personality disorder are often deceitful, lack remorse for their actions, and show an unwillingness to conform to social norms and laws.

*Borderline personality disorder.* Borderline personality disorder is characterized by a persistent pattern of emotional instability, volatile interpersonal relationships, unstable self-image, and self-destructive impulsive behaviors.

*Histrionic personality disorder.* Histrionic personality disorder is characterized by a pattern of excessive emotional expression and attention seeking. Individuals with HPD often behave dramatically in situations that do not justify this type of reaction. They have an excessive need for approval and are often inappropriately sexually seductive or provocative.

*Narcissistic personality disorder.* Narcissistic personality disorder is characterized by extreme feelings of self-importance, a high need for admiration, and a lack of empathy. Individuals with narcissistic personality disorder often exploit others for their own gain and are overly sensitive to criticism, judgment, or defeat.

***Cluster C personality disorders.*** Cluster C, also referred to as the anxious-fearful group, includes the personality disorders avoidant, dependent, and obsessive-compulsive. The common feature of the cluster C personality disorders is a high level of anxiety.

*Avoidant personality disorder.* Avoidant personality disorder is characterized by a pattern of social inhibition, feelings of inadequacy, and hypersensitivity to negative evaluation. Individuals with avoidant personality disorder are extremely shy and fearful of rejection, making it difficult for them to interact socially and professionally. Loss and rejection are so painful to those afflicted with avoidant personality disorder that they often choose to be lonely rather than risk trying to connect with others.

*Dependent personality disorder.* Dependent personality disorder is a pattern of submissive and clinging behavior related to an excessive need to be taken care of. Individuals with dependent personality disorder often feel helpless or unable to cope independently, frequently and inappropriately transferring responsibility for their situation or well-being onto another.

*Obsessive-compulsive personality disorder.* Obsessive-compulsive personality disorder is a pattern of preoccupation with orderliness, perfectionism, and control. Individuals with obsessive-compulsive personality disorder are preoccupied with details, rules, and schedules to the point that any joy in an activity is lost. Their extreme level of perfectionism often interferes with the ability to complete tasks.

## Prevalence and Age of Onset

The lifetime prevalence of personality disorders in the United States is estimated to be 9.1–14.8 percent of the population. The prevalence of the specific personality disorder clusters varies, with 2.1–6.8 percent of the population meeting criteria for a cluster A disorder, 1.5–6.1 percent of the population meeting criteria for a cluster B disorder, and 2.6–10.6 percent of the population meeting criteria for a cluster C disorder.[4] Personality disorders usually become recognizable during adolescence or early adulthood. Some personality disorders (paranoid, schizoid, schizotypal, antisocial, narcissistic, and obsessive-compulsive) are diagnosed more frequently in males while others (borderline, histrionic, and dependent) are more frequently diagnosed in females. Avoidant personality disorder appears to be equally frequent in males and females.[5] Individuals with personality disorders are likely to have co-occurring major mental disorders, including anxiety disorders, depressive disorders, bipolar disorders, posttraumatic stress disorder, attention deficit/hyperactivity disorder, and substance use disorders.[6]

## Developmental and Psychosocial Risk Factors

A number of developmental and early psychosocial risk factors have been found to increase the likelihood that an individual will meet criteria for a personality disorder in adulthood.

---

[4]DSM-5; Mark F. Lenzenweger et al., "DSM-IV Personality Disorders in the National Comorbidity Survey Replication," *Biological Psychiatry* 15 (2007): 553-64; Bridget F. Grant et al., "Prevalence, Correlates, and Disability of Personality Disorders in the United States: Results from the National Epidemiological Survey on Alcohol and Related Conditions," *Journal of Clinical Psychiatry* 65 (2004): 948-58; and Svenn Torgersen et al., "The Prevalence of Personality Disorders in a Community Sample," *Archives of General Psychiatry* 58 (2001): 590-96.

[5]DSM-5.

[6]Lenzenweger et al., "DSM-IV Personality Disorders," 553-64.

Perinatal risk factors include obstetric complications during delivery (e.g., asphyxia) and prematurity (less than thirty-seven weeks of completed gestation). Childhood risk factors related to later personality disorder diagnosis include adverse care giving, emotional and physical maltreatment or neglect, sexual abuse, and parental loss or divorce. A diagnosis of either childhood conduct disorder or attention-deficit/hyperactivity disorder also increases an individual's risk of a later personality disorder. Other risk factors include a family history of personality disorders or other mental illness, a low level of education, and lower socioeconomic status.[7]

## *Neurobiology*

**Heritability.** There is considerable evidence that genetic factors play a role in personality disorders. If we think of personality disorders, like all mental illnesses, as resulting from a combination of genetic and environmental factors (heritability + environment = disorder), then using twins we can calculate the percentage of a disorder that is accounted for by heredity and the percentage that is accounted for by environmental factors. Research has shown that the influence of heredity (60 percent) is greater than that of the environment (40 percent) in personality disorders. However, the influence of heredity does vary across the personality disorder

---

[7]Seena Fazel et al., "Perinatal Risk Factors in Offenders with Severe Personality Disorder: A Population-Based Investigation," *Journal of Personality Disorders* 26 (2012): 737-50; Shirley Yen et al., "Traumatic Exposure and Posttraumatic Stress Disorder in Borderline, Schizotypal, Avoidant, and Obsessive-Compulsive Personality Disorders: Findings from the Collaborative Longitudinal Personality Disorders Study," *Journal of Nervous and Mental Disease* 190 (2002): 510-18; Jeffrey G. Johnson et al., "Associations Between Four Types of Childhood Neglect and Personality Disorder Symptoms During Adolescence and Early Adulthood: Findings of a Community-Based Longitudinal Study," *Journal of Personality Disorder* 14 (2000): 171-87; and Jeremy W. Coid, "Aetiological Risk Factors for Personality Disorders," *British Journal of Psychiatry* 174 (1999): 530-38.

clusters: 37 percent for Cluster A, 60 percent for Cluster B, and 62 percent for Cluster C.[8]

Additional evidence for heritability in personality disorders comes from the fact that first-degree relatives of individuals diagnosed with a personality disorder have a higher risk of having a personality disorder themselves compared to the general population. Cluster A personality disorders (paranoid, schizoid, and schizotypal) show an increased prevalence in the relatives of individuals with schizophrenia.[9]

*Neuroanatomy.* Neuroimaging studies have shown a significant number of brain regions to be abnormal or dysfunctional, compared to healthy controls, in individuals diagnosed with personality disorders. The differences, however, vary across the personality disorder clusters.

Cluster A personality disordered individuals show larger lateral ventricles (fluid filled spaces in the brain) and reduced gray matter in the caudate nucleus, hippocampus, and fusiform gyrus. The caudate is a deep brain structure involved in voluntary movement, learning, memory, sleep, and social behavior. The fusiform gyrus, located in the temporal lobe, is involved in face and body recognition. In addition, functional and volume differences have been found in the prefrontal cortex (PFC) of individuals diagnosed with Cluster A personality disorders. These neuroanatomical abnormalities are similar to what is seen in individuals diagnosed with a schizophrenia spectrum disorder.[10]

---

[8]Svenn Torgersen et al., "A Twin Study of Personality Disorders," *Comprehensive Psychiatry* 44 (2000): 416-25.

[9]DSM-5.

[10]Marianne Goodman et al., "Neuroimaging in Personality Disorders: Current Concepts, Findings, and Implications," *Psychiatric Annals* 37 (2007): 100-108; and Adrian Raine et al., "Prefrontal Structural and Functional Deficits in Schizotypal Personality Disorder," *Schizophrenia Bulletin* 28 (2002): 501-13.

Studies with Cluster B diagnosed individuals have found significant gray matter reductions in the anterior cingulate cortex, amygdala, and PFC. Additionally, the amygdala seems to be overreactive in these individuals, resulting in emotional instability. Disruption in the connections between the amygdala and PFC leads to the explosiveness and lack of impulse control seen in the Cluster B personality disorders.[11]

Individuals diagnosed with Cluster C personality disorders have been found to have an overreactive amygdala as well as disruptions in the connections between the insula and areas known to be involved in the processing of emotions such as the PFC and the anterior cingulate cortex. The insula is often referred to as the emotional cortex and appears to be involved in the self-awareness of emotional states and the integration of emotional information. These neuroanatomical abnormalities are similar what is seen in individuals diagnosed with anxiety disorders.[12]

***Neurochemistry.*** Much like with the neuroanatomical differences already described, the abnormalities in the brain's neurotransmitter systems associated with personality disorders vary across the diagnostic clusters. Cluster A personality disorders have been shown to have increased activity in both the dopamine (DA) and

---

[11]Antonia New et al., "Neuroimaging and Borderline Personality Disorder," *Psychiatric Annals* 42 (2012): 65-71; Matthew S. Stanford et al., "Psychophysiological Correlates of Psychopathic Disorders," in *International Handbook on Psychopathic Disorders and the Law*, ed. Alan R. Felthous and H. Sass (New York: John Wiley, 2008); and Birgit Völlm et al., "Neurobiological Substrates of Antisocial and Borderline Personality Disorder: Preliminary Results of a Functional fMRI Study," *Criminal Behavior and Mental Health* 14 (2004): 39-54.

[12]Bryan T. Denny et al., "Elevated Amygdala Activity During Reappraisal Anticipation Predicts Anxiety in Avoidant Personality Disorder," *Journal of Affective Disorders* 172 (2015): 1-7; Harold W. Koenigsberg et al., "The Neural Correlates of Anomalous Habituation to Negative Emotional Pictures in Borderline and Avoidant Personality Disorder Patients," *American Journal of Psychiatry* 171 (2014): 82-90; and Goodman et al., "Neuroimaging in Personality Disorders," 100-108.

serotonin (5-HT) neurotransmitter systems. This likely leads to the odd and eccentric patterns of thinking seen in Cluster A disorders and is similar to neurotransmitter differences found in individuals diagnosed with schizophrenia.[13]

Individuals diagnosed with Cluster B personality disorders show reduced activity in both the 5-HT and norepinephrine systems. This neurochemical profile is thought to be related to the lack of impulse control and emotional instability seen in the Cluster B disorders. Several studies have also suggested that dysregulation in DA transmission is also related to the Cluster B personality disorders but the nature of this dysfunction is not well understood.[14]

Overactivity in both the 5-HT and DA neurotransmitter systems has been shown in the Cluster C personality disorders. Increased activity in the brain's 5-HT system leads to the extreme behavioral inhibition seen in these individuals. Increased DA activity in the basal ganglia (a set of structures deep in the brain involved in movement) results in the uncontrolled movements such as tics and compulsions that often manifest in the Cluster C disorders.[15]

---

[13]Anissa Abi-Dargham et al., "Striatal Amphetamine-Induced Dopamine Release in Patients with Schizotypal Personality Disorder Studied with Single Photon Emission Computed Tomography and [123I]iodobenzamide," *Biological Psychiatry* 55 (2004): 1001-6; and Mairead Dolan et al., "Relationship Between 5-HT Function and Impulsivity and Aggression in Male Offenders with Personality Disorders," *British Journal of Psychiatry* 178 (2001): 352-59.

[14]Birgit Völlm et al., "Neuronal Correlates and Serotonergic Modulation of Behavioural Inhibition and Reward in Healthy and Antisocial Individuals," *Journal of Psychiatric Research* 44 (2010): 123-31; Peter R. Joyce et al., "A Dopamine Transporter Polymorphism Is a Risk Factor for Borderline Personality Disorder in Depressed Patients," *Psychological Medicine* 26 (2006): 807-13; Wei Wang et al., "Cerebral Information Processing in Personality Disorders: I. Intensity Dependence of Auditory Evoked Potentials," *Psychiatry Research* 141 (2006): 173-83; and Emil F. Coccaro et al., "Norepinephrine Function in Personality Disorder: Plasma Free MHPG Correlates Inversely with Life History of Aggression," *CNS Spectrums* 8 (2003): 731-36.

[15]Peter R. Joyce et al., "Polymorphisms of DRD4 and DRD3 and Risk of Avoidant and Obsessive Personality Traits and Disorders," *Psychiatry Research* 119 (2003): 1-10; and

## Treatment

Given that personality disorders are deeply ingrained and rigid patterns of maladaptive thoughts, feelings, and behaviors, psychotherapy (talk therapy) is seen as the first line of treatment; several medications have also been found to be helpful in the treatment of specific personality disorders.

**Psychotherapy.** Two forms of psychotherapy have been shown to be effective in treating personality disorders, psychodynamic therapy and cognitive-behavioral therapy. In psychodynamic therapy, a therapist helps the person look inside him- or herself to discover and understand emotional conflicts that may be contributing to their present problems. The goal of this psychotherapeutic approach is to uncover unconscious motivations—unanswered problems from the past, particularly childhood—in order to resolve present issues by becoming aware of how those motivations influence current actions and feelings. As described in earlier chapters, the focus of CBT is to help the client eliminate negative beliefs or behaviors and replace them with positive ones. A modified form of CBT, dialectical behavior therapy, has been shown to be particularly effective in treating borderline personality disorder. In dialectical behavior therapy the therapist and the patient work on accepting uncomfortable thoughts, feelings, and behaviors rather than struggling with them. Once an identified thought, emotion, or behavior has been validated, the process of change no longer appears impossible.[16]

---

Mairead Dolan et al., "Relationship Between 5-HT Function and Impulsivity and Aggression in Male Offenders with Personality Disorders," *British Journal of Psychiatry* 178 (2001): 352-59.

[16]Joel Paris, "Clinical Trials of Treatment for Personality Disorders," *Psychiatric Clinics of North America* 31 (2008): 517-26; Falk Leichsenring and Eric Leibing, "The Effectiveness of Psychodynamic Therapy and Cognitive Behavior Therapy in the Treatment of Personality Disorders: A Meta-Analysis," *American Journal of Psychiatry* 160 (2003): 1223-32; and

***Pharmacotherapy.*** Due to their similarity to the schizophrenia spectrum disorders the Cluster A personality disorders are often treated with low-dose antipsychotic medications to help control distorted thinking. Several studies have demonstrated the effectiveness of selective-serotonin reuptake inhibitors (SSRIs) and mood stabilizers in the treatment of the Cluster B personality disorders borderline and antisocial. SSRIs help reduce depressive symptoms while mood stabilizers such as lithium control the impulsiveness and explosive anger often seen in these disorders. The fear and anxiety common to Cluster C personality disorders is often treated through the use of a wide range of antidepressant medications, including SSRIs, serotonin, and norepinephrine reuptake inhibitors, tricyclic antidepressants, and monoamine oxidase inhibitors.[17]

## *The Other Side of Borderline Personality Disorder*

Cami and Ray's was a whirlwind romance. Introduced, engaged, and married in less than a year, their union would last only slightly longer than their courtship. Cami initially noticed Ray's personality problems prior to their wedding. She said, "At first, it was just little things—inconsistencies, oddities—but I was unable to put it all together until much later, or maybe I just ignored it." Soon after the wedding it became obvious that there were problems when Ray chose to continue to live in a different state than his new bride.

---

Anthony W. Bateman and Peter Fonagy, "Effectiveness of Psychotherapeutic Treatment of Personality Disorder," *British Journal of Psychiatry* 177 (2000): 138-43.

[17]Luis H. Ripoll et al., "Evidence-Based Pharmacotherapy for Personality Disorders," *International Journal of Neuropsychopharmacology* 14 (2011): 1257-88; Joel Paris, "Clinical Trials of Treatment for Personality Disorders," *Psychiatric Clinics of North America* 31 (2008): 517-26; Sabine C. Herpertz et al., "World Federation of Societies of Biological Psychiatry (WFSBP) Guidelines for Biological Treatment of Personality Disorders," *World Journal of Biological Psychiatry* 8 (2007): 212-44; and George Kraus and David J. Reynolds, "The 'A-B-C's' of the Cluster B's: Identifying, Understanding, and Treating Cluster B Personality Disorders," *Clinical Psychology Review* 21 (2001): 345-73.

Cami described Ray as distant during those early months. "He even disappeared one weekend and no one could find him. At some point he told me that he suffered from clinical depression, which one of the therapists we would later see confirmed, as did his mother and sister." For a while Cami assumed all their problems were the result of Ray's "depression." In fact Ray had told her that he had been molested by an uncle (his father's brother) when he was five. He also said that his father was emotionally abusive and sometimes threatened physical violence. After his parents divorced when he was in college, he broke off all contact with his father. It all seemed to make sense: Ray must be depressed.

Things quickly began to spiral out of control. One night during those initial months apart, Ray called after having a nightmare and asked Cami if she ever feared that he would hurt her. Cami was understandably surprised by Ray's question. After seven months apart, Ray finally moved in with Cami. For a year he searched for a job, although Cami says he had little motivation, staying in bed until noon most days and rarely applying for jobs or going on interviews. He finally landed a job at a large law firm. Surprisingly, despite all of his problems Ray had been able to complete college and law school. Cami thought Ray's new job and their finally being together in the same house would be a new start.

The subsequent months were difficult for the couple. Ray's behavior was erratic, and their relationship suffered. He was increasingly agitated and could not sleep. He would disappear for hours at a time with no explanation. "If my family invited us to a function at their homes or we went out of town with my family, he would disappear into another room the entire time." As things continued to go downhill Ray got to a point where he wouldn't go out of the house. At Cami's insistence they sought out a marriage counselor.

Almost two years into their marriage, on the day she found out she was pregnant, Cami received a disturbing phone call from her sister, who, a lawyer like Ray, had learned from colleagues at Ray's firm that he had been practicing law without a license. Ray had been lying to his employer for a year. Around the same time Cami's accountant, who was working on their first joint tax filing, called with disturbing news. Ray had not paid his taxes in the last seven years and owed the IRS over $150,000. Cami was overwhelmed and didn't want to believe all these allegations. She searched his computer for evidence that he had completed paperwork for the bar and perhaps just forgot to submit it. She did not find what she was looking for but did discover multitudes of gay pornographic websites, and shortly thereafter even received several similar publications in the mail. During all this time Ray was out of the state serving in the Air National Guard.

Ray was immediately fired from his job. They again sought counseling, and Ray admitted his involvement with pornography. "He said that he was not gay but that he was emotionally numb and he was trying to find something that would make him not feel so numb." Through Ray's brother, Cami found out that Ray had been discharged from the Air National Guard for misconduct. She also found out that Ray had been lying all this time about being a pilot in the Guard. By the time their daughter was born, in October of the same year, they were separated. It was just prior to the separation that a marriage counselor first mentioned that Ray may have borderline personality disorder.

My first thought when he was diagnosed was relief, because there was a reason behind all the crazy behavior. Then came the fear and anxiety. Would my daughter inherit it? How would I live like this? This is not what I bargained for, and I was not sure if I could handle it.

Ray's illness has not just affected me, but everyone—our daughter, my family, his family, our friendships. It financially wiped me out due to his back taxes and because he fought the divorce. His illness has also strengthened my faith and brought me closer to my faith community. I became much more involved in my church, desperately trying to find other people who were going thru similar situations.

It amazes me that seven years later we get along as well as we do. If someone had said that would happen, I would have told them they were crazy. But we have managed, at least lately, to work well together for our daughter. I have attended a support group for family members of loved ones with BPD and it has helped me tremendously. It has taught me how to communicate with him in a way that doesn't set him off. He still doesn't go to therapy, and he has isolated himself, so I mostly feel sorry for him now. And I feel sorry for my daughter that she doesn't have an emotionally available and healthy dad. But I do know he loves her. I just wish he knew how to express it in a better way.

## Biblical Examples

The Bible describes two individuals whose thoughts and behaviors suggest they were suffering from a personality disorder. Both of these descriptions are of Cluster B personality disorders. The lack of Cluster A and C examples in the Scriptures is likely due to the fact that these disorders are expressed more as a dysfunction of inner experience, causing the individual to withdraw from social interactions and isolate themselves. Cluster B disorders, on the other hand, are more likely to have come to the attention of the biblical writers because they are outwardly expressed and highly destructive.

*Samson.* Following the death of Joshua and before the anointing of Saul as the first king, the Israelites were a loose confederation of tribes periodically ruled by judges (men and women called out by God to lead his people in times of crisis). Samson is the last judge described in the Old Testament (Judges 13–16), historically standing between the old tribal Israel and the coming monarchy. A member of the tribe of Dan, he judged Israel for twenty years, during which time he began to deliver Israel from the Philistines (Judges 13:5).

Unlike earlier judges who were called to serve as adults, God physically appeared to Samson's childless mother and father to announce his birth prior to his conception. God instructs Samson's parents that he will be "set apart to the Lord" as a Nazirite from the womb. He is never to consume alcohol, become ceremonially unclean by touching or coming into contact with a dead body, or cut his hair (Numbers 6:1-6). Another unique aspect of Samson's calling as a judge is that the Israelites do not cry out to God for deliverance or repent from their sinful ways prompting the divine selection of a judge to lead them as had happened previously. Samson's selection as judge is divinely initiated by God himself to begin the delivery of the Israelites from the Philistines.

The Scriptures tell us that as Samson grew up, the Lord empowered him, and at approximately the age of twenty the Spirit of the Lord began to control him. What most people know about Samson are his amazing feats of superhuman strength: killing a lion with his bare hands, defeating one thousand Philistines with the jawbone of a donkey, pulling down the city gates of Gaza and carrying them to the top of a nearby hill, and in his final act of strength single-handedly destroying the Philistine temple of Dagon, killing himself along with three thousand Philistines.

Perhaps more importantly, as it relates to this discussion, are the numerous bad decisions and inappropriate actions that Samson takes throughout his short life.

His first adult act detailed in the book of Judges is his selection of a Philistine girl, against the wishes of his parents, rather than an Israelite to be his bride. Following this he violates his Nazirite vow and the Jewish dietary laws by eating honey out of the carcass of a dead lion. He also gives some of the same honey to his parents but does not tell them where it came from. This causes them to unknowingly violate the dietary laws as well. Prior to his wedding ceremony he participates in a drinking party, again violating his Nazirite vow. At the same party, he deceitfully uses an impossible-to-solve riddle in an attempt to con his groomsmen out of thirty linen robes and thirty sets of clothes. When his groomsmen gain the upper hand on him through their own deception and solve the riddle, Samson in anger kills thirty innocent men and takes their clothes to pay his debt. In this act he once again violates his Nazirite vow by touching the dead men's bodies to remove their clothing.

Because of his anger at the groomsmen, Samson never returns to his new wife to consummate their marriage, causing her father to assume that he has abandoned her. To protect his daughter and his family's honor, the father gives Samson's bride to the best man as his wife. When Samson finds out about this sometime later, in retaliation he burns the Philistines' fields and grain supply. The Philistines take revenge for this act by burning alive Samson's former bride and her father. Samson, driven by revenge himself, kills those responsible.

Though a Nazirite, set apart to the Lord, and a divinely called judge of Israel, Samson visits Philistine prostitutes and at some point falls in love with a woman named Delilah. The name Delilah means "devotee" and suggests that she may have been a pagan temple prostitute. His final poor decision is to tell the deceptive Delilah the source of his strength, a final violation of his Nazirite vow, leading to his capture and imprisonment by the Philistines. If we look at Samson's thoughts and actions within a modern diagnostic context (see table 10.1) he appears to meet the criteria for antisocial personality disorder.[18]

**Table 10.1.** Biblical example of antisocial personality disorder

| CHARACTERISTIC SYMPTOMS | SAMSON'S SYMPTOMS | REFERENCE |
|---|---|---|
| **Pervasive Pattern of Disregard for and Violation of the Rights of Others** | | |
| Failure to conform to social norms | Violates dietary laws | Judges 14:9 |
| with respect to the law | Violates Nazirite vow | Judges 14:9-10; 14:19 |
| | Burned Philistine fields | Judges 15:5 |
| | Killed for revenge and was arrested | Judges 15:7-8, 13 |
| Deceitfulness | Doesn't tell parents about unclean honey | Judges 14:9 |
| | Used riddle to trick groomsmen | Judges 14:12-14 |
| Impulsivity | Married Philistine girl | Judges 14:2 |
| Irritability and aggressiveness | Killed thirty men in anger | Judges 14:19 |
| | Burned Philistine fields | Judges 15:5 |
| | Killed for revenge | Judges 15:8 |
| Reckless disregard for safety of self | Abandoned wife, burned fields | Judges 14:19–15:6 |
| and others | Visited prostitute in Gaza | Judges 16:1 |
| | Told Delilah the secret to his strength | Judges 16:4-21 |
| | Suicide | Judges 16:30 |
| Lack of remorse | Abandoned wife; returns later | Judges 14:19–15:2 |

*Gomer.* The prophet Hosea was called by God to minister to the northern kingdom of Israel. In Hosea's time (760–725 BC) Israel had turned from God to worship Baal (the Canaanite storm and fertility god). Hosea's charge was to call the Israelites to repentance for their spiritual unfaithfulness. We see in the opening scene of the book that Hosea was instructed by the Lord to marry Gomer (Hosea 1:2). I assume that Hosea was in love with Gomer at the

---

[18]Eric L. Altshuler and Ansar Haroun, "Did Samson Have Antisocial Personality Disorder?" *Archives of General Psychiatry* 58 (2001): 202.

time. God told Hosea that Gomer would be unfaithful to him but that he should marry her anyway. God used the marriage of Hosea and Gomer as an example to the Israelites of their spiritual unfaithfulness toward him. For the purposes of this description, I would like to focus on Gomer the person, removed from the broader context of her representation of Israel.

We know nothing of Gomer's history before she married Hosea. We only know that God told Hosea she would be unfaithful to him. Early in their marriage they were blessed with a son. Sometime after that, Gomer began to stray from the marriage. Emotionally she was unstable, declaring her love for Hosea one minute and her disdain the next. She gave birth to a daughter as a result of an adulterous affair. Despite her unfaithfulness, Hosea remained with Gomer. She gave birth to another illegitimate child, this time a son. At some point after the birth of her third child, she abandoned Hosea and the children. Fueled by an insatiable desire for material things, she went through a number of adulterous relationships. Adultery in ancient Israel was punishable by death, and repeated affairs would have been a risky pattern of behavior.

Despite Hosea's warnings of the consequences of Gomer's behavior and his pleas for her return, her life continued in a downward spiral. From multiple adulterous relationships she turned to prostitution as a means of supporting herself. She lost her faith, drank to excess, and may have begun cutting herself.[19] Ultimately Gomer found herself alone and emotionally broken, owned as property by another man. When viewed within a modern diagnostic context (see table 10.2) Gomer appears to meet the criteria for borderline personality disorder.

---

[19]Some Bible versions translate Hosea 7:14 as "they slash themselves for grain and wine"— a reference to pagan Canaanite cultic practices of people cutting themselves to rouse their gods. See, for example, the NET, NIV, NRSV, and NLT.

**Table 10.2.** Biblical example of borderline personality disorder

| CHARACTERISTIC SYMPTOMS | GOMER'S SYMPTOMS | REFERENCE |
|---|---|---|
| Frantic Efforts to Avoid Real or Imagined Abandonment | Sought out adulterous relationships to meet her needs<br>Multiple short-term relationships | Hosea 2:5, 7<br><br>Hosea 2:2, 7 |
| Pattern of Unstable and Intense Interpersonal Relationships | Abandoned family<br>Relational and emotional instability | Hosea 3:1-2<br>Hosea 6:4 |
| Identity Disturbance | Inconsistency in behavior and a lack of commitment to values | Hosea 2:8, 12, 17; 4:10-12 |
| Self-damaging Impulsiveness | Sexual promiscuity<br>Prostitution<br>Drunkenness | Hosea 1:2, 6, 8; 2:2<br>Hosea 1:2; 2:5<br>Hosea 4:11 |
| Self-mutilation | Cutting | Hosea 7:14 |

## Final Thoughts

The stories of Samson and Gomer are tragic tales that fully detail the pain and destruction resulting from Cluster B personality disorders. In personality disorders, not only is the person afflicted damaged but so is everyone they are in relationship with, as these two stories so clearly demonstrate.

I believe that we learn two very important lessons about personality disorders from the lives of Samson and Gomer. First, a personality disorder does not disqualify an individual from a relationship with or service to God. God used the various mistakes and poor decisions of both Samson and Gomer to draw both them and the Israelites closer to himself. God's will is clearly sovereign over the wrong thinking and inaccurate perceptions associated with personality disorders.

Second, God is actively seeking those who struggle with personality disorders and longs for an intimate relationship with them. The book of Hosea not only describes Gomer's sinful behavior and the destruction that it brought on her and her family, but it also gives us a godly process by which she was restored and healing occurred. At the end of his life Samson, broken and humbled after months of imprisonment, prays that God will give him his strength once more. God answered his prayer and in a single, divinely empowered act, Samson eliminated the entire Philistine leadership. This was a major turning point in Israel's conflict with the Philistines. Samson's faith is honored in the book of Hebrews' "roll call of faith" (Hebrews 11:32) where he is listed alongside such noted biblical figures as Gideon, David, and Samuel. Restoration and redemption are possible for those with personality disorders. In fact, it is God's will for those who are afflicted.

# NEUROLOGICAL DISORDERS

# 11

## STRICKEN IN YEARS

### DEMENTIA

*And, to deal plainly, I fear I am not in my perfect mind.*
*Me thinks I should know you and know this man, yet I*
*am doubtful: for I am mainly ignorant what place this is;*
*and all the skill I have remembers not these garments, nor*
*I know not where I did lodge last night.*

KING LEAR, WILLIAM SHAKESPEARE

NATE AND SHARON FIRST MET DURING COLLEGE. After dating on and off for three years, graduation and a job halfway across the country ended their romance. With time, they both met other people and married. Forty years later, after the deaths of their spouses due to cancer, they were reunited. Their feelings for one another were quickly rekindled, and they married after a year of dating. Theirs was a storybook romance. So much so that a local newspaper reporter published a story about the college sweethearts who had found one another after forty years. For five years, everything seemed perfect. Two people, each grieved by the death of a spouse and alone, had found love again.

One evening as he was paying their bills, Nate, a former chief financial officer for a college, said to Sharon, "I can't do math anymore!" Sharon said, "I didn't think anything of it. I thought he was just experiencing the normal effects of aging. I suggested he use a calculator in the future to make it easier for him." Several weeks later the couple went on a cruise. Nate seemed confused while on vacation and struggled to find his way around the ship. "That's when I first felt like something was wrong. I encouraged him to talk to the doctor about his memory problems at his upcoming annual physical." Testing by his primary care physician suggested that sixty-nine-year-old Nate was showing the symptoms of moderate dementia. A referral to a neurologist and further testing brought a diagnosis of frontotemporal dementia.

Over the next three years Nate's cognitive function gradually declined. Medication did little to slow the progression of the disease. During that time, Nate suggested to Sharon that they move to a retirement community. Sharon says, "He was thinking of me. He didn't want to burden me with being his caregiver or leave me alone after he passed away." By the fourth year of the disease, Nate was no longer able to care for himself. He struggled with incontinence, had trouble walking, and couldn't dress himself. Sharon had become his full-time caregiver.

To keep herself healthy, Sharon attended a weekly caregivers' support group. She also hired a home health care nurse to come in two hours a week to sit with Nate so she could run errands. "Our friends were very gracious to come and stay with Nate so that I could have time for myself. The church was also wonderful and supportive. I could feel their prayers."

While changes during the first four years of the disease had been mostly neurological in nature, emotional changes began in the fifth year. "Nate would wake up in the morning and start crying. Weeping, he would ask me, 'What's happening to me?'" During that last year, he struggled to control his emotions. In his final six months Nate was moved to a nursing unit at the retirement community so he could receive twenty-four-hour care. Sharon spent three to four hours a day with him in the room. During that time, Nate acquired a urinary tract infection that further weakened his body. On his final day, Sharon said, "We did a devotional and prayed together. I kissed him and said, 'I'll see you in the morning.'" That night Nate peacefully passed away in his sleep.

Sharon's faith was a sustaining force during those difficult five years. "My first husband's cancer and death had somewhat prepared me for what Nate and I went through. I hold on to something my mother told me when my father was dying. She said, 'Remember that this life is only the beginning.' That gives me great comfort. I know that Nate is whole again in heaven."

## Characteristic Symptoms

Dementia, also called major neurocognitive disorder, is a general term used for a decline in cognitive functioning severe enough to interfere with daily life. Dementia is not a disease itself; instead, it is a group of symptoms caused by other conditions that have damaged an individual's brain. Symptoms that signal the onset of dementia are usually subtle and may not be noticeable for a number of years. The characteristic symptoms of dementia include memory loss, communication difficulties, confusion, changes in mood, and apathy.

*Memory loss.* Memory loss in dementia is often subtle and tends to involve short-term memories. The individual may be able to remember years past, but not what they had for breakfast. Signs of memory loss may include forgetting where they left something, struggling to remember why they went into a particular room, or forgetting what they were supposed to do on any given day.

*Communication difficulties.* Communication difficulties make it hard for individuals with dementia to carry on normal conversations.

They may struggle with vocabulary, have problems finding the right word, or call things by the wrong name. To try to overcome this problem, they may talk around a word they cannot remember (circumlocution) or substitute an inappropriate word, making their statements, at times, almost incomprehensible.

*Confusion.* Confusion usually first appears as problems with more complex tasks such as balancing the checkbook or playing games that have a lot of rules. Learning how to do new things or following new routines becomes more and more difficult. As the cognitive decline progresses, they may struggle to complete familiar tasks. Sometimes they may even forget where they are or how they got there.

*Changes in mood.* Changes in mood are common in dementia. Individuals can become suspicious, depressed, fearful, and anxious. They may show increased irritability and explosive outbursts of anger when their routine or schedule is disrupted. Sudden mood swings can occur regularly. For example, it is not uncommon for individuals with dementia to become friendly and affectionate within a few minutes of an angry outburst.

*Apathy.* Apathy is frequently a problem in individuals with dementia. In the early stages, they begin to lose interest in hobbies or activities they once considered pleasurable. They may not want to go out anymore or to do anything fun. Emotionally they may appear flat and have no interest in spending time with friends or family.

## Diagnoses

The seventh-century-BC Greek physician Pythagoras is credited as being the first person to document the mental decline that can occur with advanced age. Describing the later stages of life he wrote, "The scene of mortal existence closes, after a length of time, to which, very fortunately, few of the human species arrives. The system returns to the imbecility of the first epoch of the infancy."[1]

In 1684 English anatomist and physician Thomas Willis identified a set of causes for dementia that included head injury, stroke, alcohol and drug abuse, disease, and epilepsy. Prior to this, dementia was considered a normal consequence of aging. In 1776 Scottish physician William Cullen further developed the concept of dementia by including it in his classification of diseases as a neurosis (nervous disease). This was the first time that dementia, defined by Cullen as a "decay of perception and memory in old age" was recognized as a medical diagnosis.[2]

Perhaps the most significant advance in the understanding of dementia occurred in 1906 when German physician Aloysius Alzheimer published a case study of Auguste Deter, a fifty-six-year-old patient who showed profound memory loss, unfounded suspicion, and paranoia toward her family, as well as significant psychological decline. In her brain at autopsy, he saw dramatic shrinkage and abnormal deposits in and around nerve cells. Alzheimer called Deter's condition the "disease of forgetfulness." Emil Kraepelin, a German psychiatrist who worked with Dr. Alzheimer, later named this condition "Alzheimer's Disease" in the eighth edition of his book *Psychiatrie*.[3]

For a person to be diagnosed with dementia (major neurocognitive disorder), they must show a significant cognitive decline in one or more of the following areas: attention, executive

---

[1]N. C. Berchtold and C. W. Cotman, "Evolution in the Conceptualization of Dementia and Alzheimer's Disease: Greco-Roman Period to the 1960s," *Neurobiology of Aging* 19 (1998): 173-89.

[2]Ibid.

[3]Francois Boller and Margaret M. Forbes, "History of Dementia and Dementia in History: An Overview," *Journal of Neurological Sciences* 158 (1998): 125-33.

function, learning and memory, language, perceptual motor, and social cognition. In addition, the individual's capacity for independence in everyday activities must be impaired.[4] The following are some of the most common types of dementia and their causes.

*Alzheimer's disease.* Alzheimer's disease is the most common cause of dementia, accounting for 60–80 percent of all cases. In AD a protein called tau becomes twisted inside the brain's cells (neurons) forming abnormal bundles, called neurofibrillary tangles. Plaques, abnormal clumps of the amyloid protein, also appear in high concentration in the spaces between the brain cells in AD patients. These two protein accumulations cause the neurons to stop functioning properly and die.

*Vascular disease.* Vascular disease is the second most common cause of dementia, accounting for about 10 percent of all cases. In this type of dementia, damage to the vessels supplying blood to the brain deprives neurons of the nutrients and oxygen they need to function normally. Vascular dementia can result from a number of conditions that narrow or damage the brain's blood vessels; these include stroke, diabetes, and hypertension. The associated features of vascular disease will be discussed in chapter twelve.

*Lewy body disease.* Lewy body disease (LBD) is one of the most common causes of dementia, after Alzheimer's disease and vascular disease. In this type of dementia, a protein called alpha-synuclein accumulates inside neurons, forming balloon-like structures called Lewy bodies. In LBD, cells in a region deep in the brain called the substantia nigra die or become impaired, and the brain's outer layer (cortex) degenerates.

*Frontotemporal dementia.* Frontotemporal dementia (FTD) is not a single disease but rather a group of brain disorders that

---

[4]DSM-5.

accounts for up to 10 percent of all dementia cases. The common characteristic of the diseases that cause this type of dementia is atrophy or shrinking in the frontal and temporal lobes of the brain. Types of FTD include behavioral variant FTD, primary progressive aphasia, FTD with Parkinsonism linked to chromosome 17, and Pick's disease.

*Mixed dementia.* Mixed dementia results from more than one medical condition. The most common form of mixed dementia is caused by both Alzheimer's and vascular disease.

## Prevalence and Age of Onset

The prevalence of dementia (any type) in the United States among individuals seventy-one or older is approximately 13.9 percent. The prevalence rate rises steeply with age, from 5 percent of those 71-79 years to 37.4 percent of those ninety years and older. Men and women are equally affected by dementia. Of the neurodegenerative dementias, LBD and FTD have the earliest average onset, while Alzheimer's disease has the latest. Vascular dementia can occur at any age, but the prevalence increases dramatically after age sixty-five.[5]

## Developmental and Psychosocial Risk Factors

Advanced age is the single most significant risk factor for dementia. Psychosocial risk factors that increase the likelihood that someone will be diagnosed with dementia include stress, depression, and social isolation. Individuals who have experienced a traumatic brain injury are at a higher risk of later dementia. Risk factors for vascular dementia are the same as those for cerebrovascular disease and include hypertension, diabetes, smoking, obesity, and high

---

[5]Ibid.; Brenda L. Plassman et al., "Prevalence of Dementia in the United States: The Aging, Demographics, and Memory Study," *Neuroepidemiology* 29 (2007): 125-32.

cholesterol. Many people with Down syndrome develop early-onset Alzheimer's disease, with signs of dementia by the time they reach middle age.[6]

## Neurobiology

**Heritability.** Twin studies have consistently found a higher concordance rate for Alzheimer's disease in identical twins (approximately 67 percent of twin pairs both have AD) when compared to fraternal twins (approximately 22 percent share the disease). Research has also found that those who have a first-degree relative with one of the neurodegenerative dementias are at increased risk of developing the disease. The individual's risk increases significantly if more than one family member has dementia.[7]

**Neuroanatomy.** The neurodegenerative dementias described in this chapter (AD, LBD, FTD) can all be classified as cortical dementias; meaning that the predominance of the damage caused by these disease states occurs in the cerebral cortex, the outer layer of the brain. Brain imaging studies with dementia patients have shown that dysfunction or atrophy in the cortex of the brain's right hemisphere is associated with the behavioral disturbances in these individuals. Problems with impulsive or disinhibited behavior in dementia patients has been correlated with damage in the frontal cortex, while impairment in emotional

---

[6]Elisa Neuvonen et al., "Late-Life Cynical Distrust, Risk Incident Dementia, and Mortality in a Population-Based Cohort," *Neurology* 82 (2014): 2205-12; "The Dementias: Hope Through Research," *National Institute on Aging*, NIH publication no. 13-2252, www.nia.nih .gov/alzheimers/publication/dementias/introduction. National Institutes of Health, September 2013; Kurt Jellinger, "Head Injury and Dementia," *Current Opinion in Neurology* 17 (2004): 719-23.

[7]Jonathan D. Rohrer et al., "The Heritability and Genetics of Frontotemporal Lobar Degeneration," *Neurology* 73 (2009): 1451-56; and Margaret Gatz et al., "Heritability for Alzheimer's Disease: The Study of Dementia in Swedish Twins," *Journal of Gerontology: Medical* Sciences 52 (1997): M117-M125.

processing, particularly of negative emotions like sadness or anger, is related to atrophy in the temporal cortex.[8]

*Neurochemistry.* The primary neurochemical implicated in Alzheimer's disease is acetylcholine (ACh). In the brain, ACh functions as a neuromodulator, meaning it alters or modulates the way brain structures, particularly those involved in learning and memory, transmit and process information. During the course of normal aging, ACh concentrations in the brain gradually decrease. This is thought to be the cause of the lapses in short-term memory that many elderly individuals tend to experience from time to time. In Alzheimer's disease, however, ACh levels have been shown to drop as much as 90 percent in the cerebral cortex and a deep brain structure known as the caudate nucleus. Studies have reported that dementia patients also appear to show abnormalities in the functioning of other neurotransmitter systems, including norepinephrine, serotonin and dopamine.[9]

## Treatment

While there is presently no cure for the diseases that cause the neurodegenerative dementias, a number of treatments and interventions have been shown to slow or minimize the development of symptoms.

*Pharmacotherapy.* Medications that boost the levels of ACh in the brain, called cholinesterase inhibitors, are the first line of treatment for Alzheimer's and Lewy body disease. This class of medications includes Aricept (donepezil), Exelon (rivastigmine),

---

[8]Howard J. Rosen et al., "Neuroanatomical Correlates of Impaired Recognition of Emotion in Dementia," *Neuropsychologia* 44 (2006): 365-73; and Howard J. Rosen et al., "Neuroanatomical Correlates of Behavioral Disorders in Dementia," *Brain* 128 (2005): 2612-25.
[9]Karen Ritchie and Simon Lovestone, "The Dementias," *Lancet* 260 (2002): 1759-66; and Elaine Perry et al., "Clinical Neurochemistry: Developments in Dementia Research Based on Brain Bank Material," *Journal of Neural Transmission* 105 (1998): 915-33.

and Razadyne (galantamine). Namenda (memantine), a drug that raises the levels of the neurotransmitter glutamate in the brain, has also been shown to be effective in minimizing the symptoms of dementia. Research has shown that combining Namenda and a cholinesterase inhibitor together often results in an even greater beneficial effect.

It is fairly common for people with dementia to also have depression; antidepressants are often prescribed to deal with mood issues in these patients. In addition, antipsychotics may be used to treat individuals with dementia who show disruptive behaviors (e.g., aggression).

*Cognitive stimulation therapy.* A noninvasive, psychological intervention for those with a cognitive impairment, cognitive stimulation therapy focuses on the improvement and strengthening of spared cognitive functions and resources, as well as on the maintenance of social and interaction skills, with the goal of improving mood and quality of life. Cognitive stimulation therapy involves taking part in activities and exercises designed to improve memory, problem-solving skills, and language ability.

*Palliative care.* Individuals with an incurable illness such as dementia may be offered palliative care so they are able to live as well as possible until their death. The goal of palliative care is not to cure the disease but rather to improve the individual's quality of life—not just in body but also in mind and spirit. Palliative care is as much about supporting the caregiver or family as it is about treating the patient suffering with dementia.

## The Other Side of Dementia

"It was the most difficult decision I ever had to make. At times I still feel guilty but I know it was right thing to do." Leslie, a widowed sixty-two-year-old mother of two, still struggles with her decision to place her eighty-four-year-old mother, Joyce, in an assisted living facility.

Leslie and her older sister first noticed their mother's cognitive decline about five years ago. "She started forgetting little things at first, like where she left her house keys. She would forget to eat and seemed confused when we talked to her on the phone." A neurological examination suggested the early stages of Alzheimer's dementia. Over the next year Leslie struggled to care for her mother, who insisted on living alone in the house where she and her husband had raised their family. "It got to a point where I had to visit her every day to make sure she ate, to make sure she had bathed, and to feed the cat. She became more and more confused, and I feared for her safety. What if something happened when I wasn't there?"

Leslie's fears for her mother's safety were soon realized. "I stopped by her house before work one morning. I usually stopped by in the afternoon but changed my routine that day. When I entered the house, I could smell that something was burning. Mom had put a kettle on to boil and forgotten it. The kettle had been on so long and had gotten so hot that it was starting to melt. If I hadn't stopped by when I did, she might have burned the house down." After the kettle incident, Leslie sought counsel from her pastor. "He helped me understand that caring for my mother might include help from an assisted living facility; that I wasn't abdicating my responsibility as her daughter but rather making sure that she was safe and healthy." Soon after, Leslie's sister flew into town, and together they found a placement for their mother that was close to Leslie's home.

That was two years ago, and Leslie's mother is doing well at the assisted care facility. "She is safe, healthy, and has friends that she interacts with every day. I visit her several times a week, and she comes over for dinner on Sunday evenings. She would not be doing as well if I had continued to try and care for her myself. I don't think I would be doing very well either. Now when we are together, I can just be her daughter and enjoy my mother in her last years."

## Biblical Examples

With an average life expectancy of 78.8 years (81.2 years for women, 76.4 years for men) in the United States today, it is common to encounter the elderly in daily life.[10] This was not the case in ancient times. Based on age reports in the biblical text, the average life expectancy of kings in biblical times was only in the mid-forties. In comparison, the common peasant male had to survive under harsher conditions than those enjoyed by royalty and had a life expectancy of less than thirty years. Life expectancy was even shorter for peasant women of the time who, in addition to living with poverty, disease, and violence, had to survive multiple pregnancies and deliveries.[11]

Despite the short life expectancy of biblical times, old age is a common theme throughout the Scriptures. Advanced age is considered a blessing of God (Exodus 23:26; Proverbs 10:27; 16:31), wisdom is attributed to the aged (Deuteronomy 32:7; 1 Kings 12:6; Job 12:12; 32:7), and the young are called to honor, respect, and care for the elderly (Exodus 20:12; Leviticus 19:32; 1 Timothy 5:1-4). While the biblical writers correctly recognize old age as a period of physical deterioration (Genesis 18:11; 1 Kings 1:1; Psalm 71:9; 102:26), only a few references are made to the mental decline that can occur with advanced age (Job 12:20; Sirach 3:12-13).

---

[10]Larry Copeland, "Life Expectancy in the USA Hits a Record High," *USA Today*, October 8, 2014, www.usatoday.com/story/news/nation/2014/10/08/us-life-expectancy-hits-record-high/16874039.

[11]David N. Freed man, "Kingly Chronologies: Then and Later," in *Eretz-Israel Series*, ed. S. Ahiuv and B. A. Levine (Jerusalem: Israel Exploration Society, 1993), 24:41-65; and Hans Walter Wolff, *Anthropology of the Old Testament* (Philadelphia: Fortress, 1974).

***Barzillai the Gileadite.*** In 2 Samuel we are introduced to the elderly Barzillai. During the coup led by his son Absalom, King David fled with those loyal to him across the Jordan River to Mahanaim. Barzillai, a wealthy Gileadite from the nearby town of Rogelim, and several others sustained the king and his people during their time in Mahanaim (2 Samuel 17:27-29; 19:32). Once Absalom was killed and the rebellion crushed, Barzillai is called before the king to be rewarded for his loyalty. David asks Barzillai to return to Jerusalem with him to live out the remainder of his life in the palace (2 Samuel 19:33). Barzillai, who was eighty, declined David's offer citing his age and the fact that he was no longer able to "distinguish between good and bad" (2 Samuel 19:35). Some have interpreted this as Barzillai refusing an appointment as a counselor to King David's court due to an age-related cognitive decline.[12] It is also possible that he was simply saying he was too old to enjoy the amenities of living in the palace, given that he also mentions that he had lost his sense of taste and could not hear well.

***King Solomon.*** Solomon, the son of King David and Bathsheba, succeeded his father to the throne and ruled Israel for forty years (970–931 BC). While it is never explicitly stated in the Bible how long Solomon lived, it appears he was in his sixties when he died. In the latter years of Solomon's life, the Scriptures tell us that the many foreign wives that he had taken "turned his heart away after other gods" (1 Kings 11:4). The first-century Roman-Jewish historian Titus Flavius Josephus expands on this event by stating that for King Solomon, "as he grew into years, and his reason became weaker by length of time, it was not sufficient to recall to his mind the institutions of his

---

[12]Yoram Barak and Anat Achiron, "Age Related Disorders in the Bible," *Aging & Mental Health* 2 (1998): 275-78.

own country."[13] This is a clear reference to mental decline, specifically memory problems, due to advanced age. If King Solomon was suffering from dementia and unable to remember the tenants of the Jewish faith, as Josephus implies, it may help explain how he was so easily influenced by his pagan wives to become involved in idolatry toward the end of his life.

## Final Thoughts

The Scriptures are clear: those advanced in age (over sixty years) are to be honored and cared for by the church. Their presence within the fellowship is both a reminder of our faith heritage as well as the opportunity for the wisdom of experience to be passed on to the next generation. In the face of dementia, the elderly are to be cared for (Sirach 3:12-13), and as we learn from the tragic story of King Solomon, protected from those that might take advantage of them.

---

[13]Flavius Josephus, *The New Complete Works of Josephus*, trans. William Whiston (Grand Rapids: Kregel, 1999).

# 12

# STRUCK DOWN BY VIOLENCE

## CEREBROVASCULAR ACCIDENTS

*No matter how bad things are, they can always be worse.*
*So what if my stroke left me with a speech impediment?*
*Moses had one and he did all right.*

KIRK DOUGLAS

"IT WAS THE BEGINNING OF A NORMAL SUMMER'S DAY." Frank, a seventy-two-year-old retired machinist, had just come in from getting the morning paper when the headache hit. "I had never felt anything like it. One minute I was fine, the next it felt like someone had hit me in the head with a bat." Frank's wife, Joan, heard him cry out from the kitchen and then heard a thud. By the time she found him he was on the floor unconscious. Joan called an ambulance. At the ER the nurse gathered a detailed medical history from Joan while an unconscious Frank was examined. Prior to that day Frank's only medical problem had been hypertension, which he took medication to control. A CT scan showed bleeding in the cerebellum. Frank was rushed to surgery, where doctors struggled to repair the damage and stop the bleeding.

After surgery Frank, now on a ventilator, was moved to the intensive care unit. For the next three months Frank would move in and out of a comatose state. "The doctors really didn't think I was going to make it." More than once they told Joan that she should be prepared for the worst.

Once he regained consciousness Frank had significant left side weakness (ataxia), trouble swallowing (dysphagia), and difficulty speaking (aphasia). Months of physical therapy in a rehabilitation hospital were necessary before Frank was able to return home. "At first I was so weak and uncoordinated. I couldn't stand without assistance. If I reached for a cup, I'd knock it off the table. Because I wasn't able to swallow, they had to surgically implant a feeding tube into my stomach so I could receive nutrients. It was almost a year before I could eat solid food again." Today Frank speaks with a deep, husky voice, changed by the stroke. He is able (with assistance) to move around the house using a walker but prefers a motorized wheelchair when he goes out in public. "I hate that Joan has to do so much for me. She has been wonderful. It is hard to let someone care for you. God has used this struggle to teach me humility. I count my blessings every day."

## Characteristic Symptoms

Cerebrovascular accidents (CVAs), or strokes, occur when blood flow to a part of the brain is stopped either by a blockage (ischemic stroke) or the rupture of a blood vessel (hemorrhagic stroke). In both cases, part of the brain is deprived of blood and oxygen, causing the brain's cells to die. Stroke is often referred to as a "brain attack" to denote the fact that it is caused by a lack of blood supply to the brain, very much like a heart attack is caused by a lack of blood supply to the heart.

Ischemic strokes account for about 87 percent of all strokes. An ischemic stroke can occur in two ways. In an embolic stroke, a blood clot or plaque fragment forms somewhere in the body (usually the heart) and travels to the brain. Once in the brain, the clot travels to a blood vessel small enough to block its passage. The clot lodges there, blocking the blood vessel and causing a stroke. A thrombotic stroke is caused by a blood clot that forms inside one of the arteries supplying blood to the brain. This type of stroke is usually seen in people with high cholesterol and atherosclerosis.

A transient ischemic attack (TIA), like an ischemic stroke, is caused by the blockage of a blood vessel; the difference between an ischemic stroke and a TIA is that with a TIA the blockage is temporary (the clot spontaneously dissolves). TIA symptoms occur rapidly and last a relatively short time. Most TIAs last less than five minutes; the average is about a minute. When a TIA is over, it usually causes no permanent injury to the brain. This, however, is a serious stroke warning that should not be ignored.

Hemorrhagic strokes are less common than ischemic strokes but they are responsible for about 40 percent of all stroke deaths. The most common type of hemorrhagic stroke happens when a blood vessel inside the brain bursts and leaks blood into surrounding brain tissue (intracerebral hemorrhage). A subarachnoid hemorrhage involves bleeding in the area between the brain and the tissues covering the brain, which is known as the subarachnoid space.

The symptoms of a stroke usually occur suddenly but can develop over hours. Common stroke symptoms include weakness or loss of movement in the face, arm, or leg, especially on only one side of the body, trouble speaking, vision changes, confusion, or trouble understanding simple statements, problems with walking or balance, and a sudden, severe headache that is different from past headaches. Persons with hemorrhagic strokes are more likely to have associated headaches and convulsions, while speech and sensory deficits are more common with ischemic strokes.[1]

## Diagnoses

Hippocrates, the father of medicine, was the first to recognize stroke as a medical problem more than 2,400 years ago. The Greeks called the condition apoplexy, which means "struck down by violence," because they had no explanation for this sudden onset of paralysis and change in well-being. Johann Jakob Wepfer (1620–1695), a Swiss physician, proposed that the symptoms of apoplexy were caused by bleeding in the brain. He also found that a blockage in one of the brain's blood vessels could cause apoplexy.

It is important that strokes are diagnosed as quickly as possible. The faster treatment can be administered, the less damage will be done to the brain. In order for a stroke patient to get the best diagnosis and treatment possible, they need to be seen at a hospital within three hours of their symptoms first appearing. The acronym FAST is a way to remember the signs of stroke, and can help toward identifying the onset of stroke in someone: *F*ace drooping: If the person tries to smile does one side of the face droop? *A*rm weakness: If the person tries to raise both their arms does one arm drift downward? *S*peech difficulty: If the person tries to repeat a simple phrase is their speech slurred or strange? *T*ime to call 911: If any of these signs are observed, contact emergency services.

A diagnosis of mild or major vascular neurocognitive disorder is given when the onset of cognitive decline is related to one or more

---

[1]Saif S. Rathore et al., "Characterization of Incident Stroke Signs and Symptoms: Findings from Atherosclerosis Risk in Communities Study," *Stroke* 33 (2002): 2718-21.

CVAs. Major vascular neurocognitive disorder is also referred to as vascular dementia.[2]

## Prevalence and Age of Onset

Annually, over 800,000 Americans experience a cerebrovascular accident (stroke); of these 87 percent are ischemic strokes (blood vessel blockages). Approximately 130,000 individuals die every year in the United States from stroke. Women experience more strokes than men and are more likely to die from CVAs than men. While strokes can occur at any age, the risk of having a CVA increases with age and is more common in older adults. Only 34 percent of stroke hospitalizations are individuals younger than sixty-five. The risk of having a stroke doubles each decade of life after age fifty-five.[3]

## Developmental and Psychosocial Risk Factors

A number of medical conditions and unhealthy behaviors have been shown to increase an individual's risk of having a CVA. Medical conditions shown to increase the risk of stroke include high blood pressure, high cholesterol, heart disease, diabetes, and sickle cell disease. Unhealthy behaviors such as obesity (unhealthy diet, physical inactivity), the consumption of too much alcohol, and smoking have also been shown to increase an individual's stroke risk. In addition, increased age, being an ethnic minority, and female gender are also factors that increase one's risk for CVAs.[4]

---

[2]DSM-5; and Dan Blazer, "Neurocognitive Disorders in the DSM-5," *American Journal of Psychiatry* 170 (2013): 585-87.

[3]"Stroke Facts," *Centers for Disease Control and Prevention*, accessed March 9, 2017, www .cdc.gov/stroke/facts.htm; and "Stroke Risk Factors," *American Heart Association/American Stroke Association*, accessed March 9, 2017, www.strokeassociation.org.

[4]"Stroke Risk," *Centers for Disease Control and Prevention*, accessed March 9, 2017, www.cdc .gov/stroke/risk_factors.htm.

## Neurobiology

**Heritability.** Ischemic and hemorrhagic stroke have both been shown to have moderate heritability in genotype and twin studies. Research has also shown that an individual's risk of an ischemic stroke is increased by 76 percent if they come from a family with a positive history of stroke. It is not clear, however, how much of this genetic influence is directly linked to the stroke process or indirectly associated through inherited factors that simply increase an individual's risk, such as hypertension, diabetes, obesity, and atrial fibrillation.[5]

**Neuroanatomy.** The most common site of stroke in the brain is the middle cerebral artery. However, a stroke can occur in any artery that supplies blood to the brain. The artery that is involved and the particular location of the blockage or bleed will determine the specific region of the brain affected and the resulting symptoms. In an ischemic stroke only the region of the brain's tissue that is supplied by the blocked artery develops the most severe injury, called the *ischemic core*, while the rim of tissue around the core, called the *penumbra*, which also receives blood from other arteries, sustains less severe injury.

Common effects of strokes that occur on the right side of the brain include left visual field loss (hemianopsia), difficulty or discomfort in swallowing (dysphagia), left-sided weakness (hemiparesis), or paralysis (hemiplegia), sensory deficits, denial of paralysis, neglect of objects or people on their left side (hemineglect),

[5]Sunaina Yadav and Pankaj Sharma, "The Genetics of Ischaemic Stroke," *ACNR* 15 (2015): 6-12; William J. Devan et al., "Heritability Estimates Identify a Substantial Genetic Contribution to Risk and Outcome of Intracerebral Hemorrhage," *Stroke* 44 (2013):1578-83; Steve Bevan et al., "Genetic Heritability of Ischemic Stroke and the Contribution of Previously Reported Candidate Gene and Genomewide Associations," *Stroke* 43 (2012): 3161-67; and Soren Bak et al., "Genetic Liability in Stroke: A Long-Term Follow-up Study of Danish Twins," *Stroke* 33 (2002): 769-74.

impaired ability to judge spatial relationships, impaired ability to locate and identify body parts, short-term memory impairments, and an inability to perform particular purposive actions (apraxia).

Strokes on the left side of the brain can produce right visual field loss, difficulty or discomfort in swallowing, a difficulty or inability to produce or comprehend spoken language (dysphasia/aphasia), difficulty or inability to read (dyslexia/alexia), difficulty or inability to write (dysgraphia/agraphia), right-sided weakness or paralysis, sensory deficits, short-term memory impairments, and an inability to perform particular purposive actions.[6]

*Neurochemistry.* Disruption in the flow of blood and oxygen to the cells of the brain causes a neurochemical cascade of events that include a failure in cellular energy metabolism, excitotoxicity, oxidative stress, hemostatic activation, and, finally, cell death. CVA induced cellular energy metabolism disruptions and oxidative stress follow a process similar to that seen in traumatic brain injury, which will be described in chapter thirteen.

Excitotoxicity refers to the secondary damage caused by the abnormal release of excitatory neurotransmitters, such as glutamate, from dying cells. An excessive accumulation of these substances in the extracellular fluid leads to an overstimulation of the neurons, which causes high levels of calcium ions to enter the cells. This high level of calcium has two effects: first, it activates enzymes in the cell that damage the cell's membrane and DNA, and, second, water follows the calcium ions as they move into the cell, resulting in cytotoxic edema (a destructive swelling of the cell). Hemostasis is the process by which bleeding is stopped by the body. Under conditions of ischemia, platelets and blood factors related to coagulation are abnormally activated. This leads to a state of

---

[6]Joseph R. Pare and Joseph H. Kahn, "Basic Neuroanatomy and Stroke Syndromes," *Emergency Medicine Clinics of North America* 30 (2012): 601-15.

hypercoagulation further diminishing the amount of blood and oxygen that are able to flow to the affected brain area.[7]

## Treatment

Treatment for a stroke depends on whether it is ischemic or hemorrhagic. Brain imaging (e.g., CT) will allow the physician to determine the type and location of the stroke. Ischemic strokes are most commonly treated with medications, while the repair of a hemorrhagic stroke normally requires a surgical procedure.

*Pharmacotherapy.* Tissue plasminogen activator (tPA) is a medication that dissolves blood clots and is commonly referred to as the "clot buster." This medication has been approved to treat ischemic strokes in the first three hours following the onset of symptoms. If given promptly, one in three patients who receive tPA resolve their stroke symptoms or have major improvements. If, for medical reasons, a doctor cannot give the patient tPA, they may be given a medication that limits blood clot formation. Antiplatelet medications (e.g., aspirin, Plavix) reduce blood clot formation by preventing the blood platelets from sticking together and forming clots. Anticoagulants, such as warfarin and heparin, commonly known as "blood thinners," slow clot formation by a biochemical mechanism related to vitamin K. Anticoagulants are considered more aggressive drugs than antiplatelet medications because they significantly increase the patient's risk for bleeding.

*Surgery.* As described earlier a hemorrhagic stroke occurs when an artery in the brain ruptures. In this type of stroke, surgery is often necessary to control the bleeding. If an aneurysm (a weakened, balloon-like area in an artery) is the cause of the stroke, two surgical procedures are commonly used to control the bleeding. An

---

[7]Raf Brouns and Peter P. De Deyn, "The Complexity of Neurobiological Processes in Acute Ischemic Stroke," *Clinical Neurology and Neurosurgery* 111 (2009): 483-95.

aneurysm clip is a small clamp that a surgeon places at the base of the aneurysm to block blood from getting to the rupture. The placement of an aneurysm clip requires the surgeon to open the patient's skull and make an incision in the brain.

A less complex procedure for treating an aneurysm is called coil embolization. In this procedure a catheter is placed in an artery in the patient's groin and a tube is threaded through the vessel to the aneurysm site in the brain. Using the tube, a small coil is then placed into the aneurysm. The coil causes a blood clot to form in the artery, stopping the bleeding.

If an arteriovenous malformation (AVM) is the cause of the stroke, an AVM repair may be necessary. An AVM is a malformed tangle of arteries and veins in the brain or on its surface. Brain AVMs occur in less than 1 percent of the general population. They are more common in males than in females and appear to be congenital, meaning a person is born with the malformation. Several methods are used to repair AVMs, including surgery to remove the AVM, injecting a substance into the vessels of the AVM to block the flow of blood, and using radiation to shrink the AVM.

## The Other Side of Stroke

Meg called her eighty-two-year-old mother, Shannon, at the same time every day. This day, however, was different. When Shannon answered the phone, Meg couldn't understand what her mother was saying. Her words were slurred and made little sense. Meg called her sister Bethany, who lived near their mother. When Bethany went to her mother's home, she found Shannon confused and having difficulty speaking. In addition, she had fallen at some point and her wrist was broken. Bethany called an ambulance, and Shannon was taken to the hospital. A CT scan showed a left frontal lobe ischemic stroke.

Shannon spent a week in the hospital and was then moved to a rehab facility to begin physical therapy. She was having trouble swallowing (dysphagia) and speaking (aphasia). While her swallowing improved, she was never able to say more than a word or two again. After leaving the rehab facility Shannon moved in with Meg and her husband. Meg said that "the stroke took away everything she loved." Shannon could no longer read (alexia), sew, or work in the garden. Cognitively, as Bethany put it, "she wasn't all there." She could still perform simple household chores like folding towels or washing dishes, but she didn't seem to fully understand conversations. Slowly, over the next nine years, Shannon physically and cognitively deteriorated.

Caring for Shannon became more and more difficult. Even with the help of home health care attendants Meg struggled both physically and emotionally to care for her mother. The stress often made her ill and she had little life beyond the care of her mother. As Shannon's physical strength deteriorated, it became more difficult for her to get around the house. Cognitively she showed the signs of vascular dementia. Meg cared for her mother well, but age took its toll. Ultimately, Shannon became bedridden and died at the age of ninety-three in her sleep. I asked Meg if she had ever considered moving Shannon to an assisted living facility. She said, "I would never have done that. She was my mother, and it was my responsibility to care for her."

## Biblical Examples

The ancient Israelites recognized the most common symptoms of stroke: weakness (hemiparesis) or paralysis (hemiplegia) on one side of the body, and difficulty or an inability to speak. Much like other ancient peoples of the day, they believed strokes were the result of divine punishment. This can be seen in several

Scriptures, including Psalm 137:5-6, in which the author wishes a stroke (withered right hand, tongue that clings to the roof of the mouth) upon any Israelite during the Babylonian exile that forgets Jerusalem.[8]

God causes the prophet Ezekiel to be mute (tongue clings to the roof of his mouth) as a sign of his displeasure toward the rebellious Jewish people (Ezekiel 3:26).[9] The prophet Zechariah is told by God to portray two shepherds—Israel's true messianic shepherd (Christ) and the false worthless shepherd (anti-Christ)—as a sign to the people. God curses the worthless shepherd with a withered right arm and a blind right eye (Zechariah 11:17).[10] Describing the consequences of an unrighteous life in the apocryphal book Wisdom of Solomon, the author says that God "will dash them speechless to the ground, and shake them from the foundations" (Wisdom of Solomon 4:19 RSV).

In addition to these brief scriptural references to stroke symptoms, the CVAs of five individuals are described in some detail (see table 12.1).

*Nabal.* Nabal was a wealthy sheep rancher from Maon, a small town in the Judean hill country south of the Dead Sea. He is described as being a surly and mean man, married to a beautiful woman named Abigail (1 Samuel 25:3). David and his rebel army had provided protection for Nabal's shepherds in the past. While fleeing from Saul, low on supplies, David sent emissaries to Nabal requesting provisions. Nabal refused the request and insulted David.

---

[8]Luiz Antonio de Lima Resende et al., "Stroke in Ancient Times: A Reinterpretation of Psalm 137:5,6," *Arquivos de Neuro-Psiquiatria* 66 (2008): 581-83.

[9]R. Shane Tubbs et al., "Roots of Neuroanatomy, Neurology, and Neurosurgery as Found in the Bible and Talmud," *Neurosurgery* 63 (2008): 156-63.

[10]Stephen K. Mathew and Jeyaraj D. Pandian, "Newer Insights to the Neurological Diseases Among Biblical Characters of Old Testament," *Annals of the Indian Academy of Neurology* 13 (2010): 164-66.

**Table 12.1.** Biblical examples of cerebrovascular accidents

| BIBLICAL CHARACTER | SUPPORTING CLINICAL DETAIL | TYPE OF CVA | REFERENCE |
|---|---|---|---|
| **Old Testament** | | | |
| Nabal | Sudden onset, became like stone (coma) Death | Cardioembolic brainstem stroke | 1 Samuel 25:36-38 |
| Shunammite boy | Sudden onset, intense headache, loss of consciousness, death | Subarachnoid hemorrhage | 2 Kings 4:19-20 |
| **Deuterocanonical Books** | | | |
| Alcimus | Unable to speak, paralysis, agonizing death | Left hemisphere cerebral vascular hemorrhage | 1 Maccabees 9:54-56 JA 12.10.6 |
| Ptolemy IV Philopator | Unable to speak, convulsion, paralysis, recovered quickly | Left hemisphere TIA | 3 Maccabees 2:22-24 |
| **New Testament** | | | |
| Zacharias | Unable to speak, problem comprehending language recovered after months | Left middle cerebral artery ischemic stroke | Luke 1:20-23; 62-64 |

JA = Flavius Josephus, *Jewish Antiquities*

Angered, David prepared his army to attack Nabal's clan. Without informing Nabal, Abigail interceded with David, begged him for forgiveness and calmed the situation, saving her family. The next day, after a heavy night of drinking, Nabal was told by Abigail how close he had been to death. The Scriptures tell us that upon hearing the news "his heart died within him, and he became as a stone." Ten days later he died. This seems to be the description of a coma resulting from a stroke. The presence of heavy drinking suggests that Nabal may have had an acute alcohol cardiac arrhythmia leading to a cardioembolic brainstem stroke.[11] Consistent with the

---

[11]A cardioembolic stroke results from a blood clot that forms in the heart, travels to the brain, and blocks an artery. It is likely a brainstem stroke because of the sudden coma onset and subsequent death.

common view of the day, David believed that Nabal's stroke was the result of divine judgment (1 Samuel 25:39).[12]

***Shunammite boy.*** As he traveled between Israel's religious centers of Gilgal and Bethel in the south and Mount Carmel in the north, the prophet Elisha often passed through the small town of Shunem. A wealthy woman of the town frequently provided food and shelter to Elisha and his servant Gehazi whenever they visited. At some point she and her husband even built a special guest room onto their home specifically for the prophet (2 Kings 4:8-10). Elisha was grateful for the woman's hospitality and wished to show his thanks. Recognizing that she did not have a son, he interceded on her behalf before the Lord and a year later she held a miracle child in her arms. Years passed and the boy grew healthy and strong under the watchful eye of his mother and father.

During the harvest season of his fifth year, the child went to the fields with his father. As the harvest was being gathered the small child suddenly cried out to his father, "My head, my head!" and collapsed to the ground. The servants quickly carried the unconscious boy back to his mother, who anxiously held the unresponsive child for several hours. At midday the boy died in his mother's arms (2 Kings 4:19-20). Calmly she carried her son's body to the guest room built for Elisha and laid him on the bed. Without telling him the tragic news, she called to her husband that she was going to visit the prophet and to have a servant prepare a donkey. The grieving mother and her servant quickly covered the fifteen miles to Mount Carmel, and when she found Elisha she fell at his feet. After she explained the circumstances surrounding the death of her son, Elisha ordered Gehazi to take his staff (the symbol of his prophetic office) and quickly return to Shunem to try to revive

---

[12]Mathew and Pandian, "Newer Insights to the Neurological Diseases Among Biblical Characters of Old Testament," 164-66.

the boy. Gehazi left immediately, but the heartbroken mother was not satisfied with this response. She begged the prophet himself to accompany her back to Shunem, and Elisha agreed. Hours passed as they traveled, and as Shunem came into view on the horizon Gehazi met them with discouraging news. He had been unable to revive the boy using the prophet's staff. When they arrived at the house, Elisha went into the guest room alone and closed the door. The prophet stretched himself across the boy's body and began to intercede on his behalf before the Lord. As he prayed, the boy's body grew warm but he did not "awaken." Hours passed and Elisha continued to cry out to God that the boy might be revived. As Elisha lay over him praying, the boy suddenly sneezed and opened his eyes. Elisha called for the boy's mother, and when she entered the room and saw her son alive, overwhelmed by gratitude and joy, she fell at the prophet's feet. Because of the boy's age, sudden onset of an intense headache and the subsequent loss of consciousness, it is possible that he suffered a subarachnoid hemorrhage due to an arteriovenous malformation.[13]

*Alcimus.* Alcimus served as high priest of Israel for three years (162–159 BC). A political and military opponent of the Jewish rebel leader Judas Maccabeus, Alcimus was appointed high priest by the Syrian Seleucid king Antiochus V Eupator and maintained his office through force. Alcimus was dedicated to the spread of Greek culture (Hellenization) within Israel and the persecution of those faithful to the Hebrew law. In 159 BC Alcimus gave orders to tear down the wall of the temple that divided the court of the Gentiles from that of the Israelites. He was unable to complete the act because he was stricken; "his mouth was stopped and he was

---

[13]Tubbs et al., "Roots of Neuroanatomy, Neurology, and Neurosurgery as Found in the Bible and Talmud," 156-63; and Valmantas Budrys, "Neurology in Holy Scripture," *European Journal of Neurology* 14 (2007): e1-e6.

paralyzed" (1 Maccabees 9:55 RSV). He suffered for several days before finally dying. Given the symptoms described, it appears that Alcimus suffered a left hemisphere cerebral vascular hemorrhage.[14]

**Ptolemy IV Philopator.** The details of Ptolemy IV Philopator's stroke are presented in the deuterocanonical book 3 Maccabees. Written sometime between 30 BC and 50 AD, 3 Maccabees is best described as a work of historical fiction. While characters, locations, and situations from real history do appear in the book, it does not recount a true history. However, the information it provides is important for our purposes because it gives us insight into how people of that time period viewed stroke.

Ptolemy IV Philopator was the fourth pharaoh of Ptolemaic Egypt; his reign lasted seventeen years (221–204 BC). In 219 BC the Seleucid king Antiochus III began a military campaign to take cities and lands that were part of the Ptolemaic Empire. In response Ptolemy IV Philopator readied an army of forty-five thousand and in 217 BC met the sixty-eight thousand strong Seleucid army near Raphia in Israel, just beyond the Egyptian frontier. The battle of Raphia was one of the largest battles of the ancient world. The Egyptian army was victorious, and the events of 3 Maccabees begin with a description of this battle.

After his victory Ptolemy IV Philopator decided to visit the neighboring cities of Israel, including Jerusalem. During his visit to Jerusalem he went to the temple and made offerings to the God of the Jews. Amazed by the magnificence and beauty of the temple, he asked to enter the Holy of Holies. The priests informed him that it was forbidden and that only the high priest on one day of the year was allowed to enter. This angered the pharaoh and he decided to enter against their protest. The high priest Simon cried out to the

---

[14]J. C. E. Kaufmann, "Neuropathology in the Bible: Part II," *South African Medical Journal* 3 (October 1964): 788-89.

Lord to intervene. God struck Ptolemy by shaking him "as a reed is shaken by the wind." After this "he lay helpless on the ground," paralyzed and unable to speak (3 Maccabees 2:22 RSV). His friends and bodyguards dragged him out of the temple to safety, where he recovered a short time later. The author is describing a left hemisphere transient ischemic attack as a result of divine punishment.

**Zacharias.** Zacharias was an elderly priest who served in the temple during the reign of Herod the Great. While performing his priestly duties, offering incense before the altar, he was visited by the archangel Gabriel. The angel informed him that he and his wife, Elizabeth, would soon have a child and that the boy should be named John. Zacharias did not believe Gabriel due to the couple's age and as a punishment was struck dumb (not able to speak) until the child was born (Luke 1:20). The Scriptures also tell us that Zacharias was unable to understand spoken language; his friends and relatives had to make hand gestures to ask him what he wanted to name his son (Luke 1:62). As previously mentioned, aphasia (an inability to produce or comprehend spoken language) is a common symptom of a left middle cerebral artery stroke.[15] Zacharias's stroke seems to have been supernaturally healed due to the fact that immediately upon writing the name "John" on a tablet, he was able to speak again (Luke 1:64).

## Final Thoughts

Consistent with the prevailing view of the day, four of the five CVA examples from the biblical text describe divine punishment. The sinful behavior of Nabal, Alcimus, Ptolemy IV Philopator, and Zacharias resulted in God allowing each to be afflicted by a stroke. Two recovered, two did not. The CVA of the Shunammite boy,

---

[15]Tubbs et al., "Roots of Neuroanatomy, Neurology, and Neurosurgery," 156-63; and Budrys, "Neurology in Holy Scripture," e1-e6.

however, was not a divine punishment but appears to have resulted from a congenital vascular abnormality. I believe the lesson here is that afflictions with a spiritual cause are so similar (possibly identical) in presentation to physical illnesses that they are difficult if not impossible to tell apart. Rather than be concerned about the cause (spiritual or physical) of the suffering, it is more important for us to recognize that illness and disorder always affect a person's whole being: physical, mental, spiritual, and relational. The point of origin for the affliction is not what should determine our response; our call is the same in all cases, to relieve suffering and reveal Christ.

# 13

# THE GOLDEN BOWL

## TRAUMATIC BRAIN INJURY

*Repetitive head trauma chokes the brain.*
*It turns you into someone else.*

BENNET OMALU, MD

FOR TWO YEARS, beginning in the fall of 2011, I worked with traumatized groups in the North African country of Libya. After forty-two years under the brutal rule of Colonel Muammar al-Gaddafi, the people of Libya rose up on February 17, 2011, and demanded change. The nine-month civil war that followed resulted in the deaths of approximately fifteen thousand Libyans. I first met Hassan in the eastern city of Benghazi. A thirty-two-year-old furniture shop owner, he had been quick to join the local brigade to fight in the revolution. Six months into the fighting, an artillery shell exploded twenty-five yards from his position, throwing him approximately fifteen feet and knocking him unconscious for a few minutes. When he regained consciousness, he had only minor injuries, was dizzy, and had a pounding headache. It would be several weeks before Hassan and his family realized the full extent of his injury.

After returning home, Hassan tried to go back to his life as a shop owner. Chronic headaches made it difficult for him to work. In addition, he was constantly fatigued and struggled to remember things. He went to see a doctor at his family's suggestion. The doctor suggested that Hassan may be suffering from posttraumatic stress disorder (PTSD) and referred him to a psychiatrist. The psychiatrist prescribed an antidepressant medication, which brought little relief. While Hassan may indeed be struggling with PTSD, his symptoms are much more characteristic of a mild to moderate traumatic brain injury.

Hassan's wife and close relatives struggled to keep the furniture shop open. Hassan was unable to work due to his constant headaches, memory problems, and fatigue. His relationship with his family was further strained by his angry outbursts and irritability when stressed. Due to Libya's continued political unrest and lack of a fully functioning medical system, rehabilitation services for traumatic brain injury were unavailable. Hassan's inability to work and support his family left him depressed and hopeless. Given the difficult circumstances, we were only able to offer Hassan encouragement and an opportunity to participate in one of our trauma support groups. There he was able to talk openly about his struggles while drawing strength from a group of individuals who shared a common set of experiences. After several weeks of attending the group, Hassan's mood was better and he had a more hopeful outlook for the future.

### Characteristic Symptoms

Traumatic brain injury (TBI) is an insult to the brain caused by some external physical force. TBIs most often result from a fall or a blow to the head that does not penetrate the skull (a closed head injury). This type of injury may cause bruising or swelling of the brain's tissue (referred to as a concussion). An object that penetrates the skull, such as a bullet, causes an open head injury. This type of TBI is more serious and often involves fractures of the skull and significant bleeding within the brain itself.

The Glasgow Coma Scale (GCS) is the most common measure used to gauge the severity of a TBI. The GCS is a reliable and objective way of assessing the initial and subsequent level of consciousness in a person following a brain injury. It is used by trained first responders at the scene of an accident as well as by physicians and nurses during the postinjury recovery period. The GSC is used to rate the injured individual's best eye opening response (4 = spontaneous; 3 = to voice; 2 = to pain; 1 = no response), best verbal response (5 = normal conversation; 4 = disoriented conversation; 3 = words, but not coherent; 2 = no words, only sounds; 1 = no response), and best motor response (6 = normal; 5 = localized to pain; 4 = withdraw to pain; 3 = decorticate posture; 2 = decerebrate posture; 1 = no response)[1] that an individual can make at a given time following the injury. The GCS score is the sum of the eye, verbal, and motor response numbers. The severity of a TBI is classified according to the following GCS cutoff scores: severe 3-8, moderate 9-12, and mild 13-15.[2]

Common symptoms of a mild TBI include headaches, nausea, dizziness, difficulty tolerating bright lights, fatigue, visual disturbances, memory loss, poor attention/concentration, sleep disturbances, and irritability. Moderate to severe TBI can include any of

---

[1] A *decorticate* posture is an abnormal posture that can include rigidity, clenched fists, legs held straight out, and arms bent inward toward the body with the wrists and fingers bent and held against the chest. A *decerebrate* posture is characterized by rigidity, arms and legs held straight out, toes pointed downward, and the head and neck arched backwards.

[2] Graham Teasdale and Bryan Jennett, "Assessment of Coma and Impaired Consciousness: A Practical Scale," *Lancet* 2 (1974): 81-84.

the symptoms of mild TBI as well as the following: repeated vomiting or nausea, seizures, dilation of one or both pupils of the eyes, clear fluids draining from the nose or ears, inability to awaken from sleep, weakness or numbness in fingers and toes, loss of coordination, profound confusion, agitation, combativeness or other unusual behavior, slurred speech, and coma.

## Diagnosis

As early as 500–600 BC, Assyrian and Babylonian physicians understood that injuries to the head could cause seizures, paralysis, and loss of sight, hearing, or speech.[3] The second-century Jewish rabbis of the Talmud recognized that an open head wound was a greater threat to life than a closed head injury.[4] Ambroise Paré, a sixteenth-century French military surgeon, is credited with being the first physician to use the term *concussion* in describing mild TBI.[5] Beyond the physical symptoms previously described, there are two significant concerns following a TBI, a deficit in cognitive functioning or a personality change.

When an individual experiences a deficit in cognitive functioning following a TBI, they are said to have a neurocognitive disorder (NCD). The first step in the diagnostic process following a brain injury is to differentiate between the individual's normal neurocognitive functioning and mild or major neurocognitive disorder. Mild and major NCD differ only in the degree of the impairment.

---

[3]Jo Ann Scurlock and Burton R. Andersen, *Diagnoses in Assyrian and Babylonian Medicine: Ancient Sources, Translations, and Modern Medical Analyses* (Urbana: University of Illinois Press, 2005).

[4]R. Shane Tubbs et al., "Roots of Neuroanatomy, Neurology, and Neurosurgery as Found in the Bible and Talmud," *Neurosurgery* 63 (2008): 156-63.

[5]Eugene S. Flamm, "From Signs to Symptoms: The Neurosurgical Management of Head Trauma from 1517 to 1867," in *A History of Neurosurgery*, ed. S. H. Greenblatt (Park Ridge, IL: American Association of Neurological Surgeons, 1997), 65-81.

In mild NCD, the decline in cognitive performance following the brain injury is judged to be modest, while in major NCD a significant cognitive decline is seen in one or more of the following areas: attention, executive function, learning and memory, language, perceptual motor and social cognition. In addition, the individual's capacity for independence in everyday activities is not affected in mild NCD but is impaired in major NCD.

In some instances, damage to the brain may result in a change of the individual's personality. Such changes may include affective lability, disinhibition, aggression, apathy, and paranoia. Personality changes are most often exaggerations of preexisting personality traits. If an individual displays a persistent personality disturbance following a TBI that represents a change from their personality pattern prior to the injury, they may also be given a diagnosis of Personality Change Due to Another Medical Condition.[6]

## Prevalence and Age of Onset

It is estimated that 1.7 million individuals sustain a TBI in the United States every year; of these head injuries fifty-two thousand result in death. Presently, approximately 5.3 million Americans are living with a TBI-related disability. Men are twice as likely to acquire a TBI as women. While TBI can occur at any age, there are three age ranges or developmental periods that show higher rates for head injuries: children 0-4 years old, adolescents 15-19 years old, and elders 65 years and older. Individuals seventy-five years and older are more likely to be hospitalized or die as the result of a TBI than any other age group.[7]

---

[6]DSM-5.

[7]Mark Faul et al., "Traumatic Brain Injury in the United States: Emergency Department Visits, Hospitalizations and Deaths, 2002–2006," *Centers for Disease Control and Prevention*, updated February 9, 2016, www.cdc.gov/traumaticbraininjury.

## Developmental and Psychosocial Risk Factors

A number of factors have been found to increase the risk that an individual will sustain a TBI. These include male gender, ethnic minority status, being age fifty-five or over, and the consumption of alcohol. Alcohol is involved in approximately 50 percent of all TBIs. Falls are the leading cause of TBI (40 percent) in the United States, followed by unintentional blunt trauma (being hit in the head by something) (16 percent), motor vehicle accidents (14 percent), and assaults (11 percent). Falls are the leading cause of TBI-related death for those sixty-five years and older. Motor vehicle accidents are the leading cause of TBI-related death in children and young adults ages 5 to 24 years, while assaults are the leading cause of TBI related death in children ages 0 to 4.[8]

## Neurobiology

**Neuroanatomy.** There are two types of brain damage due to TBI: focal damage and diffuse injury. Focal damage occurs in a specific area and is caused by a direct impact on the brain. For descriptive purposes, the brain can be divided into four areas or lobes: frontal, temporal, parietal, and occipital. The frontal lobe is the largest and the most common area of injury following mild to moderate TBI.[9] Focal damage to the frontal lobes can produce a wide variety of symptoms and problems, including disturbances in motor functioning, difficulty speaking, changes in social behavior and personality, and deficits in attention and cognitive flexibility.

---

[8]Bob Roozenbeek et al., "Changing Patterns in the Epidemiology of Traumatic Brain Injury," *Nature Reviews: Neurology* 9 (2013): 231-36; Faul et al., "Traumatic Brain Injury in the United States."

[9]Harvey S. Levin et al., "Magnetic Resonance Imaging and Computerized Tomography in Relation to the Neurobehavioral Sequelae of Mild and Moderate Head Injuries," *Journal of Neurosurgery*, 66 (1987): 706-13.

The temporal lobes are involved in the primary organization of visual and auditory sensory input. Focal injury to the temporal lobe may produce disturbance of auditory and visual sensation and perception, impaired organization and categorization of verbal information, problems with language comprehension, long-term memory deficits, altered personality and affective behavior, and abnormal sexual behavior. The parietal lobe, located under the crown of the skull, is responsible for the processing of visual images and the ability to multitask using information from more than one of the senses. Focal damage to the parietal lobe results in problems recognizing people and objects as well as a loss of awareness of one's body and limbs and their position in space. Located at the back of the brain, the occipital lobe is responsible for visual perception. Focal damage to the occipital lobe can result in a loss of visual ability (in some cases total blindness), an inability to identify colors, and hallucinations.

A diffuse injury is caused by the stretching and tearing of the brain tissue, which results in damage over a wide area. The most common form of diffuse injury is called diffuse axonal injury, which is due to differential motion of the brain within the skull (acceleration-deceleration) that leads to the shearing of axons.[10] Diffuse axonal injury occurs in about half of all severe head traumas. The symptom that is most evident from this type of brain injury is mainly unconsciousness. If the individual is unconscious for more than six hours, they could have experienced a diffuse axonal injury.

*Neurochemistry.* Two of the most damaging biochemical events that occur in the brain's tissues after an injury are oxidative stress and alterations in cellular energy metabolism. Oxidative stress is an imbalance between the production of free radicals and the ability

---

[10]Every nerve cell in the brain has an axon. An axon is a long projection that comes out of one side of the nerve cell's main body. Nerve cells send signals to one another through their axons.

of the body to counteract their harmful effects through neutralization by antioxidants.[11] Free radicals are unstable molecules that chemically interact with other cellular components such as DNA, proteins, or lipids to steal their electrons in order to become stabilized. This, in turn, destabilizes the cellular components, which then seek and steal electrons from other molecules, therefore triggering a large damaging chain of free radical reactions. Antioxidants, such as ascorbic acid (vitamin C), are molecules present in cells that prevent these reactions by donating an electron to the free radicals without becoming destabilized themselves. An imbalance between oxidants and antioxidants is the underlying basis of oxidative stress.

Immediately after the damage caused by the physical trauma, the brain's cells indiscriminately release neurotransmitters, and the neural cells' carefully maintained electrolyte balance is disrupted, resulting in uncontrolled ionic fluxes across the cell membrane. In a desperate attempt to correct these neurochemical disruptions, the brain's cells activate additional systems and resources. This increase in activity requires an increased amount of cellular energy, so there is a dramatic jump in the brain's glucose metabolism. This increase in cellular energy metabolism occurs in the setting of diminished blood flow within the brain due to the trauma, and the disparity between glucose supply and demand triggers a cellular energy crisis.[12]

## Treatment

Once an individual who has sustained a TBI is medically stabilized through emergency trauma care and inpatient medical treatment, rehabilitation begins.

---

[11]A free radical is an oxygen containing molecule that has one or more unpaired electrons, making it highly reactive with other molecules.
[12]Stefano Signoretti et al., "Biochemical and Neurochemical Sequelae Following Mild Traumatic Brain Injury: Summary of Experimental Data and Clinical Implications," *Neurosurgery Focus* 29 (2010): 1-12.

*Acute rehabilitation.* As early as medically possible in the recovery process, individuals with brain injuries should begin acute rehabilitation. During acute rehabilitation, a team of health professionals with experience and training in TBI work with the patient to regain as many activities of daily living as possible (e.g., dressing, eating, toileting, walking, speaking).

*Postacute rehabilitation.* When TBI patients are well enough to participate in more intensive physical therapy, they may be transferred to a postacute rehabilitation setting, such as a rehabilitation hospital or a residential rehabilitation facility. The goal of postacute rehabilitation is to help the patient regain the most independent level of functioning possible. Rehabilitation involves both strengthening weaknesses as well as learning new ways to compensate for abilities that may have permanently changed due to the brain injury.

*Outpatient physical therapy.* Following acute and postacute rehabilitation, a person with a brain injury may continue to receive outpatient physical therapy to maintain or enhance their recovery. Individuals whose TBI was not severe enough to require hospitalization or who were not diagnosed as having a brain injury when the incident occurred may attend outpatient physical therapy to address functional impairments.

*Cognitive rehabilitation.* Cognitive problems associated with TBI may be the greatest barrier to returning to normal life. These difficulties involve memory, attention, social behavior, judgment, and planning. *Cognitive rehabilitation* is a broad term used to describe treatments and interventions that address the cognitive problems that can arise after a brain injury.

*Pharmacotherapy.* A number of psychiatric conditions can manifest following a TBI. These include depression, anxiety, agitation and irritability, posttraumatic stress disorder, and psychosis. To treat these co-occurring conditions, psychiatric medications are often prescribed and may include antidepressants, anxiolytics, antipsychotics, psychostimulants, and anticonvulsants.

## The Other Side of TBI

Brad was only twelve when the accident happened. A family outing to ride go karts suddenly turned tragic. His mother, Clare, said, "Our lives stopped for a while; he wasn't expected to live. I quit my job that moment and ever since our world has taken many detours and hit a lot of obstacles. Every moment is a moment of uncertainty. We never know what to expect. Life after TBI is not and never will be the same." Many family and friends were present during Brad's one-month coma, but after he woke up there was little support for the family. "At first a few folks came around and asked, 'How are you doing?' . . . As time went by, fewer people came by, and now no one asks or seems to care anymore. We have been left alone to pick through the pieces of our life and try to rebuild." The first year with Brad at home was the most difficult for Clare. "A grieving process had to take place. The old Brad was no longer there; a new, different person had invaded his body." Prior to the accident Brad was active, outgoing, happy, and very social. Nothing held him back; he lived life to the fullest. "Brain injury took my child away from me. My son has missed out on everything. While others his age are enjoying their lives, he is stuck with his mom taking care of all his needs. I hurt so much for him! I love him more than anyone could imagine and would take his place in an instant."

## Biblical Examples

While the ancient Hebrews did not have an accurate scientific understanding of the functions of the brain, they certainly understood its importance to life and that damage to it brought serious consequences and often death. This connection between the brain and life is beautifully described by Solomon in Ecclesiastes. Using poetic language, Solomon refers to the skull as a golden bowl and the spinal cord as the silver chord (Ecclesiastes 12:6). This language is used metaphorically to compare the bowl of a lamp that holds oil and the cord that suspends it from the ceiling to illuminate a darkened room with the skull that contains the brain and the spinal cord that connects it to the body and through which the light of life shines. Four detailed examples of TBI are reported in the Scriptures (see table 13.1).[13]

**Sisera.** A Canaanite general during the time of the judges, Sisera led the army of King Jabin against the Israelites. Deborah and Barak were called by God to oppose him. God delivered Jabin's army into the hands of the Israelites, and Sisera had to flee the battlefield. He chose to hide from the Israelites in the tent of Jael, the wife of Heber the Kenite, a family he believed to be his ally. After Sisera fell asleep, Jael made her allegiance to the Israelites clear by using a hammer to drive a tent peg through the general's temple and into the ground below him (Judges 4:17-22; 5:26-27). Sisera sustained a severe perforating brain injury and died quickly.[14]

**Abimelech.** Abimelech was the son of Gideon (Jerubbaal), a judge who delivered the Israelites from the Midianites. After the death of his father, Abimelech killed his seventy brothers and made himself king of Israel. Three years into his illegitimate reign, the leaders of Shechem rebelled against him. Abimelech attempted to put down the uprising by force. After taking control of Shechem,

[13]Valmantas Budrys, "Neurology in Holy Scripture," *European Journal of Neurology* 14 (2007): e1-e6; and Moshe Feinsod, "Three Head Injuries: The Biblical Account of the Deaths of Sisera, Abimelech and Goliath," *Journal of the History of the Neurosciences* 6 (1997): 320-24.

[14]A perforating brain injury is a wound in which an object passes through the head/brain and leaves an exit wound.

Abimelech and his army attacked the town of Thebez. During the battle, a woman threw a millstone from the top of a tower, striking Abimelech in the head. The Scriptures tell us that the blow "crushed his skull" (Judges 9:53). Realizing that the wound was mortal, Abimelech ordered his armor bearer to thrust him through with his sword, so that it might not be said he had been killed by a woman. The armor bearer did as his king had requested. Abimelech sustained a moderate to severe penetrating brain injury, from which he would likely not have recovered.[15]

**Goliath.** Goliath was the legendary Philistine giant who challenged the Israelite army led by King Saul. When none of the Israelite warriors nor King Saul were willing to fight the Philistine champion, the young shepherd boy David volunteered. Taking a sling and five smooth stones, the boy engaged the Philistine warrior in the Valley of Elah. David's first stone struck the giant in the forehead, knocking him unconscious. The Scriptures tell us that the stone "sank into his forehead" (1 Samuel 17:49), while the Jewish historian Josephus says that it "sank deeply into his brain."[16] Both of these descriptions suggest a depressed skull fracture.[17] While Goliath was unconscious, David took the giant's sword and cut off his head. It appears that Goliath sustained a moderate penetrating brain injury from which he likely would have recovered.

**Eutychus.** Eutychus was a young man from the port city of Troas on the northwest coast of Asia Minor, 125 miles southeast of Philippi. On a visit to Troas during his third missionary journey, the apostle Paul was teaching a large group in the upper room of a home. Eutychus was there, sitting in the window listening to Paul.

---

[15] A penetrating brain injury is a wound in which an object breaches the skull but does not exit it.

[16] Flavius Josephus, *The New Complete Works of Josephus*, trans. William Whiston (Grand Rapids: Kregel, 1999).

[17] In a depressed skull fracture part of the skull is actually sunken in from the trauma.

Late into the evening, while Paul was still teaching, Eutychus dozed off and fell out of the window, hitting the ground three stories below (Acts 20:9-12). Knocked unconscious, the people initially thought he was dead. Paul examined him and found that he was still breathing. Sometime later Eutychus regained consciousness and went home with his family. It appears that Eutychus sustained a mild head injury, what we today might call a concussion, from which he quickly recovered.

**Table 13.1.** Biblical examples of traumatic brain injury

| BIBLICAL CHARACTER | SUPPORTING CLINICAL DETAIL | ESTIMATED LEVEL OF TBI | REFERENCE |
|---|---|---|---|
| **Old Testament** | | | |
| Sisera | Perforating brain injury, death | Severe | Judges 4:17-22 |
| Abimelech | Skull fracture, no loss of consciousness | Moderate–severe | Judges 9:52-53 |
| Goliath | Depressed skull fracture, loss of consciousness | Moderate–severe | 1 Samuel 17:41-49 JA 6.9.5 |
| **New Testament** | | | |
| Eutychus | Loss of consciousness | Mild | Acts 20:7-12 |

JA = Flavius Josephus, *Jewish Antiquities*

## Final Thoughts

Most of these biblical descriptions of TBI offer us little more than the opportunity to see the consequences of evil. Sisera, Abimelech, and Goliath were wicked men who attacked God's chosen people and were punished for their actions. Their stories are reported to us both as a warning against sin and to remind us of the sovereignty of God. The story of Eutychus, however, is different, and I believe there is a profound lesson the church can learn from this description of brain injury.

When Eutychus fell from the window, it is clear that Paul stopped teaching and went to the unconscious young man

(Acts 20:10). In fact, from the text it appears that the entire group took a break to eat a meal and comfort the family of Eutychus while he recovered (Acts 20:11-12). Paul and these early Christians understood that the most important thing to the heart of God at that moment was Eutychus and his family.

Brain disorders are messy things; they don't fit well into our rigid and highly structured churches. Far too often, we choose ritual and tradition over broken people and families. The story of Eutychus teaches us that in God's economy, people are most important. I pray that the families of individuals struggling with brain disorders will leave our churches the same way that Eutychus's family left that home in Troas centuries ago, "greatly comforted" (Acts 20:12).

# CARING

*for those who are*

# SUFFERING

# 14

# A FATAL DECISION

## SUICIDE

*Suicide is what the death certificate says*
*when one dies of depression.*

PETER D. KRAMER, MD

SUICIDE IS A WORD THAT PROVOKES FEAR, shame, and sadness. Some have called suicide "a selfish act" and "a permanent answer to a temporary problem." Both of these statements wrongly imply that suicide is a reasoned and rational decision to take one's life. Since its beginning, the church has struggled with understanding the spiritual consequences of suicide, at times even refusing burial and religious rites to the victims because they were thought to have committed an unforgiven (mortal) sin, damning them to hell. Suicide is neither reasoned nor rational, and mental illness is the most common cause.

## Warning Signs

Communicating ideas of suicide or a desire to die is the single strongest indicator of increased suicide risk. This warning sign may present as threats to hurt or kill oneself, actively looking for ways to kill oneself (seeking access to pills, weapons, or other means), or talking or writing about death, dying, or suicide. Immediate help from a mental health provider or emergency personnel should be sought if any of these overt expressions of heightened suicidality are displayed by an individual.

Additional warning signs of heightened suicide risk include increased drug or alcohol use; no reason for living (no sense of purpose in life); anxiety, agitation, inability to sleep, or sleeping all of the time; feeling trapped (like there's no way out); hopelessness; withdrawal from friends, family, and society; rage, uncontrolled anger; seeking revenge; acting recklessly or engaging in risky activities, seemingly without thinking; and dramatic mood changes. It is important to remember that warning signs are only meaningful as a collection or group. The presence of a single, isolated warning sign is usually not reflective of increased suicide risk.[1]

Although suicide is often preventable, it is important to understand that when a loved one sadly follows through with their suicidal thoughts, no one is to blame. Sometimes no matter how hard we try, those we love still act on their hopeless feelings and end their lives.

## Prevalence and Age of Onset

Each year, approximately forty thousand individuals die by suicide in the United States. It is estimated that there is one suicide death for every twenty-five attempts. Suicide is the tenth most common cause of death for all ages (for comparison, homicide is seventeenth) with middle-aged adults accounting for the largest proportion of suicides (56 percent). Suicide is the third most common cause of death among children and adolescents ages 10-14

---

[1]M. David Rudd et al., "Warning Signs for Suicide: Theory, Research, and Clinical Applications," *Suicide and Life-Threatening Behavior* 36 (2006): 255-62.

and the second among those 15-24 years old. While women are more likely to have suicidal thoughts and three times more likely to attempt suicide, men die by suicide at nearly four times the rate of women and represent 77.9 percent of all suicides. This gender difference is due to the fact that men tend to use more lethal means when attempting suicide, such as firearms or hanging, while the most common method of suicide in women is poisoning (overdose).[2]

## Risk Factors

Individuals living with mental illness are at a greatly increased risk of suicide. Approximately 90 percent of those who die by suicide are suffering from a psychiatric disorder at the time of death.[3] The abuse of alcohol or other drugs coupled with depression exponentially increases an individual's likelihood of suicide. Stressful life events such as divorce, a death in the family, or the loss of a job, and prolonged stressful circumstances, such as harassment or bullying, all increase an individual's risk of suicide. A serious or chronic health condition, chronic pain, and a family history of suicide attempts are all factors that increase suicide risk. Once an individual has attempted suicide, they are at an increased risk for future attempts.

## Neurobiology

**Heritability.** Family studies have clearly demonstrated that suicide runs in families. The relatives of suicidal individuals are five times more likely to display suicidal behavior themselves

---

[2]"Suicide Statistics," *American Foundation for Suicide Prevention*, accessed March 10, 2017, https://afsp.org/about-suicide/suicide-statistics; and "Suicide: Facts at a Glance," *Centers for Disease Control and Prevention*, updated October 28, 2016, www.cdc.gov/violenceprevention /suicide.

[3]Jonathan T. O. Cavanagh et al., "Psychological Autopsy Studies of Suicide: A Systematic Review," *Psychological Medicine* 33 (2003): 395-405.

compared to the general population.[4] Twin studies have consistently found higher concordance rates for identical twins (monozygotic) compared to fraternal twins (dizygotic), suggesting a genetic effect. Heritability for suicidal thoughts (ideations) and attempts appears to be greater than death by suicide.[5] While the transmission of heritable psychiatric disorders likely accounts for much of the genetic effect related to suicide, it does not fully explain it. Recent studies suggest that the heritability of suicidal behavior may be independent of mental illness.[6]

*Neuroanatomy.* A number of neuroanatomical abnormalities have been found in the brains of individuals who have committed and attempted suicide. Postmortem studies have found reductions in the size of the parahippocampal gyrus, a region of the brain that surrounds the hippocampus and is part of the limbic system,[7] in the brains of those who have died by suicide.[8] Several studies have also found reductions in both gray and white matter, as well as increased numbers of subcortical gray matter hyperintensities in the brains of individuals who have attempted suicide.[9] Reductions

[4]Ross J. Baldessarini and John Hennen, "Genetics of Suicide: An Overview," *Harvard Review of Psychiatry* 12 (2004): 1-13.

[5]Nancy L. Pedersen and Amy Fiske, "Genetic Influences on Suicide and Nonfatal Suicidal Behavior: Twin Study Findings," *European Psychiatry* 25 (2010): 264-67.

[6]Enrique Baca-Garcia et al., "Variables Associated with Familial Suicide Attempts in a Sample of Suicide Attempters," *Progress in Neuro-Psychopharmacology & Biological Psychiatry* 31 (2007): 1312-16.

[7]The limbic system is a set of structures deep within the brain that controls our most basic emotions (e.g., fear, pleasure, anger) and drives (e.g., hunger, sex, care of offspring).

[8]Lori L. Altshuler et al., "The Hippocampus and Parahippocampus in Schizophrenic, Suicide, and Control Brains," *Archives of General Psychiatry* 47 (1990): 1029-34.

[9]Hyperintensities are thought to be dilated perivascular spaces or demyelination caused by reduced local blood flow. Jen-Ping Hwang et al., "Cortical and Subcortical Abnormalities in Late-Onset Depression with History of Suicide Attempts Investigated with MRI and Voxel-Based Morphometry," *Journal of Geriatric Psychiatry and Neurology* 23 (2010): 171-84; and Eileen P. Ahearn et al., "MRI Correlates of Suicide Attempt History in Unipolar Depression," *Biological Psychiatry* 50 (2001): 266-70.

in prefrontal cortex activity have also been shown to correlate with suicidal behavior.[10]

**Neurochemistry.** Serotonin (5-HT) has been the most commonly studied neurotransmitter in relation to suicide. Several postmortem studies have found 5-HT abnormalities in the prefrontal cortex of suicide victims, particularly the ventromedial prefrontal cortex. Low serotonin activity in the ventromedial prefrontal cortex impairs inhibition, creating a propensity to act on suicidal thoughts. Diminished levels of norepinephrine (NE) have also been found in the brains of individuals who have died by suicide. Low NE functioning can generate feelings of hopelessness and pessimism.[11]

## Prevention Strategies

As mentioned at the beginning of this chapter, individuals at risk of suicide often show warning signs prior to an attempt. In addition, individuals with mental illness, particularly mood issues such as depression or bipolar disorder, are at particularly high risk for suicide. Knowing these facts allows us an opportunity to put preventative measures in place to protect our loved ones.[12]

**Talking.** If you are concerned that your loved one may be suicidal, talk to them! Ask specifically if they are (1) having suicidal thoughts/ ideas, (2) devising a plan to do so, and (3) if they have access to lethal means (e.g., pills, weapons). Asking an individual the "suicide question" does not increase the risk of suicide and may save their life. If the response makes you believe that the person is suicidal,

---

[10]Maria A. Oquendo et al., "Positron Emission Tomography of Regional Brain Metabolic Responses to a Serotonergic Challenge and Lethality of Suicide Attempts in Major Depression," *Archives of General Psychiatry* 60 (2003): 14-22.

[11]J. John Mann, "Neurobiology of Suicidal Behavior," *Nature Reviews* 4 (2003): 819-28; and Masoud Kamali et al., Understanding the Neurobiology of Suicidal Behavior," *Depression and Anxiety* 14 (2001): 164-76.

[12]J. John Mann et al., "Suicide Prevention Strategies: A Systematic Review," *Journal of the American Medical Association* 294 (2005): 2064-74.

take them to an emergency room, call the police, or help them contact their mental health care provider.

*Screening.* If your loved one falls into an at-risk suicide group (e.g., serious mental illness, substance abuse) get them to a physician or mental health care provider sooner rather than later to be assessed. Contact with a primary care physician or mental health care provider is not uncommon for those having suicidal thoughts. Research shows that 75 percent of suicide victims had contact with their primary care physician in the year of their suicide. Forty-five percent of those had contact in the month of their death.[13] Being aware of the warning signs, getting the at-risk individual to professional help early, and being available to provide additional information when needed will make your loved one's interactions with medical personnel more effective at preventing suicide.

*Treatment.* Psychiatric disorders are present in at least 90 percent of suicides and more than 80 percent of those individuals are not receiving treatment at the time of their death.[14] As described in the previous chapters, pharmacotherapy with antidepressants and mood stabilizers is effective in treating mood disorders such as depression and bipolar disorder. Psychotherapeutic approaches, such as cognitive behavioral therapy, are also highly effective at treating mood disorders and have been shown to reduce reattempt rates in suicide attempters.[15]

*Means restriction.* Restricting an at-risk individual's access to lethal means is a common suicide prevention strategy. Given that nine out of ten suicide attempts occur at home, making the home

---

[13]Jason B. Luoma et al., "Contact with Mental Health and Primary Care Providers Before Suicide: A Review of the Evidence," *American Journal of Psychiatry* 159 (2002): 909-16.

[14]Jouko K. Lonnqvist et al., "Mental Disorders and Suicide Prevention," *Psychiatry and Clinical Neuroscience* 49 (1995): S111-S116.

[15]Gregory K. Brown et al., "Cognitive Therapy for the Prevention of Suicide Attempts: A Randomized Controlled Trial," *Journal of the American Medical Association* 294 (2005): 563-70.

environment as safe as possible is paramount. Guns are the leading means of death for suicidal individuals, accounting for nearly 60 percent of suicide deaths per year. Guns should be taken out of the home and secured. While guns are the most common way that people complete suicide, poisoning (overdose) is the most common means by which people attempt suicide. To minimize the risk of overdose, keep only small quantities of medication in the home or consider keeping them in a locked cabinet. Remove all unused or expired medication. Remember that over-the-counter medication, such as Tylenol or Advil, can also be lethal if misused. Alcohol use or abuse can decrease inhibitions and cause people to act on their feelings more freely. Only small quantities (or none at all) of alcohol should be kept in the home.

## The Other Side of Suicide

"A wound that never seems to fully heal" is how Helen describes the lingering pain associated with the death of her husband, Curtis, by suicide. It was the week before Thanksgiving, and Curtis, a forty-one-year-old elementary school coach and teacher, left the house to go for a walk. Several hours later Curtis returned home to a worried Helen. He admitted to her that he had walked down to the river with the thought of killing himself. Helen encouraged Curtis to call his psychiatrist. Curtis had been diagnosed with obsessive compulsive disorder in his early twenties and took medication daily to manage his symptoms. Prior to that day, Curtis had never struggled with suicidal thoughts. Because Helen was nine months pregnant and scheduled to deliver soon, the psychiatrist decided not to hospitalize Curtis but did make a change in his medication. A week later, on Thanksgiving Day, Curtis once again left the house. Several hours later, he was found dead in an empty field a few blocks from the house. The cause of death: a self-inflicted gunshot wound. Helen delivered their second child the next day. Curtis's funeral was an amazing event; hundreds attended the celebration of a man who had lived his life for others. Person after person moved to the microphone to share how Curtis had positively impacted their lives. Heavy with grief, many silently wondered how a man so loved by others could take his own life.

Looking back, Helen believes that Curtis began having problems after a stillbirth during the couple's second pregnancy two years earlier. "He became more fearful and anxious about everything after we lost the child." In addition, for a week or two prior to his death, Curtis was prescribed a steroid for his allergies. "It seemed to make his anxiety even worse," Helen said. In her mind, Curtis's obsessive compulsive disorder, his inability to deal with the loss of their child, irritability caused by the steroid, and the sudden medication change by the psychiatrist was the perfect storm that resulted in Curtis's suicide. Today, Helen works as an elementary school teacher and is raising her two young sons. She says that "special days like birthdays and anniversaries are hard," but she has been able to begin to live again despite the pain. "The body of Christ was incredible; they loved us well. I don't know what I would have done without that support. God truly showed his love for us through his people."

## Biblical Examples

A diverse group of individuals mentioned in the Bible considered suicide during periods of distress, while twelve actually took their own lives. Men and women, rich and poor, young and old, prophets, kings, and tyrants all found themselves in hopeless circumstances from which they believed that suicide was their only way out.[16]

---

[16]B. M. Barraclough, "The Bible Suicides," *Acta Psychiatrica Scandinavica* 86 (1992): 64-69; and Horst J. Koch, "Suicides and Suicide Ideation in the Bible: An Empirical Survey," *Acta Psychiatrica Scandinavica* 112 (2005): 167-72.

*Suicidal ideations.* The suicidal thoughts (ideations) of seven individuals are described in the Scriptures (see table 14.1). Six of those individuals cry out directly to God, asking him to kill them or allow them to die. The seventh, the Philippian jailer, differs in that he was preparing to commit suicide when Paul and Silas stopped him. In each case, rather than grant their desire to die, God intervenes and provides comfort in their time of crisis. All seven individuals were transformed by their interaction with God or his chosen representatives and no longer desired to die.

**Table 14.1.** Biblical examples of suicidal ideations

| BIBLICAL CHARACTER | REASON FOR SUICIDAL IDEATIONS | GOD'S RESPONSE | REFERENCES |
|---|---|---|---|
| Moses | Stress of leadership | Appointed others to help lead, sent quail for the people | Numbers 11:10-17 |
| Elijah | Fear of Jezebel | Sent an angel with food and water, came near to Elijah, called Elisha to be his disciple | 1 Kings 19:1-20 |
| Job | Loss, physical suffering | Appears to Job in the whirlwind | Job 6:8-11; 38–41 |
| Jonah | Fear, anger | Sent a great fish, provided shade from a bush | Jonah 1:12-17; 4:1-11 |
| Tobit | Poverty, loss of sight | Sends the angel Raphael | Tobit 3:6, 16-17 |
| Sarah | False accusations, deaths of husbands | Sends the angel Raphael | Tobit 3:10-13, 16-17 |
| Philippian jailer | Fear, escaped prisoners | Paul and Silas share the gospel | Acts 16:25-34 |

*Suicidal deaths.* The twelve suicidal deaths that are detailed in the Scriptures fall into three broad categories: heroic martyrdom, battle or conflict related, and personal distress (see table 14.2).

*Heroic martyrdom.* In heroic martyrdom, a person knowingly sacrifices his life in order to further a belief, cause, or principle.

There are four examples of this type of suicide in the Bible. Samson's death during his destruction of the Philistine temple is the most well known. All four biblical characters are described as courageous for their sacrifice and considered heroic examples to be emulated. Even today, individuals who commit this type of suicidal act, such as a soldier who falls on a live grenade to save his comrades or a follower of Christ who willingly dies for their faith, are honored for their sacrifice and remembered as heroes. Jesus himself speaks to this type of sacrificial act, foreshadowing his own death on the cross, when he says, "Greater love has no one than this, that one lay down his life for his friends" (John 15:13).

*Battle or conflict related.* The motivation behind battle- or conflict-related suicides in the Scriptures is to maintain honor by avoiding capture and subsequent torture at the hands of one's enemies. The most well-known battle- or conflict-related suicide in the Bible is likely that of King Saul during his final battle with the Philistines. Individuals who committed suicide in this manner are eulogized in the Bible based on the quality of the life that they lived. If they were evil individuals during their lifetime (e.g., Abimelech, Saul, Zimri), their suicide is seen as a divine punishment (Judges 9:54; 1 Chronicles 10:13-14; 1 Kings 16:19), while those who had lived righteously (e.g., Razis), are remembered with honor (2 Maccabees 14:43).

*Personal distress.* People are most commonly driven to suicide when they view their current situation as being completely hopeless and feel as if they have no way to change things for the better. Three examples of suicide resulting from personal distress are found in the Scriptures. The most well-known example is that of Judas Iscariot, who became distressed as a result of betraying Jesus and hung himself. He was seen as a pariah by the Jewish leaders and a traitor by Jesus' followers, and his body was left hanging in the tree until the rope broke and his bloated and rotting body burst open on the ground (Acts 1:18). This extreme example should not be taken as representative of how those whose personal distress led them to suicide were seen in biblical times. In the other two scriptural examples, Ahithophel is shown honor after his death by being buried in the tomb of his father (2 Samuel 17:23), while no information is given of the events following Ptolemy Macron's death (2 Maccabees 10:13). It is also important to realize that all of these biblical examples of suicidal ideations described here happened during personal distress. In each of those instances, God drew near and offered comfort, not condemnation.

**Table 14.2.** Biblical examples of suicide

| BIBLICAL CHARACTER | MEANS OF SUICIDE | SUICIDAL MOTIVATION | REFERENCES |
|---|---|---|---|
| **Heroic Martyrdom** | | | |
| Samson | Crushing | Revenge | Judges 13:5; 16:28-30 |
| Eleazar Avaran | Crushing | Save his people; honor | 1 Maccabees 6:43-46 |
| Seventh brother | Burning | To maintain faith | 4 Maccabees 12:16,19; 13:9-10, 13 |
| Mother of seven brothers | Burning | To maintain faith | 4 Maccabees 17:1 |
| **Battle/Conflict Related** | | | |
| Abimelech | Stabbing | Not to die by a woman | Judges 9:54 |
| Saul | Stabbing | Fear of capture and torture | 1 Samuel 31:3-4; 1 Chronicles 10:4 |
| Saul's armor bearer | Stabbing | Fear of capture and torture | 1 Samuel 31:5; 1 Chronicles 10:5 |
| Zimri | Burning | Fear of capture | 1 Kings 16:18 |
| Razis | Evisceration | Fear of capture and torture | 2 Maccabees 14:41-46 |
| **Personal Distress** | | | |
| Ahithophel | Hanging | Disrespect; fear of the king | 2 Samuel 17:23; JA 7.9.8 |
| Ptolemy Macron | Poisoning | Loss of respect, called traitor | 2 Maccabees 10:13 |
| Judas Iscariot | Hanging | Distressed over betrayal | Matthew 27:3-5 |

JA = Flavius Josephus, *Jewish Antiquities*

*Is Suicide an Unforgivable Sin?*

While both Jewish and Christian traditions consider suicide a serious sin, there is no direct prohibition of suicide in either the Old Testament or New Testament. In Judaism, those who take their own lives are not entitled to Jewish burial and mourning rites. In the Talmud, the ancient Jewish rabbis based the prohibition against suicide on Genesis 9:5-6:

> Surely I will require your lifeblood; from every beast I will require it. And from *every* man, from every man's brother I will require the life of man.
>
> "Whoever sheds man's blood,
> By man his blood shall be shed,
> For in the image of God
> He made man."

This is interpreted to mean, "I will require your blood if you yourselves shed it."

Saint Augustine (AD 354–430), perhaps the most influential church father in Western Christianity, considered suicide a sin that violated the sixth commandment, "You shall not murder" (Exodus 20:13; Deuteronomy 5:17). Thomas Aquinas (AD 1225–1274), the thirteenth-century theologian and philosopher, furthered this line of thinking by arguing that suicide was a sin because life is God's gift and only God has the right to take it away. He based his thoughts on Deuteronomy 32:39: "It is I who put to death and give life." Aquinas's argument for the sinfulness of suicide is further strengthened by 1 Corinthians 6:19-20: "Do you not know that your body is a temple of the Holy Spirit who is in you, whom you have from God, and that you are not your own? For you have been bought with a price: therefore glorify God in your body."

While these are all sensible interpretations of Scripture in relation to suicide, there is one significant caveat that must be mentioned. The Talmudic rabbis, Augustine, and Thomas Aquinas all considered suicide to be a reasoned and freely chosen act. They believed that the suicidal individual was making a rational choice to violate God's will and plan for their life. Their thinking was, at least in part, based on a faulty understanding of suicidal motivations. Understandably, they had no appreciation for the role that mental illness plays in suicide. That being said, their scriptural arguments appear theologically sound and suggest that suicide is indeed a sin. But is it unforgivable and does it affect an individual's eternal destination?

Our good behavior does not get us to heaven, just like our sinful behavior does not send us to hell (Ephesians 2:8). We are all born dead in our sins, separated from God with no hope of eternal life (Psalm 51:5). Only through the death and resurrection of Christ can we have an opportunity to be reconciled to our heavenly Father. When an individual comes to a saving faith in Jesus, they are made righteous and forgiven for every sin; past, present, and future, including suicide (Ephesians 1:7). If that individual, for whatever reason, dies by suicide, they are ushered into the presence of Christ because they are a redeemed child of God (John 3:16). Suicide is not the determining factor for eternal life; a saving faith in Jesus is.

## Final Thoughts

We can learn a number of important principles from the reports of suicidal behavior in the Bible. First, having faith, even a strong faith, does not guarantee that during times of extreme distress an individual will not consider suicide as a way out. Moses, Elijah, and

Job are some of the most revered heroes of the faith, yet they became hopeless and longed for death.

Second, God promises to comfort those in distress who feel hopeless. God drew near to each individual in the Bible who considered suicide when they called out to him in their distress. He did not rebuke them for their suicidal thoughts but offered them physical and spiritual comfort and support.

Third, the Bible does not condemn those who commit suicide, but in many instances it reports that the individual was shown honor after their death. Suicide does not appear to have been an event that would tarnish a righteous individual's legacy in biblical times.

Finally, suicide does not disqualify an individual from eternal life with God. Samson is our best example for this principle. Although he struggled staying true to his faith and ultimately took his own life, the Bible records him in the Hebrews 11 "roll call of faith."

The gospel is a message of forgiveness, redemption, and hope. When psychological distress overwhelms an individual and the person takes their life, our response should be one of grace toward their legacy while showing sympathy and compassion toward their family. The gospel makes no room for fear, shame, and condemnation; we must do the same in the church when we lose a brother or sister to mental illness.

# 15

## A HOLISTIC APPROACH
## TO RECOVERY

*The best way out is always through.*

ROBERT FROST

*THERE IS HOPE!* These are easy words to say but difficult words to believe when you are in the midst of the storm. If you or your loved one is struggling with a mental disorder, you may have lost hope. After numerous medications and hospitalizations, you may no longer believe that your present circumstances will ever change. At one time you had dreams for yourself and your family. Those dreams now seem impossible. You can't remember the last time you laughed or felt real joy. Each day brings more fear, stress, shame, moods swings, strange thoughts, abnormal behavior, and rejection. Unfortunately, this scenario is all too common for individuals living with mental illness and their families.

Every day I work with men and women whose lives have been destroyed by mental illness. It doesn't matter what their diagnosis is or how many failed treatments they may have tried in the past: my statement to them during the first meeting is always the same. "No matter how difficult your circumstances may presently be, you (or your loved one) can recover. With proper care and support you can be better than you are today. There is hope!" This is not an empty statement that I say to make people feel better but a fact based on the miracles I see every day; lives are being transformed and families are being restored.

"There is *hope*," is a statement for you or your loved one today. While I may not know your particular story, a better tomorrow is possible. If this all sounds too good to be true to you, or you think your situation is different or more difficult than others, just keep reading. What do you have to lose?

## Recovery Versus Cure

Mental disorders are chronic conditions, meaning that while we are presently able to treat or manage the afflicted individual's symptoms, we are unable to cure them. For other chronic conditions such as type 1 diabetes, asthma, and hypertension, treatment is equivalent to symptom management. The same is true for mental disorders. The good news, however, is that a majority of individuals with mental illness (60–80 percent) who receive treatment do report some level of symptom reduction.[1] I imagine that you or your loved one are looking for more than simply symptom reduction; you are seeking recovery.

The Substance Abuse and Mental Health Services Administration defines recovery as "a process of change through which individuals improve their health and wellness, live a self-directed life, and strive to reach their full potential."[2] The goal of recovery goes far beyond symptom reduction but aims at equipping the

---

[1] National Mental Health Advisory Council, "Health Care Reform for Americans with Severe Mental Illnesses," *American Journal of Psychiatry* 150 (1993): 1450-52.
[2] "SAMHSA's Working Definition of Recovery: 10 Guiding Principles of Recovery," *SAMHSA*, updated October 5, 2015, www.samhsa.gov/recovery.

individual to live beyond their illness. The most important thing to remember is that recovery is a process. It takes time, can be messy, and differs from person to person, but people with mental illness can and do recover.

### What Does the Recovery Process Look Like?

Figure 15.1 is a simple diagram I use with families to explain the mental health recovery process. The top line is the process for a person struggling with mental illness. The bottom line shows how the family's relationship with their loved one is affected by the stage of their recovery.

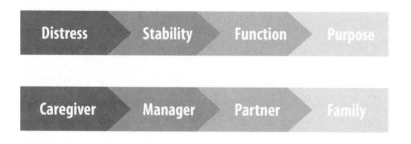

**Figure 15.1.** The mental health recovery process

Let's look at the top line first. At the far left side of the process we have *distress*. When an individual is in distress they are often delusional and unable to care for themselves. They may be having suicidal or homicidal thoughts, and often require hospitalization. This is the beginning of the recovery process. Family members at this point in the process are reduced to little more than *caregivers* tending to the individual's basic needs (e.g., food, safety, shelter).

As the afflicted individual begins to receive treatment, their symptoms are lessened and they become stable. *Stability* is defined as no longer a danger to self or others, and corporative with some level of treatment. At this point in the recovery process, the individual is likely living with a family member or in a residential setting with some type of assistance. The family's relationship has changed from one of caregiver to *manager*, meaning they are managing their loved one's treatment. Without the family's support (management), it is likely that the individual would not continue with their treatment and deteriorate back into distress.

As the individual continues to improve, they move to the point in the recovery process I call *function*. Here the individual begins to take an active role in planning and managing their own recovery. At this point in recovery, both the individual and his family are less concerned about pathology, illness, and symptoms, but instead start to focus more on the individual's strengths and wellness. The family's relationship with their loved one is now that of a *partner* in their recovery. No longer is the individual fully dependent on another for care but is empowered to get better through the support of others.

At the last stage in the recovery process we find *purpose*. Here the individual has rediscovered a sense of personal identity separate from their disorder. The person is beginning to participate in the local community and is striving to build a meaningful and satisfying life. At this point in the process, the *family* has regained their familial relationship with the individual. In other words, Mom can be Mom again, not a caregiver or manager.

As I said before, this process takes time and is messy. It is never a steady progression from one stage to the next. There will be setbacks and challenging periods, but recovery is possible. Understanding where you are in the process, as well as what the family relationship is at any given point, helps define more realistic expectations for you and your loved one.

## A Holistic Mental Health Recovery Plan

A holistic approach to mental health recovery relieves physical and psychological suffering while revealing the unconditional love and limitless grace available only through a personal relationship with Jesus. The following is a brief overview of what a holistic mental health recovery plan involves.[3] The physical, mental, spiritual, and relational needs described on the following pages are issues and problems common to mental health problems. The needs should be viewed as broad general principles to be implemented into a daily or weekly routine or schedule.

Recovery is a process, not a quick fix. You should be thinking in terms of months and years rather than days and weeks. As the afflicted individual heals and gains more stability, they will be able to do more and will move beyond a highly structured daily routine or schedule. The recovery plan should be adjusted accordingly as the individual becomes more independent and successful at navigating daily life.

### Physical Needs

The physical needs associated with a mental disorder go far beyond simply taking medication but also include sleep, nutrition, and exercise. Keeping the body (and brain) healthy will help lessen the severity of symptoms related to the disorder and can enhance the action of psychiatric medication.

*Sleeping well.* Chronic sleep problems affect 50-80 percent of individuals living with mental health difficulties, compared to 10-18 percent of the general population.[4] While excessive sleep

---

[3]For a detailed holistic recovery curriculum, contact the Hope and Healing Center & Institute (hopeandhealingcenter.org) or the Grace Alliance (mentalhealthgracealliance.org).

[4]"Sleep and Mental Health," *Harvard Health Publications*, July 2009, www.health.harvard .edu/newsletter_article/sleep-and-mental-health.

(hypersomnia) can be a problem for those living with mental health difficulties, the two most common complaints are not being able to fall asleep (onset insomnia) and waking up early and not being able to go back to sleep (late insomnia). Sleep deprivation has been shown to trigger symptoms such as suicidal thoughts, paranoia, agitation, and hyperactivity. Activities that can increase restfulness include having a set bedtime and routine, regular exercise, avoiding the use of caffeine and nicotine, and talking with your doctor about the effects of your medications on sleep.

*Medication.* The primary function of psychiatric medications is to alter the way that the nerve cells (neurons) in the brain function. This is done by changing the amount of chemical messenger (called neurotransmitter) the cells release or by changing the electrical properties of the cells' membrane. Every person responds to medications differently, and it is normal to try many different psychiatric medications until the best one is found for you. Educate yourself about the psychiatric medications that have been prescribed to you or your loved one. Know what they do, their potential side effects, interactions with food and other medications, and how sensitive the effects of the drug are to missed doses or noncompliance. Organize the medications in such a way that they can be taken regularly and with ease (e.g., weekly pill dispensing boxes).

*Leaning to relax.* The physical symptoms of stress and anxiety (heart racing, sweating, shortness of breath, nausea) can be overwhelming. Relaxation techniques such as paced breathing or progressive muscle relaxation can be helpful during these episodes of panic, but can also help when done on a daily basis to bring down your or your loved one's general level of stress. As you learn relaxation techniques, you'll become more aware of muscle tension and other physical sensations of stress. Once you know what your stress response feels like, you can make a conscious effort to practice a relaxation technique the moment you start to feel stress symptoms. This can prevent stress from spiraling out of control. If one relaxation technique doesn't work for you, try another; everybody is different.

*Eating healthier.* A balanced and nutritious diet promotes brain health and stabilizes moods. In addition, a healthy diet combats increased appetite and weight gain, common side effects of psychiatric medication. A diet that includes fruits, vegetables, whole grains, lean meats, poultry, fish, beans, eggs, and nuts (much like the "Paleo" or "Whole Food" plan) replenishes electrolytes and amino acids. This in turns affects neurotransmitters in the brain and can enhance the effects of medication. In some cases, nutritional supplements such as essential fatty acids may be helpful. These supplements should be used in addition to, but not in place of, medication. Always check with your doctor before taking a nutritional supplement.

*Being more active.* Some sort of daily physical exercise is recommended for those living with a mental illness. This does not need to be an intense workout at the gym, but something that gets them moving and is easy to maintain (e.g., a fifteen-minute walk or thirty minutes working in the garden). The goal is to be regularly active in order to strengthen the body and relieve anxiety and depressive symptoms. Regular exercise also offsets common troublesome medication side effects such as constipation, drowsiness, weight gain, fatigue, and irritability.

## Mental Needs

Mental disorders are often a battle between reality and wrong or negative thoughts that overwhelm a person's mind. A structured approach to psychological needs is just as important as physical needs and includes regular psychotherapy, healthy thinking, positive coping strategies, and enjoyable mental activities.

*Psychotherapy.* Talk therapy in conjunction with medication has been shown to be the most effective approach to treating mental illness. Psychotherapy is done by a licensed therapist or clinical psychologist and focuses on managing symptoms related to the disorder and improving an individual's general quality of life. Be sure your loved one's therapist is using a psychotherapeutic intervention that has been shown to be effective in treating their particular disorder.

*Healthy thinking.* Our emotions and behaviors are the result of what we think or believe about ourselves, other people, and the world (thinking = feeling). These thoughts shape how we interpret and evaluate what happens to us, influence how we feel about it, and provide a guide to how we should respond. Unfortunately, sometimes our interpretations, evaluations, underlying beliefs, and thoughts contain distortions, errors, and biases. The more a person's thinking is characterized by these distortions, the more likely they will experience negative emotions and engage in maladaptive behaviors. Simple tools to address ongoing negative thinking are essential to the recovery process. Developing a process of healthy thinking helps the individual identify how negative thoughts and stressors are affecting their moods and behaviors.

*Coping with problems or stress.* Coping mechanisms are learned patterns of behavior used to cope. We learn from others as well as from our own experiences how to deal with stress. Negative coping choices reduce our feelings of stress at the time we are experiencing the stressful event. However, with time they usually create their own problems and are best avoided (e.g., substance use). Positive coping choices, when done in a balanced way, diminish stress and enhance the quality of life (e.g., routine relaxation techniques). We can actively confront a problem by gathering information, cultivating skills, or changing a situation in order to adapt. A more passive coping strategy is to regulate our emotional response to a challenge by suppressing negative thinking, distracting our thoughts, or learning to accept a negative situation. When individuals struggling with mental health difficulties take direct, positive action to cope with their disorder, they put themselves in a position of power. Active positive coping is empowering and takes away feelings of helplessness. Examples of this type of coping include setting reasonable and flexible goals, practicing relaxation techniques, developing a schedule and routine, and regular exercise.

***Recognizing cycles and triggers.*** We all have good days and bad days, and it is no different for individuals living with mental health difficulties or disorders. A recovery-oriented lifestyle requires understanding and being educated about the predictable cycles and triggers of mental illness in order to better manage them. During times of stability, common signs often appear that reveal a more difficult cycle (episode) is coming (e.g., losing sleep or oversleeping, increasing irritability, not eating or overeating, racing thoughts or slower cognitive processing, increasing anxiety or nervousness). Negative cycles triggered by seasonal changes, events, or transitional times (e.g., holidays, end of school semester) can be predicted and minimized. Without a plan or process to help minimize these cycles or triggers, life will be driven by the symptoms affecting your thoughts, emotions, and behavior. Taking a preventative, proactive approach when these signs appear will assist you in helping your loved one maintain greater stability and health.

***Engaging the mind.*** Cognitive (neural) reserve is the complexity and redundancy of neural networks in the brain that provide a buffer against loss of function following aging, brain injury, or mental illness. This reserve is affected by a multitude of

factors, including genes, childhood environment, education, oc-
cupation, physical health, health behaviors, lifestyle, and mental
activities. Evidence suggests that mental activities have a healing
and protective effect on mental well-being. They provide a means
of self-expression and reduce blood pressure while boosting the
immune system and reducing stress. In other words, cognitive
(neural) reserve can be built up. The symptoms associated with
mental health difficulties often cause an individual to become
sedentary and isolated, resulting in a lack of mental activities.
Within a recovery-oriented lifestyle the brain should be viewed
as a muscle that requires exercise and activity to function at its
best. These activities may be done individually or in a group
setting. When working to build up your cognitive (neural) reserve,
involve yourself in mental activities that are associated with
hobbies or enjoyment. These could include painting, drawing,
reading, photography, music, gardening, word games or puzzles,
or other hobbies. Mental activities are just that, active! Avoid
passive, mindless activities such as watching TV.

*Living a structured life.* The ups and downs of mental health
difficulties can be very chaotic. A daily structure and routine helps
one gain stability and thrive. The goal of a routine and schedule is
to establish habits that allow your loved one greater control over
what they're doing and greater freedom to focus on what's important in their life. Routines and schedules reduce stress and
anxiety. They help us live more relaxed lives. They allow us to stop
constantly making decisions or guessing about the future. Within
a recovery process, routines do not bring boredom or monotony.
Rather, they bring peace and a sense of safety. When starting to
implement a routine or schedule into your loved one's recovery, do
not overburden them with too much in the beginning. Start off
slowly. During the first month or so of recovery, tend to only what's

absolutely necessary. Because of cognitive confusion and memory problems (due to their disorder or medication), some individuals living with mental illness may need to physically see a schedule of things they are going to do that day to be successful.

## Spiritual Needs

The church has a significant role to play in the lives of those struggling with mental illness. Studies have shown that religious support offers resources, which are unavailable from general social support, to the psychologically distressed individual.[5] Religious support is vital to recovery and wholeness. More importantly, we serve a God who loves us deeply, hears our desperate cries, and responds with sustaining mercy and grace.

**Discovering hope.** Hope is believing the promise of better things to come despite challenges. It is not simply wishing that something bad or negative would somehow change. Hope is positively associated with perceived ability and self-worth, while negatively associated with the symptoms of depression. Hope energizes people and gives them strength to endure in a way that nothing else does. People without hope become defeated, broken, and unable to cope with adversity. Hopeless people give up.

Christian hope is confidence that something will come to pass because God has promised it will come to pass. Faith and hope are overlapping realities: hope is faith in the future tense. Hebrews 11:1 says, "Faith is confidence in what we hope for and assurance about what we do not see" (NIV). We must be careful to not allow circumstances to break down our hope. Circumstances change, God does not. Christian hope comes from the promises of God rooted in the work of Christ. The Scriptures

---

[5]William E. Fiala et al., "The Religious Support Scale: Construction, Validation, and Cross-Validation," *American Journal of Community Psychology* 30 (2002): 761-86.

were written to encourage us and to give us hope. Use God's Word to rebuild your loved one's hope.

Show them that heroes of faith like David (Psalm 13), Job (Job 3), and Jeremiah (Lamentations 3) struggled with times of intense hopelessness. Remind them that while deep despair and hopelessness can occur in believers, God is faithful. Demonstrate to them how focusing on that single truth brought hope to the prophet Jeremiah at his lowest point:

This I recall to my mind,
Therefore I have hope.
The Lord's lovingkindnesses indeed never cease,
For His compassions never fail.
*They* are new every morning;
Great is Your faithfulness. (Lamentations 3:21-23)

Use the Scriptures to make clear that as children of the living God our hope is built on Christ (suggested verses: Romans 5:1-5; Colossians 1:27; 1 Timothy 1:1; Hebrews 6:17-20), who chose us, saved us, sealed us with the Holy Spirit, and promised to return and take us home.

**Knowing your identity.** Your loved one's identity is not their diagnosis or mental health difficulty! Their true identity, who they really are, is based on what they mean to God. Circumstances and struggles do not define them; God does. One of the common difficulties for people living with mental illness is a disconnection or loss of emotional control. It is very common for them to feel unable to connect emotionally in important relationships or even with God. Because faith is not tangible like bodily sensations, individuals living with mental illness may feel condemnation or that their faith is not "strong enough." They may begin to think that God does not care for them or is distant and silent. They may even question their salvation! Feeling disconnected from God can be frustrating and common, but it is not a reflection of our access to God. As his children, God has given us access to him through prayer in all circumstances, both good and bad. He wants us to share our feelings, our thankfulness, and our requests for what we need. The Bible says that he "longs to be gracious to you" (Isaiah 30:18). Your loved one must be continually reminded of this truth so that they will have a strong foundation on which to rebuild their life.

*Finding your purpose.* God's purpose and plan for all believers includes knowing him more fully through his Word, following his commands and being a witness for Jesus wherever God has placed us. Since God is good, his purposes and plans for us are also good. Likewise, since he sets our paths, no one's purpose is more or less important than another's; they are all part of God's greater plan. God has given each of us different talents and gifts so that we might be equipped to fulfill the specific purpose and plan he has ordained for our life (1 Peter 4:10-11). To help us recognize our purpose and fulfill his plan for our lives, God has bound all believers together in his church and sent us the Holy Spirit to guide us. Your loved one's mental disorder does not hinder God's purposes, nor does it in any way affect God's plan for their life. We all must learn and recognize that a mental health difficulty may be an opportunity for the works of God to be manifested in one's life.

*Growing spiritually.* The Scriptures call us to "grow in the grace and knowledge of our Lord and Savior Jesus Christ" (2 Peter 3:18). Grace is unmerited love freely given. You don't have to be perfect to receive God's grace, only willing. Receiving God's grace is the first step in the process of spiritual growth. God desires to know your loved one in such a way that blesses them and brings rest to their faith.

For those living with mental health difficulties, brief daily encouragements from Scripture are often better than in-depth Bible study. The focus of study should be on God's character and their identity and approval in Christ, not references that imply what they must do to get better. Meditating on a single verse of Scripture is often better than a long, detailed Bible study or devotional. Studying Scripture should be a time for them to be loved by God, not a time to fight their disorder (which they cannot cure on their own). Worship is a time to come into the presence of God in a very physical sense. It should not be a time of mental condemnation and overwhelming physical stimulation for your loved one.

*Living in community.* An active and supportive faith community cultivates life, while isolation brings frustration and fatigue. God has called us to "rejoice with those who rejoice, and weep with those who weep" (Romans 12:15). A strong faith community offers comfort and support, gains wisdom as it learns from one another, shares and upholds common values, strengthens one another, takes risks together, and always looks to encourage one another. Many times, because of certain cycles or difficult symptoms, staying consistent with community events can be difficult for those living with mental illness. Others may not understand this inconsistency and back away. The key is staying connected to a few trusted and supportive people, not trying to keep up with the gathering or community events that are wearing them down. Living in community is more about being connected to life-giving relationships than trying to attend events with people a person doesn't know well.

## Relational Needs

Mental illness affects more than just the person with the disorder; it affects all of their relationships. Difficulties, stigma, and shame often isolate whole families trying to care for a mentally ill loved one from the world around them. In addition, high levels of stress and difficult symptoms can result in relational conflict requiring forgiveness and reconciliation.

*Family and friends.* The symptoms of mental health difficulties and disorders can interfere with trust, emotional closeness, communication, and effective problem solving. At the beginning of symptoms, family members and friends often look for answers or reasons for the problems other than mental health difficulties, hoping that the symptoms are caused by physical problems, a spiritual problem, or external stressors that can be easily removed. Mental health difficulties do not just affect individuals but affect entire families. It is imperative that the family and friends of an individual living with mental illness gain understanding about the disorder and receive support from others. Without information to help families learn to cope with mental health difficulties, they can lose hope and withdraw. Supportive family and friends are an important part of recovery. They can be there to listen and to help during the rough times.

*Resolving conflict.* Every relationship will have some conflict, therefore it's important to learn and grow from them. Resolving conflicts is more about compromising for a healthy conclusion, not proving a point. If you push for your point of view, it creates more tension and can come across as manipulative. If you find yourself in conflict with your loved one, ask yourself whether the disorder may be clouding their judgment of the situation. If so, allow yourself (and them) to take a break and return later to follow up with a more appropriate perspective and emotions. When you do engage them, use an active listening approach to defuse tension. First, validate the emotions and feelings they are experiencing. Next, affirm their faith in Christ and as a valued friend or family member. Finally, offer an opportunity for reconciliation by providing grace to find a point of common ground to restore harmony. With time, you will learn to respond rather than simply react with offense in these situations.

*Overcoming stigma.* Stigma is always born out of fear and misinformation, and can only be overcome by truth and education. The purpose of stigma is to minimize, disgrace, or dehumanize someone so inaction and a lack of compassion can be justified. Others' wrongly held views and beliefs (stigma) are hurtful and are not your loved one's fault; don't own them. Mental health difficulties are not the result of personal sin, having a weak faith, or demonic oppression. All believers struggle with sin and weakness of faith at times, but God still chooses to love and care for us. Educate your loved one's family and friends about the causes and treatments of your loved one's mental disorder.

*Opportunities to serve.* When we serve others, we are actually serving God: "Then the King will say, 'I'm telling the solemn truth: Whenever you did one of these things to someone overlooked or ignored, that was me—you did it to me'" (Matthew 25:40 *The Message*). We are most like Jesus when we're serving others. After washing his disciples' feet, Jesus said, "I have given you an example to follow. Do as I have done to you" (John 13:14-15 NLT). As your loved one gains stability, look for simple ways for them to serve and bless others. Whether it is at home, for a neighbor, or at church, serving provides a healthy way to look beyond personal difficulties and engage others with compassion. Serving others builds value and worth.

*Choosing to forgive.* Forgiveness is not choosing to inflict the price for an offense. The wrongful act that hurt or offended your loved one might always remain a part of their life, but forgiveness will lessen its grip on them and help them focus on other, positive parts of their life. Forgiveness is a choice we make through a decision of our will (not a feeling), motivated by obedience to God and his command to forgive. Just as we have received forgiveness from God, he has called us to forgive those who hurt us. That does not mean we are required or even able to forget the offense. We are simply to forgive the person who has wronged us and trust God for justice, leaving the events in his hands. Forgiveness is a choice we make through a decision of our will (not a feeling), motivated by obedience to God and his command to forgive. Just deciding to forgive will not strip away all of the pain of the incident. Help your loved one forgive those who may have wronged him or her because of the disorder and to ask forgiveness from those your loved one may have wronged.

## Recovery Can Be Messy

People living with mental illness can behave in strange and bizarre ways. Their perception of the world and those around them can be very different. They may even perceive your attempts to help them as a threat. They may deny that they have a problem. They may refuse to be involved in treatment. These are difficult issues—long-term and messy—requiring a steadfast commitment on your part. Don't expect appreciation; in fact, you might receive just the opposite. This is as much your trial as it is that of the person with the disorder. God wants to use it to draw you and your loved one closer to him.

There are no easy answers, and there is no quick fix. This is real life, and sometimes it will seem like you are feeling your way in the dark, but you are not alone. God is present in the midst of this storm, and he will provide sustaining grace as you and your loved one walk toward hope, recovery, and healing.

# 16

# MENTAL ILLNESS
# AND THE CHURCH

*Is anyone among you sick? Then he must call for the elders
of the church, and let them pray over him, anointing him
with oil in the name of the Lord.*

JAMES 5:14

THE HOPE AND HEALING CENTER & INSTITUTE, the organization I lead, sits on the campus of a large Episcopal Church. Recently, the church's receptionist called and asked if I could come over because there was a suicidal woman in the front office. I walked to the church and found Kate talking with one of the clergy. Kate, a disheveled forty-five-year-old woman was obviously in distress. We spoke for about an hour.

During our conversation, she told me she was afraid to go home because she might hurt herself. She shared with me that she had struggled with depression in the past but was presently not receiving any treatment. That morning she and her boyfriend, with whom she lives, had a heated argument about their financial difficulties. I helped her calm down and then provided connections to local resources that could help with her employment and financial problems. I also assessed her suicidality and found that while distressed, she was not actively suicidal. I scheduled an appointment for her with one of our mental health coaches at the HHCI, and she began seeing her the following week for depression. Kate told me she did not attend a church, leading me to ask her why she had come to this particular congregation for help. Her parents had been married there fifty years earlier.

This story is repeated daily in churches across the country. Research shows that individuals struggling with mental health problems are more likely to go to a clergy member before a mental health provider or physician.[1] A survey of pastors by author Amy Simpson for her book *Troubled Minds: Mental Illness and the Church's Mission* found that 44.5 percent of pastors report being approached two to five times a year for help with mental illness while 32.8 percent report being approached six or more times.[2] Unfortunately, the average faith community is not equipped to effectively assist or support individuals with mental health problems. A recent LifeWay Research study found that only 28 percent of churches surveyed maintained a referral list of local mental health care providers.[3] How would your church have assisted Kate?

Viewed through the eyes of faith, the fact that those struggling with mental health problems are seeking assistance from the church first is a divine opportunity. God is sending those broken by mental illness to us so that they might receive hope and healing. Given that 450 million individuals in the world are presently struggling with a mental health problem, it is time that the church

---

[1]Philip S. Wang et al., "Patterns and Correlates of Contacting Clergy for Mental Disorders in the United States," *Health Services Research* 38 (2003): 647-73.

[2]Amy Simpson, *Troubled Minds: Mental Illness and the Church's Mission* (Downers Grove, IL: InterVarsity Press, 2013).

[3]"New Study of Acute Mental Illness and Christian Faith: Research Report," *LifeWay Research*, accessed March 13, 2017, http://lifewayresearch.com/wp-content/uploads/2014/09/Acute-Mental-Illness-and-Christian-Faith-Research-Report-1.pdf.

recognized its role in what may be the great mission field of the twenty-first century.[4] The involvement of the church in mental health is the missing piece necessary to transform our broken system, making it accessible and more effective.

## Why the Church Is Important

Our present mental health care system is not a true system of care. Rather, it is a set of disjointed resources that individuals and families find difficult if not impossible to access. Existing resources are critically important, but on their own they do not provide a holistic approach to meeting the needs of people struggling with mental illness. In addition, many people who would benefit from professional care do not receive it, largely because they are unable to find an open door to the mental health care system. The body of Christ offers four things the mental health care system presently lacks: (1) a hope that transcends circumstances, (2) a holistic view of humans, (3) accessibility, and (4) supportive community.

Hope is the fuel that drives the engine of mental health recovery. As long as one has hope, there is motivation and opportunity for change. Historically, severe mental illness has been conceptualized as a chronic medical condition in which stability is the best possible outcome for treatment. The hope presently offered by the mental health care system is symptom reduction and illness management. The church, however, understands that hope is more than a feeling; hope is a person, Jesus Christ. Hope in Christ transcends circumstances and sustains us when the world around us sees the situation as hopeless.

Second, the person struggling with a mental health problem needs a holistic approach to treatment that takes into account all

---

4"Mental Disorders Affect One in Four People," *World Health Organization*, October 4, 2001, www.who.int/whr/2001/media_centre/press_release/en.

aspects of their being: physical, mental, spiritual, and relational. Treatments and interventions that focus solely on a single aspect of a person's being can bring limited relief at best. A holistic mental health approach, however, is comprehensive, addressing the whole individual: physical needs (e.g., sleeping well, medication, relaxation, nutrition, and exercise), mental needs (e.g., healthy thinking, coping with problems or stress, mindfulness, cycles and triggers, and mental activities), spiritual needs (e.g., hope, knowing your identity, finding purpose, spiritual growth, and living in community), and relational needs (e.g., family and friends, resolving conflict, overcoming stigma, opportunities to serve, and forgiveness). The church's holistic view of being human offers those struggling with a mental health problem a more complete framework for recovery.

Third, accessibility is perhaps the biggest problem with our present system, but imagine what would happen if churches were equipped to effectively serve as front doors to mental health care? This would mean that individuals in psychological distress who seek assistance from the church would be quickly identified and referred to professional care. What if churches were equipped not only to be effective front doors but also places where peer-led mental health services were available onsite? These services would not replace professional mental health care, but instead would serve as an adjunct to those resources. Basic helpful interventions, such as psychoeducation and support groups, are ideal for implementation in a church setting. Services such as these, led by non-professionals, have been shown to be effective in managing symptoms and maintaining stability, and have the added benefits of minimal cost and maximum accessibility.

Finally, a supportive community is a necessary factor in successful mental health recovery. Churches offer individuals and their families an accepting and supportive environment in which they can pursue healing and wholeness. The church is called to "love one another"; this makes available to the afflicted and their family a community of care and respite from the struggles associated with mental health problems.

## A Mental Health Equipped Church

Every church is different; each has a specific set of needs and available resources. For the church to transform the mental health care system, it is not necessary for every congregation to be involved at the same level. It is only necessary that each congregation become involved. The following are suggestions of how churches might become more equipped to serve those struggling with mental health problems.

**Clergy mental health training.** Research shows that over 70 percent of pastors report feeling inadequately trained to recognize mental illness.[5] If all churches would simply train their staff to recognize the signs and symptoms of mental illness, then clergy would become effective mental health gatekeepers, and access to the system would be increased. A number of organizations (e.g., National Alliance for the Mentally Ill, Mental Health America) offer mental health training that clergy and their ministry staff can easily access.

**Collaborative professional relationships.** It is important that clergy build professional relationships with mental health care providers in their local community. When a clergy person has a relationship with a professional mental health provider, their referrals

[5]William M. Hunter and Matthew S. Stanford, "Adolescent Mental Health: The Role of Youth and College Pastors," *Mental Health, Religion and Culture* 17 (2014): 957-66; and Jennifer L. Farrell and Deborah A. Goebert, "Collaboration Between Psychiatrists and Clergy in Recognizing and Treating Serious Mental Illness," *Psychiatric Services* 59 (2008): 437-40.

are more meaningful to the person being referred. A referral should not be seen as passing the buck but rather as a collaborative opportunity in which the pastor and mental health provider work as a team to care for and support the struggling individual. Clergy should vet a wide range of mental health professionals in the community as potential referrals, including psychiatrists, clinical psychologists, clinical social workers, and counselors. The pastor should seek mental health providers who are willing to work collaboratively on cases and who affirm the Christian faith.

**Congregational education and awareness.** Stigma and shame are barriers that keep suffering individuals from receiving the care and support they need to recover. It is the responsibility of the clergy and ministry staff to educate the congregation that the church is a safe place to discuss our problems, including mental illness. This can be done in a number of ways. Place brochures, information regarding mental illness, and other available resources in the church entry or main office. Invite a local mental health professional to speak or offer a seminar on mental illness.

Perhaps even more important, the congregation must be educated about the process the church has put in place to care for and support those who are struggling with mental health problems. Do not assume that they know. A recent LifeWay Research study found that while 68 percent of pastors reported their church kept a list of local mental health referrals for members, only 28 percent of their congregants reported that they knew about it.[6]

**Pastoral care team.** All followers of Christ are called to "bear one another's burdens" (Galatians 6:2). The care and support of those who are struggling is not only the responsibility of a few hired clergy but also the congregation as a whole. Establish and develop

---

[6]"New Study of Acute Mental Illness and Christian Faith."

a pastoral care team or ministry within your church. God has placed individuals within your congregation that are supernaturally gifted in mercy. Seek them out. Also recruit individuals with personal experiences to offer counsel in areas such as marriage, parenting, addiction, or divorce. A strong pastoral care ministry is vital when ministering to individuals with mental health problems.

*Support groups.* There is strong evidence for the clinical efficacy of peer-led support groups in mental health recovery. It requires few resources for the church to allow organizations that offer mental health support groups (e.g., National Alliance for the Mentally Ill, Depression/Bipolar Support Alliance, and Alcoholics Anonymous) to use the church's facility to hold weekly meetings. If the faith community is interested in being more directly involved in the delivery of support groups, partner with faith-based organizations such as Grace Alliance (mentalhealthgracealliance.org) or Celebrate Recovery (celebraterecovery.com) to have congregants trained to lead groups. Support groups are not just beneficial to individuals living with mental illness, but are also helpful to their caregivers as well.

*Sunday morning.* Breaking the silence is the first step in developing an environment that promotes hope and healing in those living with mental illness. The weekly corporate gathering of the congregation is a great place to begin. As a faith community, pray in a general way each week for anyone who is struggling with a mental or emotional disorder. If your church has a time of prayer at the end of the service, explicitly invite individuals with mental health problems to come forward for prayer. Prepare sermons that acknowledge the struggle experienced by those with mental illness; consider inviting a member of the church who has struggled with mental illness to share their story with the congregation during the service.

**Special populations.** Many churches have special ministries for groups known to have higher than normal rates of mental illness. These groups include substance abusers, prison inmates, the homeless, victims of human trafficking, and individuals traumatized by natural disaster. It is imperative that the individuals who serve in these ministries be educated about mental health problems.

**Prevention.** I have tried to emphasize that mental disorders result from a complex interaction of biological vulnerabilities and environmental factors. As you may have noticed, risk factors such as divorce, family conflict, physical or sexual abuse, low self-esteem, and a negative outlook on life are common to a number of disorders. I suggest that in addition to offering help to those presently suffering with mental disorders, we in the body of Christ also have an opportunity to help prevent or limit the development of these disorders. We may not be able to do much about our biology, but we can certainly alter our environment. We can do this by making Christ the central focus of our families and teaching our children how valued they are in the eyes of God.

## Challenges

As the body of Christ we are called to share the good news, to make disciples, to love one another, to bear one another's burdens, and to pray for one another. Unfortunately the response within the church toward the mentally ill has been to withdraw, either by characterizing them as sinful or by ignoring the problem altogether. That makes it easy for us: either these people are unclean and not deserving of our help, or they are invisible. The Scriptures do not give us qualifiers about who we should minister to; they simply say we should love one another (John 13:34; 1 John 3:11), bear one another's burdens (Galatians 6:2), and pray for one another (James 5:16). They tell us that if we see people in need and do nothing to help, the love of God does not abide in us (1 John 3:17) and our faith is of no value (James 2:14-17).

I don't think I'm being self-righteous. I will be the first to admit that I fall short. On more than one occasion I have grown so frustrated with mentally ill individuals in my own church that I wished they would change churches! These things are impossible to do in our own strength (John 15:5), but the good news is that we don't have to. By grace through faith we have been changed (Ephesians 2:8-10). We are a new creation (2 Corinthians 5:17). God has placed the Spirit of his Son within each of us. He is now our very life (Colossians 3:4). He wants to love through us (1 John 5:1-2). He wants to bear burdens through us. He even prays for us when we don't know how to pray (Romans 8:26). Our part in all this is to simply keep our heart submissive to his leading. That is the first step in ministering effectively to those with mental disorders.

Remember that God has called us to "rejoice with those who rejoice, and weep with those who weep" (Romans 12:15). This is as much our trial as it is that of the person with the mental illness. God wants to use it to draw us closer to him. This is also not something you should try to do all on your own. We are a community, a body. With the permission of the one you are ministering to, recruit other believers to help. The same Spirit that connects us to God also connects us to one another, so we should be eager to offer assistance. Sharing the burden lightens the load for all.

## Final Thoughts

The fact that individuals living with mental illness are seeking assistance and counsel from the church should prompt us to rise up and be the hands and feet of Christ to a suffering people. This is best done through the application of both biblical truth and mental health resources. God is leading his hurting children to us. It's time that the church stopped abdicating its role in mental health and started leading.

My hope is that this book has given you a better understanding of the clinical and spiritual aspects of mental disorders. As I've said before, with mental illness there are no easy answers, and there is no cookie-cutter set of action points that will be effective in every situation. The best advice I can give you is simply to let grace be your guide. If God has placed a mentally ill person in your life and you in theirs, how will you respond?